MODERNISM AND THE CULTURE OF CELEBRITY

Aaron Jaffe investigates the relationship between two phenomena that arrived on the historical stage in the first decades of the twentieth century: modernist literature and modern celebrity culture. Jaffe systematically traces and theorizes the deeper dependencies between these two influential forms of cultural value. He examines the paradox that modernist authors, while rejecting mass culture in favor of elite cultural forms, reflected the economy of celebrity culture in their strategies for creating a market for their work. Through collaboration, networking, reviewing, and editing each other's works, T. S. Eliot, James Joyce, Ezra Pound, and Wyndham Lewis, among others, constructed their literary reputations and publicized the project of modernism. Jaffe uses substantial archival research to show how literary fame was made by exploiting the very market forces that modernists claimed to reject. This innovative study illuminates not only the way High Modernist reputations were constructed, but also the cultural impact and continued relevance of the modernist project.

AARON JAFFE is Assistant Professor of English at the University of Louisville. He has previously taught at Indiana University and the University of Illinois. This is his first book.

MODERNISM AND THE
CULTURE OF CELEBRITY

AARON JAFFE

CAMBRIDGE
UNIVERSITY PRESS

CAMBRIDGE UNIVERSITY PRESS

Cambridge, New York, Melbourne, Madrid, Cape Town, Singapore, São Paulo

Cambridge University Press
The Edinburgh Building, Cambridge CB2 2RU, UK

Published in the United States of America by Cambridge University Press, New York

www.cambridge.org
Information on this title: www.cambridge.org/9780521843010

First published 2005

Printed in the United Kingdom at the University Press, Cambridge

A catalogue record for this book is available from the British Library

Library of Congress Cataloging in Publication data
Jaffe, Aaron.
Modernism and the culture of celebrity / Aaron Jaffe.
Includes bibliographical references and index.
1. English literature – 20th century – History and criticism.   2. Modernism (Literature) –
English-speaking countries.   3. Literature and society – English-speaking countries – History – 20th
century.   4. Literature publishing – English-speaking countries – History – 20th century.
5. Authors and readers – English-speaking countries – History – 20th century.   6. American
literature – 20th century – History and criticism.   7. Authorship – Marketing – History – 20th
century.   8. Celebrities – English-speaking countries.   I. Title.
PR478.M6J34   2004
820.9′112 – dc22   2004051947

ISBN-13 978-0-521-84301-0 hardback
ISBN-10 0-521-84301-4 hardback

For Tatjana and Elias

Contents

Illustrations

Acknowledgments

I wish to acknowledge and thank my teachers at Colgate University, Indiana University, and elsewhere. Michael Coyle and John Gery introduced me to modernism. Steve Watt guided me through this project's formative stages and its development. Along with Steve, I would like to thank Pat Brantlinger, Jim Naremore, and Helen Sword for invaluable suggestions and critique. Memorable discussions with Rob Richardson, Cristina Iuli, James Davis, Chris Raczkowski, Stacy Thompson, and Ed Comentale influenced various parts of this work. The intelligent criticism provided by the readers selected by Cambridge also helped shape its final form.

The generosity of a Project Completion Grant from the Office of Senior Vice President for Research at the University of Louisville hastened this book's completion. I also acknowledge the kindness of my new colleagues and the graduate students at the University of Louisville and the assistance of Bill Kehrwald in the last stages of the project.

I wish to thank especially my parents, Stephen and Wilhelmina, and my brothers, Neil and Ben, on whom I count when it matters.

My EU family, Anica, Čedo, and Dejan: *hvala*.

Above all: Tatjana Soldat-Jaffe, who has helped me in innumerable ways. This book is for you and Elias.

Parts of this book have appeared elsewhere in print. A version of chapter two appeared as "Adjectives and the Work of Modernism in an Age of Celebrity," *The Yale Journal of Criticism* 16.1 (2003), 1–37. Portions of the introduction appeared in *Key Words: A Journal of Cultural Materialism* 4 (2003), 156–67.

Introduction

Das Werk ist die Totenmaske der Konzeption.
– Walter Benjamin[1]

Although Marilyn Monroe and James Joyce never met in person, they met each other and posterity in one of Monroe's publicity photos: Monroe pictured reading Joyce (see Figure 1).[2] Each cultural entity – the celebrity and the modernist – assumes its characteristic form as cultural capital. One signifies the woman at the keyhole, the cipher of celluloid, the celebrity star image; the other signifies the objective correlative of her brains, the magisterial book-in-print, the modernist's textual imprimatur. The homology lies at the crux of this book. Like the star image, the textual imprimatur is a metonym for its subject, a metonym that represents it as an object of cultural production, circulation, and consumption. Strictly speaking, modernists like Joyce were not cut from the same celebrity cloth as movie stars like Monroe. Unlike movie stardom, the matrix of associations supporting their reputations is not intrinsically image-based but predicated instead on a distinctive textual mark of authorship, a sanction for distinguishing a high literary product from the inflating signs of consumption.

For all the revisionist work about the canon during the last decades, only a dozen or so names and texts remain in heavy rotation when modernism is discussed.[3] Paradoxically, the expanded modernist canon shows that the rule of scarcity remains a powerful principle for organizing literary reputations, a rule which dovetails perfectly with the limited resources and meager shelf-space devoted to "serious literature." This operating principle, I submit, was founded during the interwar period on modernist works and doctrines as certain modernists worked to create and expand a market for elite authorial signatures. As F. M. Marinetti cast his defiance unto the

Figure 1 Monroe and Joyce, 1955.

stars, modernists like T. S. Eliot, Ezra Pound, James Joyce, and Wyndham
Lewis cast their reputations against an increasingly indifferent, transna-
tional culture of celebrity, which unraveled traditional modes of literary
self-fashioning. Hedging against celebrity and its fetish of biography, they
transformed the authorial signature itself into a means of exposing – indeed,
publicizing – modernist work in a variety of extramural generic and cultural
registers.

Scrutinizing the "High Modernists" in their two characteristic haunts – canonical masterpieces and literary apocrypha – this book is interested in why, when, and how modernist visions and revisions of reputation inflect the production of modernist texts, their politics, and literary history. My concern is neither modernist celebrities in pop culture nor celebrity sightings in modernist texts; instead, I seek to account for two seemingly paradoxical, yet interrelated phenomena: the capacity of modernist texts to sustain an exclusionary notion of literary reputation, and the capacity of certain modernist careers to fix "masterpieces" in emerging economies of cultural prestige by calling upon a matrix of secondary literary labors. Prominent modernists – Eliot, Pound, Joyce, Lewis, to name the four under sustained consideration – were more canny about fashioning their careers – indeed, fashioning the very notion of a literary career – than is often appreciated. Even as literary *self*-fashioning became increasingly inscrutable, figures like Lewis, Eliot, and Pound mobilized their textual signatures – their authorial imprimaturs – into durable promotional vehicles for their careers, hybridizing bodily agency and textual form.

That is to say, Lewis, Eliot, and Pound had a stake in offering their imprimaturs and those of selected contemporaries like Joyce, Djuna Barnes, and Marianne Moore as the embodiment of representative distinction: it was a means to economize and thus monopolize the plenitude of the literary firmament and uphold a two-tier system of modernist labor. For the duration of their careers – and with particular intensity during the interwar period – modernists and their allies, working to create and expand a market for elite literary works, transformed the textual signature itself into a means of promotion. Imprimatur fashioning informed the *ad hoc* infrastructure of modernist production from its elite durable goods to its sanctioned, masculinist frameworks of reviewing, introducing, editing, and anthologizing to its kinds of devalued, feminized collaborative work apocryphally documented in modernist memoirs.

My first chapter traces the descent of this form of capital from the rise of professionalism at the end of the nineteenth century to the fall of modernist careerism in the early forties. Thus, beginning with examples from Henry James's stories of literary life, I examine the messages about public literary persona, authority, and politics coded in expert narrative about authorship. I compare the Jamesian example with Joyce's *Portrait of the Artist as a Young Man*, perhaps the most frequently invoked modernist author–novel. Finally, considering Lewis's *Revenge for Love*, Evelyn Waugh's *Vile Bodies*, Edward Upward's *Journey to the Border*, and Christopher Isherwood's *Prater*

Violet, I show the modernist model being remade and undone during late modernism.

My second chapter examines the relationship between the critical wings of modernism, the making of modernist reputation, and the circulation of modernist names as rarefied, fungible commodities in economies of great names. Specifically, I compare the uses and abuses of the authorial adjective (for example, "Jamesian," "Joycean," etc.) in modernist and practical criticism. The modes of criticism inaugurated by Eliot and Pound and elaborated by I. A. Richards and F. R. Leavis were predicated on certain assumptions about the scarcity of elite literary reputation. In the second chapter, I analyze how many of these assumptions – in particular, impersonality of critical method and autonomy of the objects of criticism – in fact disguise deep resemblances between public literary persona and the ideal, magisterial author presupposed in modernist theories of literary production.

By and large, women literary figures have been ill served by this apparatus. In my third and fourth chapters, I pursue this topic by investigating the recourse among modernists to the feminized, collaborative work of publicity. The key ingredient in elite modernist reputation, I argue, is not only the demonstration of high literary labor through imprimaturs and extant masterpieces, but also the capacity to frame work against contrastingly lesser labors of contemporaries, a scenario documented in accounts of modernist work in women's memoirs. The third chapter considers individual relationships staged between modernists. Examining the precarious position of women writers in Eliot's introductions and Pound's editing activities, I argue that their shared approach to the work of others calls for a revised interpretation of their celebrated shared work on *The Waste Land*. The fourth chapter turns to modernist intergroup relations and the dynamics of the new anthology system established in the 1910s and 1920s for advancing literary brands like the Georgians, the imagists, and Edith Sitwell's *Wheels* group. Here, I extend the thesis of the third chapter to the mechanisms of lionization, investigating a tendency in the anthologies' promotional logic to "find" certain figures and "lose" others, which I attribute, in part, to the factionalist ethos of its futurist origins.

My fifth chapter concerns the symbiosis of modernist reputation and the arts and culture superstructure emerging in interwar England. It examines the tension between Wyndham Lewis's prewar disdain for existing cultural institutions and his postwar bid to transform the London museum establishment into a modernist portrait gallery. I show how Lewis revises the prevailing portraiture ideal to accommodate the promotional logic of imprimaturs. Again, as in the four other case studies, modernism is already at work crossing the border, closing the gap, and bridging high/low cultural divides. What is more, the purchase placed on managing a version of public notoriety increases as the duration of this notoriety increases, the growing span between the notoriety of the present and the original narratives of prewar lionization. Progressively, modernists strove to get the most effect from their existing renown in the popular press, over national radio, and from associations with cultural institutions, practices which served as feedback loops for publicizing and sustaining their careers, reputations, and imprimaturs.

"How did this book get into my series?"

On Amazon.com, someone pretending to be Henry McBride – the seminal, long-deceased critic of modernist art – asks this of Lawrence Rainey's *Institutions of Modernism*, published in Yale's Henry McBride Series in Modernism and Modernity. Strangely enough, this joke, however recondite, seems to characterize a recent pattern of response to materialist accounts of modernism. The idols of the modernist past – according to certain latter-day ventriloquists, at least – are outraged. The presumption figures prominently in a particularly indignant review of Rainey's book by Roger Kimball. McBride's criticism, Kimball writes,

> was the polar opposite of the grim, politicized irrelevancies that Rainey provides. The fact that Rainey is General Editor of the Henry McBride Series adds insult to injury. McBride was famous for his easygoing humor, so perhaps he is smiling at the irony of it all instead of rolling over in his grave . . . [F]or the patrons of this series commemorating the achievement of a great critic – *Institutions of Modernism* must be regarded as an impertinence that is as offensive as it is calculated to be.[4]

Best known for his anti-academe jeremiads, Kimball is no friend to the modes of intellectual inquiry current in academic discourse. His misrepresentation of the genesis of cultural studies, for instance – a "popular pseudo-discipline that resulted from crossing Marxist animus with deconstructionist verbiage" – is so procrustean it is best read as a barometer of his intellectual bad-faith.[5] Given such conspicuous ill will, it is less noteworthy that Kimball finds a work like Rainey's objectionable than that he singles it out as representative: the arch-symptom of the purported vices of "chic academic criticism."[6]

Rainey's fevered brand of archival materialism and altogether measured theoretical claims hardly exemplify recent trends in academic criticism (let alone Kimball's caricatured sense of a "discipline in crisis").[7] In fact, Rainey makes a far more specific intervention – all the more offensive to Kimball because its specific purchase on the material underpinning of modernist culture threatens the *ex nihilo* brand of cultural authority he cherishes. It entails telling the unofficial, often all too commonplace stories of modernist cultural production, tracing a selection of modernist masterpieces – *The Waste Land, Ulysses, A Draft of XVI Cantos, The Collected Poems of H.D.* – to their initial sites of patronage, promotion, and publication. The case studies exhibit an astonishing pattern: modernism's crowning successes often depend on their promotion among non-readers, a network of cultural producers not necessarily concerned with putting the aesthetic artifacts themselves first. "Not-reading," he provocatively suggests, is instrumental to modernism's "institutional profile," and, thus, he cautions his readers with "literary critical training" to expect "little of the detailed examination of actual works that is sometimes held to be the only important or worthwhile form of critical activity."[8]

This *caveat emptor* anticipates the consternation of readers like Kimball who complain that "Rainey is really not interested in novels or poems."[9] What's really off the table, though, is the presumption that modernist novels and poems are self-positing works. Rainey's achievement is his recognition that understanding modernism as a mode and means of cultural production means moving beyond the hard carapaces of modernist masterpieces, beyond both the critical practices founded on a "unilateral focus on [their] formal devices" and sifting them for residue of "ideological constellations." Bracketing these concerns for "the actual works" – that is, the actual contents strictly defined – allows Rainey to move his examination to "the intervenient institutions that connect works to readerships, or readerships to particular social structures."[10] In practice, then, what Rainey calls "not reading" actually means reading other things and interpretation by other means. In his over-saturated end-notes, one finds a prodigious amount of reading: lecture programs, travel-guides, bibliographies, biographies, mass distributed periodicals, publishers' ledgers, newspapers, little magazines, family histories, memoirs, exhibition catalogues, letters, reviews, and criticism. As this course in *reading other things* implies, the history of modernism's "structural logic and development" is embedded in the very types of writing its logic and development tended to erase, that is, the kinds of discourse it habitually marks as subordinate, minor, un-literary, or, worst of all, commercial. Further, the full range and extent of the practices, conventions, and institutions that regulate modernist cultural production remain one of the principal blind spots of contemporary criticism.

This form of neglect pinches modernist studies especially hard, and the kind of outrage Kimball directs at *Institutions of Modernism* helps explain why.

The presumed offense boils down to this: modernist culture is ordinary. We arrive at the unthinkable formulation: modernist cultural production is, in fact, cultural production. One imagines paroxysms in the offices of the *New Criterion*. No formula seems more at odds with the familiar accounts of modernist cultural activity – from the "extraordinary literary and critical authority" and elite pretensions of minority culture Kimball finds so beguiling to its claims to aesthetic autonomy and purported resistance to the mass marketplace.[11] Yet, surely modernism is also, among other things, ordinary. As producers of culture, modernists were keenly involved with the exigencies of making a place for themselves in the world and for their products in the cultural marketplace. Look at Pound's letter to Eliot's father in 1915, for example, anxiously making the case that Eliot's prospects for a career abroad in "unpopular writing" actually constitutes sound economy.[12] Not only does being an unpopular writer provide a living equal to that earned by practitioners of respectable professions like law, medicine, or the clergy, but, Pound reckons, it also provides the added benefits of "an infinitely more interesting life."[13]

Modernist culture is ordinary, then, in the particular sense Raymond Williams obtains in "Culture Is Ordinary." Modernist culture pairs descriptive claims about a whole way of life with prescriptive formulas about arts and culture. Modernism is more than just the instances of conscious "modernist" artistry. The "ordinary" idioms, practices, and institutions by which modernist aesthetic objects became known – that is, the ubiquitous tissue of promotion – are "modernist," too. Williams's famous polemic hinges on the synthesis of these descriptive and prescriptive meanings of the word "culture." On the one hand, the sociological, culture is "a whole way of life – the common meanings"; on the other, the axiological, it is "the arts and learning – the special processes of discovery and creative effort." "Some writers," Williams writes, "reserve the word for one or the other of these senses; I insist on both, and on the significance of their conjunction . . . Culture is ordinary in every society and every mind."[14] Modernist culture is ordinary yet everywhere mystified; that is where my book starts: the sociology of modernist axiology.[15]

Pound, for example, proves he is not detached from this logic of material causes when he tells Eliot's father in 1915 that a "man succeeds either by the scarceness or the abundance of copy."[16] Four years on, Eliot has the promotional strategy all worked out: there are only two ways in which a writer can become important – to write a great deal, and have his writings appear everywhere, or to write very little. It is a question of temperament. I write very little, and I should not become more powerful by increasing my output. My reputation in London is built upon one small volume of verse, and is kept up by printing two or three more poems in a year. The only thing that matters is that these should be perfect in their kind, so that each should be an event.[17]

As I have already proposed, one of the chief obstacles to materialist accounts of modernism is the very critical apparatus erected by modernist writers like Pound and Eliot; publicists like John Middleton Murry, Edward Marsh, and Edwin Muir; and, eventually, academic allies like I. A. Richards, the Leavises, and the *Scrutiny* writers. That is to say, a critical regime that fetishizes peerless originality and conjures forth free-floating aesthetic artifacts obscures the difficult passage of the modernist text to its readers: not only the promotional uses of criticism but also a host of other necessary cultural labors. For this reason in particular – contrary to Rainey's emphasis on pseudo-aristocratic prerogatives of patronage – we should perhaps look to modernism's critical idioms for its most formidable institutions. These services were its most effective means of promotion. While such labors have never been wholly hidden from view, they have never been on display in modernism's canonical masterpieces either. Swept to one side of its arch literary compositions, books-in-print, and collected works, they have been nevertheless enshrined in the bibliographic record.[18] Prominently documented in the host of bibliographic endeavors modernists undertook in the period in addition to high literary labor, the collaborative promotion of modernist idiom is documented in modernist limited editions, small magazines, little reviews, introductions, editing, anthologies, and other cultural furnishings.

My book shares in a new turn in modernist studies towards what could be described as a post-romantic phenomenology of "influence" and the concomitant materialities of promotion: "influence" and promotion as imbricated vectors of cultural input and output.[19] The chapters that follow persistently emphasize authors and forms of authorship over, say, formalist or post-formalist accounts of modernist canons of masterpieces. Be warned, though – after an examination of the imprimatur in chapter one, more "not-reading" than "reading" (to appropriate Rainey's critical terms) of modernist masterpieces follows. While these matters do not quite represent a sea-change for modernist studies, they serve instead as fragments shored against its ruins, older critical constellations which merit rewriting, renewed scrutiny, and reformulation. When it comes to "influence" and promotion, causation is complex, sometimes even multidirectional, mediated by a system of "exchanges" – to choose a suitably multidirectional and economic term – which is made possible by the warrants of literary names. The focus here is what could be roughly described as modernist self-fashioning, the instrumentality of signs of "authorship" not only for modernist projects and idioms but also for its critical posterity. When it comes to modernist studies, it seems, the name of the author won't go away. As so many entrance and exit visas, authorial names warrant the exchanges, the translations, the bearing of bodies and discourses. At best, authors are forever elusive, off-stage paring fingernails, feigning disinterest.[20] In their "diminished" capacities, however, they're arranging a host of contacts, ordinary labors, and promotional exchanges.

In any case, the usual suspects are well represented here. This book makes the looming presence of the familiar exchanges of modernist author-geniuses in modernist studies the very object of its analysis – those figures who fit into Pound's famous taxonomy of literary posterity as "masters" and "inventors," or who Foucault might have called the founders of modernist discursivity.[21] More tellingly, perhaps, the rest of Pound's taxonomy is also well represented: "the diluters," "the workers in 'the style of the period,'" "the belle lettrists," "the starters of crazes." To the Poundian rogues' gallery, we should add the indispensable literary workers Robert McAlmon disparagingly refers to as "intriguers" and "politicians" in the unexpurgated version of *Being Geniuses Together*.[22] Demystifying the mysterious processes between modernist bodies and discourses entails a quite literal and rigorous understanding of exchange, I think, one that directly accounts for the regulative institutional, technological, and, yes, economic frameworks that make modernist culture possible.

TOWARDS AN AXIOLOGY OF MODERNISM

Undertaking no less than a unified field theory of symbolic equivalence and exchange, Jean-Joseph Goux writes that in the

drift of value objects, of interchangeable parts, a hierarchy (of values) develops, a principle of order and subordination which places the great (manifold and polymorphous) majority of "signs". . . under the sacred command of a select few among them. In certain points of condensation, value seems to gather, capitalize, centralize itself investing certain elements with a privileged representativeness and even with a monopoly on representativeness within the diverse set of which they are members. The mysterious genesis of this privilege is effaced, leaving their monopoly absolute, absolved, exempted in their transcendent role as standard and measure of values.[23]

Plug modernist names in the foregoing as so many condensation points and the cunning of Goux's formulation for modernist studies becomes apparent. Condensation – a word with suggestive chemical, meteorological, and psychoanalytic connotations – both points to the accumulation of exaggerated hierarchy around *certain privileged* authors and undermines it as a kind of bogus sublime from which underpinnings of denser states of matter can be recovered ("the genesis of this ascendancy," "the genesis of every *institutionalization*," "to reconstitute the dictates of this stage direction"). Conceptually speaking, condensation is materialist; unlike sublimation, it moves from the immaterial to solid states of matter. Thus, it provides a keen analytic razor for seemingly incorporeal problematics such as modernist authorial immanence. Modernist imprimaturs condense (capitalize from the cultural field at large to *privileged representativeness* to *monopoly on representativeness*) because of an incentive-laden hoarding of value that was a deliberate part of its promotional logic.

Certainly, at the individual level, the assignment of literary value can be volitional, as, at communal level, it can be communicative.[24] In the history of the drift of value objects, it is also possible to track more comprehensive forms of interestedness, the promotional will to value as a form of modernist agency, for instance. I propose, in other words, to track the points of origin and terminus of drifts by better studying recent currents. The agents of modernist value are numerable and specifiable. The condensation of exaggerated cultural value around them depends not only on necessary promotional work but also on its habitual effacement. My contention is that something akin to surplus value, to invoke the specter of Marx, brings modernists into being as spectral forms of exaggerated hierarchy and confers upon them exchangeability. The materialist message is, to be brief, that modernist value capitalizes. It capitalizes through the systematic devaluation and effacement of a host of promotional and other literary labors first by modernist others and later in multiple scenes of reading and assorted cultural encounters. Detached, disembodied reputations have the visionary appearance of bodily agency and textual form, because of a host of necessary literary and semiotic labors. Whether reputations serve as capital or coins comes down to issues of availability. In their more solid form, they serve as capital, stores of value, hoarded assets available for use in the production of further value, expertise, and prestige. As coins, liquid assets, they serve as a medium of exchange and unit of account – standards for defining value relationally. That reputations serve both cultural roles – means to hoard and to exchange value – is borne out through the second current alluded to earlier, namely the drive to inexorable devaluation.

A brief detour from the specter of Marx to the specter of Nietzsche helps explain this: Nietzsche's famous aphorism likening linguistic denotation to money – dead metaphors to worn coins – is not just a noteworthy early observation about the commodity character of language; it is also a suggestive meditation about the ghostly figure of reputation as the misplaced mediator of the process:

> What . . . is truth? A mobile army of metaphors, metonymies, and anthropomorphisms – in short, a sum of human relations which became poetically and rhetorically intensified, metamorphosed, and adorned and after long usage seem to a nation fixed, canonic, and binding: truths are illusions about which one has forgotten that they *are* illusions; worn-out metaphors which have become powerless to affect the senses; coins which have their obverse effaced and now are no longer of account as coins but merely as metal.[25]

As Goux points out, this passage itself has become something of a dead metaphor, if only because now, having dismantled the gold standard, we are twice dead from commodity money. Yet, for all the inquiry into this theme, the discussion tends to fly over one of its most provocative implications: the inevitable role of devaluation and decay as a driving force in the circulation of both words and things.[26] The connection depends on the uncanny appearance of a third term from someplace beyond words and things: the haunting image of embodied authority as a regulative idea. "Faces" are the defining features of coins; wearing them away removes their sensuous power. Like coins themselves, reputations are media of specular exchange. Like coins, they devalue. Like coins, they lose their powers of sensuous specularity through both over-use (handling, shaving, clipping, proofing, counterfeiting) and, yes, hoarding (more about which shortly).

Reputations are like coins, and coins are like reputations. The two share a foundational mythos from which Nietzsche draws his aphorism, one blurring any handy distinction of metaphoric tenor and vehicle.[27] Reputation is, at bottom, face value. Face value, the value signifier, defines itself beyond the value signified, just as the face value of the coin defines itself beyond the signified value of a coin as so much precious metal. Once out of the box, it is undermined by its signified, for circulation entails wear, bag marks, chop marks, counterfeiting, corrosion, and so on. Once circulated, face value – returning more deliberately to Nietzsche's analogy – stands as a harbinger of inevitable debasement; denotation gives way to the coming loss of denotation. Nietzsche's "worn coin" calls to mind Gresham's law – the idea that worn coins chase away unworn ones. With time, the impression, or what is left of it, becomes a standard for departing with worn coins and hoarding unworn ones. More and more unworn coins are hoarded. More and more worn coins circulate. Eventually, it is not just the aggregate quality of circulated currency that decays but the reputation of the whole and finally the premise of denotation as such. What holds for the reputation of coins holds for elite modernist reputation in the age of celebrity: its value, its very visionary appearance, comes together, with a nod to Beckett, at once astride a grave and a difficult birth.

If celebrity presents a kind of authorial self-fashioning *in extremis*, then modernism may be best understood in terms of its struggle for dead cultural authority, its complex material intersection of practices, protocols, and institutions conveying ostensible cultural continuity and legitimacy, on the one hand, and internal instability and bogus pretension, on the other.[28] Redefined thus, modernism is less a periodizing term or a bundle of formal concerns than a historically circumscribed mode of presenting value and prescribing frameworks of expectations. It resembles, in this regard, what Peter Osborne calls a "real abstraction," "a social relation, constituted through, but by no means exhausted by, historically specific but socially diverse practices of recognition."[29] The real difficulties of the modernist rubric are now so well known that the point has become all but perfunctory. John Harwood's observation that modernism, "in any of the reified versions now deployed in academic debate, did not exist in 1909, or 1922 [but] is an academic invention . . . retrospectively imposed on the works and doctrines it supposedly illuminates," makes sense, but it requires a qualification: the historical "modernism" played an active part in its own reification.[30] Stan Smith, for instance, argues that – on an empirical basis, at least – the now familiar claim that "modernism" is a retroactive construction is erroneous. Although it only took hold after the "appearance of the usurping tanist, 'postmodernism,'" the usage "in our current restricted sense has in fact surfaced and disappeared with equal rapidity in every decade of this century."[31] From *in or about December 1910* (as Woolf punches the clock with notorious elusiveness in "Mr. Bennett and Mrs. Brown"), it seems we've always been modernists; it's just we can't help forgetting.

To remember means distinguishing "historical modernism" from "existing" modernism from the start. By "historical modernism," I mean modernism posed as a kind of inductive category, particular "facts" from which generalizations follow. The problem here is that more often than not, the "facts" pan out to be particular names – brands, if you will – and the bundle of associations, qualities, and properties they organize. "Historical modernism" finally amounts to the product descriptions invented to contain stylistics adduced in, say, Eliot, Joyce, Pound, Woolf, or Stein. It is "historical" – prone to fixation on born-on and expire-on dates – because it is over, and, because it is ultimately tied to an idea of generation, it carries a robust notion of the author as the productive source for cultural work yet remains critically blind to it.[32] By contrast, the concept I aver, "existing" modernism, proceeds from the general premise that the conditions of production, circulation, and consumption at work in the so-called "historical modernism" still exist. However attenuated, these conditions, in one form or another, still obtain. So conceived, a critique of "existing" modernism can help modernist studies account for its blind spots vis-à-vis the author function and the afterlife of "historical modernist" value. So conceived, the critique would also have important things to tell us about "the organization of cultural value in the advanced capitalist world," taking a page from John Frow's *Cultural Studies and Cultural Value.*[33]

"Existing" modernism, then, speaks from a new way of cultural valuation, a way in which knowledge of labor processes – in particular, a collector's knowledge of how cultural labor regulates the flow of value to cultural commodities – becomes preeminent. The impetus here is doubly post-Marxist, motivated partly by Harold Perkin's historical account in *The Rise of Professional Society* and partly by a qualified version of Pierre Bourdieu's cultural theory.[34] From Perkin, I borrow an account and a late nineteenth-century timeline for an emergent fraction of professionals (experts, managers, knowledge workers, academics, intellectuals, etc.) who depend on managing flows of expert knowledge, prestige, and technical know-how for affecting privileged status within certain market exigencies (as opposed to, say, merely hoarding them for class ornamentation). From Bourdieu, I borrow a methodological emphasis on material practices and mediators and a recognition of "the economic world reversed" – that certain economics are at work within professional society in spite of – and also because of – a sheen of preservation from the market.

Several key modifications of Bourdieu are in order, though, especially with respect to his trademark concept, cultural capital. I agree with Frow that the modes of high culture central to Bourdieu's thesis rate here and now (and, thus, in "existing" modernism) as little more than a latter-day irrelevancy. Due to the rise of mass audience structures and competencies, coupled with the sheer proliferation and serial ubiquity of mass commodity culture, elite cultural capital understood as distinction no longer carries the class legitimating functions Bourdieu ascribes to it.[35] But, rather than frame this as a triumph of mass over elite, it makes sense to me to follow Perkin's lead and recast the critical scene as an infiltration of micro-techniques of hierarchy throughout the social system, a process well underway if we return to the alleged scene of the "historical modernism" in the twentieth century's first decades. The point is that, at the same moment elite becomes irrelevant as elite, the system surreptitiously trades from top to bottom on its afterimage; a kind of "high regard" permeates and, after a fashion, guarantees the inner workings of the system, even if it takes the form of "covert" prestige.[36]

Here is the strategic relevance both of Goux's metaphorics and of a more literal turn to Marx's labor theory of value. Unlike Bourdieu, Marx makes the following clear about capital creation: it concentrates productive value in the hands of the few and expropriates surplus value from the many.[37] Like Frow, I want to hold more closely to this conception than Bourdieu does, but doing so begs two questions of the notion of cultural capital. First, to borrow from Frow, where is "the axis of exploitation"? If we posit that "the possession of skill assets . . . does not *in itself* constitute an exploitative relation to those without them," then exploitation is hard to find.[38] Second, following the classic Marxist opposition between living and dead labor: isn't cultural capital – incorporated as modernist imprimaturs, for instance – stored value and therein non-productive labor?

Modernists help us past these theoretical impasses, insofar as modernists are *not* possessors of cultural capital. Despite significant elective affinities and a shared provenance (discussed in detail in chapter one), modernists are *not* professionals – not exactly anyway. If not as possessors of professional knowledge, they are better understood as aspirants to the status of capital. They (their names, their reputations) comprise so much embodied professional knowledge – bodies-in-texts, signatures of value, imprimaturs. Their scarce, meticulously maintained cultural imprints bear capital for others *ab initio*. If the axis of "exploitation" is necessarily cast with production, the producers of regimes of modernist value cannot be the modernist authors, not in any biographically reductive sense, at any rate. Instead, this axis is produced by the signs of the authorial value mobilized by cadres of reverent "readers," those who all too readily play the part of modernism's alienated labor. Modernists are, in these terms, positioned as real abstractions for a reorganization of value in which reputation itself – as so much condensed of surplus value – becomes productive: modernist value is experienced as a labor of the living dead.[39]

VISIONARY OTHERS

"Would it not be an excellent thing if this sense of presence, impelling one to speak only as though the author were here at one's side listening to one's every inflection, could become a universal rule in criticism?"[40] This question comes from I. A. Richards' obituary for Eliot: Richards explicitly experiences Eliotic "influence" as a labor of the living dead. No longer suffering the absent author's personality means stamping the mind which creates into portable proof coin. Without question, other proof coins circulate besides Eliot and his fellow Men of 1914. Rather than counterexamples these may be seen as alternate configurations of the promotional dynamics within a shared cultural system. We can look to Virginia Woolf, for instance. "Other than Eliot," Stephen Spender writes, "the only two older writers who made themselves *present* to contemporaries twenty years younger were E. M. Forster and Virginia Woolf."[41] Adam Parkes argues that Woolf's late entrée into public *engagement* in the 1930s – her move from domestic to political tyranny in *Three Guineas*, especially – comes as she vets the "problems of representation and selfhood that preoccupied [her] throughout her career" through haunting visions of the personalities of Bloomsbury as she writes and revises *Roger Fry: A Biography*.[42] Having Bloomsbury's resident theorist of formalism and aesthetic disinterestedness as a subject, Parkes argues, raises a kind of flaming sword over all matters of personality in ways that led Woolf's writing to a new synthesis. A phrase in the Woolf diaries captures a significant leitmotif of this process:

I have been thinking about Censors. How visionary figures admonish us . . . If I say this So & So will think me sentimental. If that . . . will think me Bourgeois. All books now seem to me surrounded by a circle of invisible censors. Hence their selfconsciousness, their restlessness. It wd. be worth while trying to discover what they are at the moment. Did Wordsworth have them? I doubt it.[43]

Visionary figures admonish us. And being admonished is, *pace* Harold Bloom, something altogether different than being made anxious. Being admonished entails bringing the presence of visionary others into the open – in both senses, into consciousness and into publicity.[44] As the comments above indicate, the presence of Fry, Forster, Eliot, Joyce, Mansfield, and others is a part of the public record in Woolf's mind and work.[45]

The summonsing of visionary censors is revealing. The presence of visionary others made Woolf, above all else, self-conscious about the self-possessiveness of modernist idiom. As Parkes notes,

Fry himself warned Woolf against the dangers of a stylistic egotism – a tendency toward unbridled self-expression, or personal self-assertion – that he detected in *her* work. In a letter to Marie Mauron (21 December 1926), Fry expressed doubts about the "Time Passes" section of *To the Lighthouse* (1927), doubts that Woolf later recalled in her diary, where she agreed with Fry that she overdid "the prose lyric vein." Woolf added: "That was by the way the best criticism I've had for a long time: that I poetise my inanimate scenes, stress my personality; dont let the meaning emerge from the matiere – Certainly I owe Roger #150." Message gratefully received, in other words, and carefully – though perhaps only half-jokingly–priced.[46]

There are two ironies here. The first is that Fry levels the charge at Woolf's least inhabited piece of writing: all subjectivity in "Time Passes" being strictly parenthetical, it is the sample of her fiction most assiduously devoid of personality (the exception of the lingering subaltern housekeeper noted). Nevertheless, the charge should sound familiar: modernist technique generates literary artifacts that are over-wrought with authorship, durable goods heavily marked with the surplus value of imprimaturs. The surfeit of absent personality folds back on personality, the departing author returning as if per Möbius strip. The second irony is that it takes a visionary other to raise the charge.

Modernist handiwork is at once too, too clever (by turns, too self-conscious, too experimental, too obscure, too indecent) to be denied as a form of personality – as a highly personalized, even outré, form of showing off. In "Mr. Bennett and Mrs. Brown," Woolf herself admonishes Eliot and Joyce for such excesses – even as she felt her own work standing in the dock likewise accused. Modernist authorial immanence starts to seem worryingly indistinguishable from the forms of publicity and promotion best left to secondary literary work. This sentiment was by no means the sole property of Bloomsbury: from another direction, with Joseph Conrad over his shoulder, Ford Madox Ford came up with the following observation in 1914: "the Impressionist author is sedulous to avoid letting his personality appear in the course of his book. On the other hand, his whole book, his whole poem is merely an expression of his personality."[47] The publicizing function of modernist authorship must be everywhere observed yet everywhere denied. Ford's impressionism is roughly synonymous with Woolf's Georgianism, and, as with Woolf's comments on Eliot and Joyce, Ford lodges his assessment in the course of a conflicted, somewhat disingenuous discussion of possible objections to modern literary technique. Variously, there are elements of national chauvinism, gender privilege, and class-bound elitism bound up in these apprehensive responses, elements which even Fry, Woolf, and Ford cannot resist, but the overarching objection, I think, expresses resistance to an unavoidable kinship between modernism's exaggerated forms of authorial immanence and the exaggerating work of publicity, promotion, and celebrity.

Thus, the critical problem at stake in the work of modernism in an age of celebrity is not detecting "influence" internalized as a hidden mechanism in the dual creation of literary artifacts and authorial egos. Rather it involves noticing the ubiquitous and all too conscious materiality of imprimaturs in scenes of reading and promotion. The point is that these visions render themselves external as promotional vehicles whatever their provenance, be it in primary and secondary literary work, up- or downstream in literary production. This is the way "Eliot" makes use of the coinage of Yeats, naming him as "part of the consciousness of an age which cannot be understood without [him]" and in the same essay describing him as "a contemporary and not a predecessor."[48] It is also the way numerous figures use "Eliot" (Pound, Barnes, Richards, Auden, Spender, Crane, Ellison, Chandler, and Waugh, for starters), and numerous others link their reputations to an experience of "Joyce" (Barnes, Upward, Hemingway, Fitzgerald, Beckett, Behan, for starters). We can see this with "Joyce" in Michael Arlen's *Green Hat*; "Woolf" in the novels of Henry Green; "Hemingway" in Kerouac's *On the Road*; "Lawrence" in Dangarembga's *Nervous Conditions*; "Yeats" in Achebe's *Things Fall Apart*; and on and on. Though linked to notions of authorial agency through the coincidence of the will to self-promotion and capitalized aggregate hierarchy, the phenomenon exceeds any individual scene of authorial self-fashioning. In effect, it is always the modernist coin that authors its own recirculation – not least in the work achieved when the coin circulates through the work of others. Brendan Behan travesties this supreme abstraction in the early 1960s in a lecture before the James Joyce Society. Having made conspicuous his promotional use of "James Joyce" all night, Behan caps off the event with the following specimen of mock solemnity: "in praising James Joyce we all praise ourselves and we all hope that some of the glory that is his . . . rubs off on us, and, ladies and gentlemen, I have nothing further to say on the matter."[49]

CHAPTER I

Imprimaturs

In London in 1915, the young T. S. Eliot asked Ezra Pound to write a testimonial to his father stateside to assure him about his prospective career choice: "I can only cite my own case as proof," Pound wrote,

> that it is possible to exist by [literary work], not only by popular fiction but by unpopular writing . . . I have made enough to live on with some comfort . . . I am now much better off than if I had kept on my professorship in Indiana, and I believe I am as well off as various of my friends who had plugged away at law, medicine, and preaching.[1]

The letter documents an improbable twist in literary employment history. Conditions are such that it all but goes without saying that the so-called serious literary life – based upon, to cite Pound's phrases, "unpopular writing," "a few grave articles in the heavier reviews," and "a certain amount of current criticism" – is improbable, a material non-starter. Eliot certainly has his doubts. Only two days before this letter was written, upon marrying Vivienne Haigh-Wood, he recorded with the marriage registrar that he had "no occupation." Yet, against the prevailing view – that literary life is no occupation – modernists insisted again and again that ostensibly unpopular writing could provide compensable work by offering another order of compensation altogether, compensation enhanced, as it were, by speculation in the signifiers of elite literary authority.

In the rising ethos of professionalism in the nineteenth century, a terrible beauty is born – one which we might also call a rough beast: the modernist. In *Modernism, Mass Culture, and Professionalism*, Thomas Strychacz adduces a number of striking resemblances between modernists and professionals. Both have "de facto monopolies" on certain forms of speech and technique. Both attempt "to demarcate a space that exists culturally, economically, and linguistically apart from mass culture and the imperatives of the mass market."[2] Both offer their expertise *sui generis* – accessible, by definition, to only a few initiates. More than anything else, the link between the two domains rests upon this last resemblance, the role of "esoteric knowledge" in both modernist literature and professional protocol as a means of keeping the "mass public" at arm's length.[3]

Despite the similarities, however, we should hesitate to classify the modernist as but another species of the professional genus. As Pound tells Eliot's father, being a modernist is not quite the same as being a professor, a lawyer, a doctor, or a clergyman. The main reason is this: whereas shared protocols, languages, and institutions make it possible – even economically rewarding – for most professionals to work "outside the exigency of market forces," modernism largely did not compensate its practitioners either with significant social power or with significant material rewards.[4] Ultimately, the payoff of expert knowledge accrued among modernism's readers rather than its practitioners. Demanding rigor and high seriousness, the casting off of amateurish reading habits, the institution of disciplined canons of literary studies, modernism, in a sense, professionalized its readers. Taken to extreme, it enabled its most attentive readers to become professional academics, forsake mass culture, and take up the thesis, the Ph.D., and the professorial chair instead. In return, academic professionals supplied modernist discourse with a secure place in emerging institutions – a "market shelter" in universities, specialized academic presses, and high culture canons. In short, literary critics and scholars rewarded modernist discourse with the career, prestige, and institutional placement modernism's originators and practitioners were largely denied among the shouts of the marketplace.[5] This substitution of modernist discourse for modernist authors – texts for bodies – is a habit worth pausing over. The cunning passage of the modernist career often depends on such transpositions of agency. When Wyndham Lewis, for example, calls his memoirs an autobiography of a career, the phrase lets him hybridize a body of texts and a text of bodies while eschewing both biographical self-fashioning and bibliographical text-fashioning. In effect, modernists like Lewis were putting "the new insistence on the power of experts and their possession of symbolic capital" to decidedly different ends than professionals. They did not become professional experts *per se*; instead, they became objects of professional expertise. The very insistent, taxing character of expert knowledge follows an epistemological fault line that resonates with Andreas Huyssen's "Great Divide."[6] Under these conditions, romantic notions of authors as active and resisting social agents appear superfluous; modernist texts themselves seem to have their own agencies. If the notion of the author does not disappear, reference to it ceases to be constitutive of the reader's work. Across the fault line, however, the notion of elite literary authority takes on a regulative function, providing tacit guidelines for how the work is to be used as an object of knowledge but without seeming to play any fundamental role in the make-up of that knowledge.

So, unlike professionals – yet partly because of them – modernists had no reason to play the role of agents of knowledge. Instead, the same modernists, often so critical of the destructive consequences of capitalist valuation, helped create a shadow economy, itself based on the scarcity of a commodity, the manifestation of artistic identity in textual form. With modernism, authorship instead resembles a kind of textual imprimatur. "The great modernisms," as Fredric Jameson writes, were "predicated on the invention of a personal, private style, as unmistakable as your fingerprint, as incomparable as your own body."[7] By the word "imprimatur," I mean the sense Jameson's statement invokes, one familiar from countless accounts of modernism, that the modernist literary object bears the stylistic stamp of its producer prominently. At once as a distinctive mark and a sanctioning impression, the imprimatur, as I define it, turns the author into a formal artifact, fusing it to the text as a reified signature of value. The imprimatur, then, represents a moment of clarity to all takers against the apparent obscurity of modernist meaning and the phenomenal disappearance of the author's body.[8]

The concept of imprimaturs is useful because it lets us examine modernist authorship without relegating it into a structural enigma. Imprimaturs sanction elite, high cultural consumption in times when economies of mass cultural value predominate. For this reason, they serve as effective cultural capital for the academic professionals who presented themselves as agents of arbitrage between high and low. The same imprimaturs that set modernist texts apart from the mass marketplace also set modernist authors apart from writer-professionals, who believe that they produce texts not according to a principle of distinction but to one of professional standards.

What I seek to do in this chapter is, first, sketch a narrative genealogy of the imprimatur; and, second, suggest how, interposed in the scene of reading fictions of literary life, the imprimatur acts to regulate the scene that occasions it, while making political agency a particularly troublesome remainder. The line of descent of the imprimatur of modernist authorship begins with the modernists themselves for whom this imprimatur, laid out in the text itself, came to represent a sovereign site for artistic consciousness in lieu of other representations of authorial mind and body. As a means of literary promotion, the imprimatur signified a repudiation of the reified personality of the "real-life" author and a willful refusal of (and alternative to) the ethos of literary professionalism. Beginning with examples from

Henry James's middle period, I want to discuss the cues about reading the imprimatur embedded in modernist fictions of literary life. In such narratives, modernists explore the social and political possibilities of the imprimatur as an ethos of artistic consciousness, an ethos made visible by comparing the Jamesian precedent to the most frequently invoked High Modernist author–novel, James Joyce's *A Portrait of the Artist as a Young Man*. Finally, considering stories of literary life set in the 1930s, Edward Upward's *Journey to the Border*, Christopher Isherwood's *Prater Violet*, and Evelyn Waugh's *Vile Bodies*, I want to investigate how these notions about authorship begin to break down as fictions of literary life are subsequently rewritten.

Pound's sanguine letter to Eliot's father aside, being an author in modern times, especially the kind publishing *unpopular writings*, is a distinctly problematic occupation – not least, financially problematic. James had a private income, which fortuitously increased as his ability to place his work in magazines decreased. Joyce, on his employment record in Trieste, describes himself as an *insegnante privato*, a private teacher, yet, on the same document, clearly represents his primary activity as literary production, listing stories, poems, and literary essays under the section for relevant publications.[9] Waugh, who eventually crosses the great divide by living exclusively from best-seller royalties, planned his epitaph to read "Evelyn Waugh, Writer," a reminder lest they forget.[10] Indeed, as his overcompensation counsels, the occupation of the author looks least bumpy, least fragmentary, in retrospect. The five authors under consideration here paid for their literary lives in ways that were often *ad hoc*, short-lived, and heterogeneous: some relating to literary production directly (selling stories, journalism and occasional writing, book advances, sales, royalties, and screenwriting), others less so (inheritance, patronage, teaching, soldiering, working in a bank or as an advance agent for a cinema). For twenty years, Upward stopped publishing altogether. Is the sustained hiatus part of literary life, too?

"Authors may be dead, literarily and theoretically," writes Joyce Piell Wexler, "yet we continue to believe that the literature we value is grounded in the lives of the people who wrote it."[11] Equally obstinate is the mythology that the lives of authors culminate in literature we value. As the biographical details above suggest, authors such as James, Joyce, and Waugh were laboring, like Pound and Eliot, in an ill-formed occupation, a lack to which their narratives about authorship repeatedly and productively return. James – a literary career moving from well-consumed, early fiction to increasingly indigestible later writings – is a logical beginning point for this genealogy. His stories of literary life are among the first strategic interventions of imprimaturs in the crisis over the occupational possibilities extracted from the production of unpopular writing. Joyce's *Portrait* is the *locus classicus*. The Joycean imprimatur – drawn from the reader's experience of Stephen Dedalus – transforms the possibility of exemplary artistic consciousness that James was after in his stories of literary life to a new language of selfhood, one that conveys certain social and political possibilities. Upward's *Journey to the Border*, Isherwood's *Prater Violet*, and Waugh's *Vile Bodies* do not mark end points in the genealogy but rather places of branching off. In these works, new exigencies strain the kinship with the versions of literary life presented by James and Joyce, but they continue to draw on an archly modernist scene of reading, strategically delimited by imprimaturs.

DIFFICULT IMPRESSIONS

The prefaces to *The New York Edition of the Works of Henry James* are staged like an archeological hoax. Loading an oeuvre's worth of literary artifacts at once, James seems to have set them up with the coy awareness of the scholars, biographers, and critics to come. As several essays collected in David McWhirter's *Henry James's New York Edition: The Construction of Authorship* attest, the prefaces do more than supply an authoritative and extremely subtle framework for his work; they also form an "extraordinary, [yet] deeply ambiguous act of self-presentation."[12] The *New York Edition* prefaces provide James with an expansive staging area to assemble various authorial personae for his oeuvre and his readers. The typical artifact deposited there is an account of the *donnée*, the provoking cause for each story's composition, the story of the story.

One of James's most famous descriptions of this story of the story is in the preface to *The Spoils of Poynton*, volume seven of the New York Edition. He compares it to a wind-borne seed:

[A] lady beside me made in the course of talk one of those allusions that I have always found myself recognizing on the spot as "germs." The germ . . . has ever been for me the germ of a "story," and most of the stories straining to shape under my hand have sprung from a small single seed, a seed as minute and wind-blown as that casual hint for "The Spoils of Poynton" dropped unwittingly by my neighbour, a mere floating particle floating in the stream of talk.[13]

As a rule, James places the provoking cause beyond the author, traced to one foreign body or other, a fragment of conversation, a bit of gossip. Yet, in the preface to volume fifteen, the volume which contains a selection of stories of literary life – "The Lesson of the Master," "The Death of the Lion," "The Next Time," "The Figure in the Carpet," and "The Coxon Fund" – there is a crucial exception. The impetus for a story of literary life, he explains, is different in kind from others:

[W]hereas any anecdote about life pure and simple . . . proceeds almost as a matter of course from . . . some pencilled note on somebody else's case, so the material for any picture of personal states so specifically complicated as those of my hapless friends in the present volume will have been drawn preponderantly from the depths of the designer's own mind.[14]

Stories of literary life are not drawn from foreign bodies but from the author's mind in autopoesis, its own provoking cause. For the story of literary life, the story of the story *is* the story in it. His "hapless friends" – the specimens of the high literary life, Neil Paraday, Ralph Limbert, Hugh Vereker, John Delavoy and "other such supersubtle fry" – are the curious products of artistic consciousness reflecting on itself.[15]

James set these stories apart from his other work explicitly, calling them, for example, his "homogeneous group."[16] Stories like "The Death of the Lion" (1894), "The Next Time" (1895), "The Figure in the Carpet" (1896), and "John Delavoy" (1898) also maintain a level of thematic uniformity that justifies their closer scrutiny together. James wrote other fiction concerning authorship, but these four tales, written in a four-year stretch spanning his involvement with the *Yellow Book* and the *Guy Domville* fiasco, share a common critical object, the worthy author; a common narrative voice, the untrustworthy critic; and a common "antagonist," the crassness of modern public life. Their variations on the common theme, artistic consciousness *in extremis*, all end with the artist's frustration, death, and dubious posterity. The stories, he writes,

deal all with the literary life, gathering their motive, in each case, from some noted adventure, some felt embarrassment, some extreme predicament . . . [I]f they enjoy in common their reference to the troubled artistic consciousness, they make together, by the same stroke, this other rather blank profession, that few of them recall to me, however dimly, any scant pre-natal phase.[17]

James links his troubles accounting for the genesis of these stories with their troubled subject-matter, distressed authors: both represent blank professions, both document the difficulty of making impressions. Having to describe where his literary coevals come from leads James, somewhat awkwardly, to confront the provisional basis of his magisterial estimation of artistic consciousness. The difference between the two Jamesian accounts

of literary composition underscores how modernists like James view authorship, as a separate domain of consciousness with its own rules.

Faced with the ordinary material, the experience and consciousness of
others, authorship for James functions as a kind of superhuman aesthetic
instrument. It confers high aesthetic value upon everyday social life, by
recording and making public the "speck of truth, of beauty, of reality,
scarce visible to the common eye."[18] This notion of authorship, however,
makes the story of literary life somewhat perplexing. With authorship as its
own subject matter, the external, provoking cause disappears. It becomes
necessary for James to *postulate* literary eminence – for the author to postulate his own conditions of possibility. James frames this public exposure
in decidedly political terms.

In the preface to volume fifteen, he confesses that, some ten years after
writing the stories of literary life, he still finds himself troubled by a technical
hitch in their composition. The effect he was after in the stories required the
literary eminence of the authors, but, he acknowledges, such eminence can
be warranted in the stories themselves only by tendentious circumstantial
evidence, the testimony of an untrustworthy narrator. For the "emphasized effect," readers must simply take the great writer in each of the tales
on face value – as a representative of exemplary "artistic consciousness" –
evidence unseen. Readers, in effect, are asked to take literary genius "on
trust": to suppose "the 'importance' of the poor foredoomed monarch of
the jungle" without reading "chapter and verse for the eminence." At first,
James attributes this to the problems of stylistic economy, but, in the course
of his exegesis, it becomes clear that postulating literary eminence is the
founding premise of a political–aesthetic logic. Representing the belea-
guered circumstance of the literary genius, he claims, makes it a technical
necessity to postulate literary eminence. He even refers to his gallery of
"eminent cases" as "postulates." Thus, he willingly pleads "guilty to the
critical charge" of postulating literary eminence, "citing celebrities without
analogues and painting portraits without models," because he takes "the
charge" to mean that the actual literary scene no longer supports the notion
of the exemplary artist.[19]

As a group, these stories suggest, among other things, why the politics of
modernist authorship appears most pronounced contemplating its failures.
When the modernist imprimatur is thrown into ironic relief against an
indifferent literary marketplace and the indiscriminate fatuity of public
life, the backdrop elicits the imprimatur's political pretensions. The need
to postulate literary eminence, its implicit implausibility, shows, for James,

the degradation of exemplary "artistic consciousness" in an unresponsive mass marketplace:

> If the life about us for the last thirty years refuses to warrant for these examples, then so much the worse for that life. The *constatation* would be so deplorable that instead of making it we must dodge it: there are decencies that in the name of general self-respect we must take for granted, there's a kind of rudimentary intellectual honor to which we must, in the interest of civilisation, at least pretend.[20]

Civilization itself, it seems, rests upon postulating the existence of literary genius, postulating the possibility of "sensibility fine enough" to penetrate, if not counteract, "all the stupidity and vulgarity and hypocrisy" associated with public life as a mass marketplace. If public life systematically negates artistic consciousness, postulating it becomes public duty, described in language surprising (for James) in its civic concern:

> What one would fain do is to baffle any such calamity, to *create* the record, in default of any other enjoyment of it; to imagine, in a word, the honourable, the producible case. What better example than this of the high and helpful public and, as it were, civic use of the imagination? . . . How can one consent to make a picture of the preponderant futilities and vulgarities and miseries of life without the impulse to exhibit as well from time to time, in its place, some fine example of the reaction, the opposition or the escape?[21]

In order for the artist to illustrate the "preponderant futilities and vulgarities and miseries of life," the possibility of what James calls a "sensibility fine enough to react against these things" must be instantiated and recorded.

Because James characterizes the postulate of exemplary artistic consciousness in such heroic terms, it is a curious twist that each of his stories of literary life illustrates the undoing of literary eminence. Before, during, and sometimes even after their demise, James's author characters are subjected to public indignities, chiefly involving their debasement before the marketplace. This systematic debasement exposes the failings of authorial identity, as it is understood strictly within the narrative frame. Being an author, it seems, offers James's author characters no romantic inheritance – no hope of liberation from social conventions and no shelter from the marketplace. Only outside the discrete narrative frame, in the context of the imprimatur, do James's stories of literary life suggest the social and political potential promised in the prefaces.

For the reader who grants James three High Modernist stipulations, the fictional death of the author occasions a return for artistic consciousness in a more durable form. These stipulations are the necessary ingredients for a relationship between the reader and the literary work regulated by imprimaturs, a literary condition in which textual form represents a hypothetical mediation with artistic consciousness. First, the author's work is worthy of renown. Second, sympathetic perspectives (of narrators, critics, and readers) are misguided. Third, public renown, when awarded, is awarded thoughtlessly, indifferent to the intrinsic merits of the author's work.

The first stipulation: the author's work is worthy of renown. James himself, as we have seen, identifies this stipulation as the postulate *sine qua non* of the stories. Famous or not, misunderstood or not, the author is, in fact, a specimen of literary genius, a "lion," "a worthy," an instance of exemplary artistic consciousness, whose eminence is not determined by the external arbitration of professional standards or mass consumer satisfaction. In a notebook entry dated 3 February 1894, James asks

could not something be done with the idea of the great (the distinguished, the celebrated) artist – man of letters he must, in the case, be – who is tremendously made up to, *fêted*, written to for his autograph, portrait, etc., and yet with whose work, in this age of advertisement and newspaperism, this age of interviewing, not one of the persons concerned has the smallest acquaintance? . . . The phenomenon is one that is brought home every day of one's life by the ravenous autograph-hunters, lion-hunters, exploiters of publicity; in whose number one gets the impression that a person knowing and *loving* the thing itself, the work, is simply never to be found.[22]

Here, contemplating the beginnings of "The Death of the Lion," James reveals a paradox, which is central to the imprimatur, namely, that the exemplary artist retains value *in spite of* success.[23] The point takes for granted the bankruptcy of external valuation in an age of advertisement, newspaperism, and interviewing. For James, success correlates with high artistic value only by accident. Such is the case with Neil Paraday in "The Death of the Lion" – the embrace of coterie society not only occasions his death but also worsens it. The salon-goers carelessly and irretrievably mislay Paraday's final manuscript, which "would have been a glorious book": "if such pages had appeared in his lifetime," the narrator says regretfully, "the Abbey would hold him today."[24]

In these stories, success either antagonizes artistic consciousness or marks its demise. In "The Next Time," James contrasts the logic of success, measured by external arbiters, with the intrinsic, absolute value he postulates in artistic consciousness. The story begins with Jane Highmore, a best-selling novelist, retaining the services of a critic "to write a notice of her great forthcoming work."[25] The critic is perplexed by her errand: why would a popular writer solicit critical approbation when her "great works . . . come forth so frequently" without it?

"One of the most voluminous writers of the time," she has often repeated this sign; but never, I dare say, in spite of her professional command of appropriate emotion, with an equal sense of that mystery and that sadness of things which to people of imagination generally hover over the close of human histories.[26]

He suggests here what scornful blurbs he might have offered for the jacket of her forthcoming book. Voluminous but not subtle. A command of appropriate emotion conditioned by the marketplace. Highmore has not come, of course, to solicit negative reviews; quite remarkably, she has come to solicit what she takes as the negative effects of a good review.

She seeks to retain the critic's services as a means of rescue from "the age of trash triumphant."[27] In such times, Jamesian authors necessarily experience prolific sales as bad conscience, longing for a kind of esteem that depends upon "exquisite failure":

There was something a failure was, a failure in the market, that a success somehow wasn't. A success was as prosaic as a good dinner: there was nothing more to be said about it than you had had it . . . It made, if you came to look at it, nothing but money; that is it made so much that any other result showed small in comparison. A failure now could make . . . such a reputation! She did me the honour . . . to intimate that what she meant by reputation was seeing *me* toss a flower. If it took failure to catch a failure I was by own admission well qualified to place the laurel.[28]

This is "the perplexing lesson" of her visit: Highmore seeks the critic's laurels only to anoint her with popular failure, or the reputation for popular failure. She seeks the approval of the critic to spoil her place in the literary marketplace and her popular success. With dismal sales now indicating intrinsic artistic merit, her "ingenious theory of [the critic's] influence" places the critic's work at the center of the process of high cultural valuation.

To achieve high cultural preeminence her reputation as a popular novelist must be annihilated. In a sense, two cultural operators for success lay claim on her work: she is subject to two modes of success – popular success, which works in spite of her ("[t]he public *would* have her," even if she would not have it), and "artistic" success, which she desires but which eludes her. The high cultural formula, dependent on elitist scorn of *vox populi*, is familiar. Popular and artistic are inversely linked: the greater a work's popular success, the less its artistic merit, and vice-versa. Having Highmore, the best-selling novelist, voice elitist scorn for mass culture shows that James was not beyond a measure of self-parody. It also suggests that his sense of a cultural divide was at odds with Highmore's, which is finally like the mass marketplace it claims to flee. It "mistakes" contingent valuations (of the critic) for absolute standards (of Jamesian artistic consciousness).

If Highmore cannot fail in the marketplace despite her best efforts, Ray Limbert, the story's postulated literary genius, cannot succeed despite his. "When he went abroad to gather garlic," the narrator comments, "he came home with heliotrope."[29] Because James locates artistic consciousness in the work rather than the person, the work has its own agency regardless of the person's desires for failure or success: Highgate's work is intrinsically popular; Limbert's, intrinsically rare.

Limbert tries to secure popular success, to make some money by writing something that will make an "impression . . . on the market."[30] He writes an adventure novel, he writes a serialized novel, he writes a column for the *Blackport Beacon*, he retains the services of the admiring critic. Yet, his own artistic consciousness defies him to the last:

> The voice of the market had suddenly grown faint and far: he had come back at the last, as people so often do, to one of the moods, the sincerities of his prime. Was he really, with a blurred sense of the urgent, doing something now only for himself? . . . What had happened . . . was that he had quite forgotten whether he generally sold or not. He had merely waked up one morning again in the country of the blue and had stayed there with a good conscience and a great idea. He stayed till death knocked at the gate, for the pen dropped from his hand only at the moment when, from the sudden failure of his heart, his eyes, as he sank back in his chair, closed for ever. "Derogation" is a splendid fragment; it evidently would have been one of his high successes. I am not prepared to say it would have waked up the libraries.[31]

"Derogation" is an evocative title for Limbert's final fragmentary work, yet it remains unclear from the narrator's account whether, in fact, the work signals the end to Limbert's tenure of derogation, prostrate to the market, or his final capitulation. The ambiguity lies in the narrator's use of the word "success" – in which cultural domain would "Derogation," if brought to completion, be successful? Evidently, the narrator is "not prepared to say" (syntax indeterminate) whether Limbert would find esteemed company in the libraries, those repositories of high aesthetic absolutes. The interceding influence of the untrustworthy narrator – a technique which is characteristically Jamesian and which brings us to the second stipulation – creates a dilemma for readers, which leads to the invocation of the imprimatur as a form of resolution.

The second stipulation: the narrative perspective is sympathetic yet misguided. The narrator in each story is a young devotee, sometimes comprehending, usually indignant at others for not taking more notice, never quite perceptive enough to grasp the full splendor of his literary idol. Not so perceptive as James's ideal reader "on whom nothing is lost," he is instead one of the anonymous critics whom James often called little writers.[32] Nevertheless, as James writes in his notebooks, the figure provides the reader with a "critical reflector," an imperfect perspective on literary greatness.[33] "Say *I'm* a 'critic,' another little writer, a newspaper man," he writes in his initial jottings for "The Figure in the Carpet." "I'm in relation with [the eminent author], somehow – relation, admiring, inquisitive, sympathetic, mystified, sceptical – whatever it may be."[34] Wayne Booth, Wolfgang Iser, and other reader-response critics have cautioned readers against confusing the narrator, "who communicates with the reader," with the implied author, "whose attitudes shape the book," or the real author, "who writes the book."[35] Yet, for even the most diligent readers, the stories of literary life make it a troublesome task winnowing one from the others. The reader's relationships with Henry James the narrator, Henry James the implied author, and Henry James the real author are fraught with difficulties. Given the simultaneous existence of an exemplary artistic consciousness, how can the narrator represent the author's voice? How would James, real or implied, communicate if not through the narrator's voice? Does the implied doubling of the narrator and his literary idol with the reader and Henry James put the reader in a position of ironic distance or shared purpose with Henry James? And, if so, with which James?

In "The Figure in the Carpet," the narrator seeks the elusive "general intention" of the author Hugh Vereker, the so-called figure in the carpet of the story's title. He reads Vereker's work and interviews Vereker himself, but neither supplies him with the "general intention" he seeks. In fact, both only serve to heighten his desire to find the general intention. Vereker, for instance, tells him that

there's an idea in my work without which I wouldn't have given a straw for the whole job. It's the finest fullest intention of the lot, and the application of it has been, I think, a triumph of patience, of ingenuity. I ought to leave that to somebody else to say; but that nobody does say it is precisely what we're talking about. It stretches, this little trick of mine, from book to book, and everything else, comparatively, plays over the surface of it. The order, the form, the texture of my books will perhaps some day constitute for the initiated a complete representation of it.[36]

It exists, Vereker affirms, but it's your task to find it. Vereker proves tantalizingly unhelpful about the exact nature of his intention. At once, Vereker veils and unveils it to the narrator, seducing him with the secret. Both

Vereker and the narrator seem, moreover, to recognize that the secret and the work are really "the same thing."[37] The circular movement – away from Vereker, back to Vereker – becomes part of a seduction which affects the narrator and the reader as well.

Like the "something or other" structuring Vereker's oeuvre for the narrator, the "something or other" structuring James's story eludes the reader, saddled with the same cache of metaphoric ciphers, each conveying a surface/depth structure – the "general intention," the "hidden structure," the "silver lining," "the string the pearls were strung on," "the buried treasure," "the figure in the carpet" – all of them asking, "What is the tenor of my vehicle?" For the reader, like the narrator, the hidden (lining, string, treasure, figure) holds forth the semblance of the object of desire. The object alone amounts to nothing, existing only as far as it is veiled for one who desires to see it unveiled.

What's at stake in "The Figure in the Carpet" is, in effect, the classic metonym substituting the author's name for the author's work. The narrator mistakes Vereker the person for Vereker the work – a misrecognition illustrated when the critic asks the author point blank "What . . . may your 'little point' happen to be?" Vereker, refusing to answer for his work, exemplifies the modernist authorial subject, but not because a true "general intention" lies beneath his entire oeuvre. Rather, the persistent assumption that a hidden "general intention" must exist retroactively positions Vereker's work as an oeuvre and Vereker as a specimen of magisterial artistic consciousness. Fittingly, for a short story so often read as a foundational text of High Modernism, the narrative path appears to lead back to the author as the master technician, a version of authorship which cannot help to invoke the sign of the master himself, Henry James. Of course, this last interpretive step beyond – the move from the story's technical mastery to James the Master – remains unavailable to the fictive narrator. For the reader, however, like a modernist sleight-of-hand, the notion of James's technical mastery immanent in the text fills in the gaps of the narrator's metonymic search for Vereker's general intention. Magisterial authorial subjectivity slips in where the author told him to look for the "something or other" that holds it all together, and the idea of James's technical and stylistic virtuosity forecloses the ominous if not impossible task of unveiling *das Ding an sich*.

Modernists and modernist texts repeatedly index literary work to authorial consciousness. Such indexing can be encouraged in different contexts – prefaces, introductory matter, notebooks, internal cues such as narrative irony – but the imprimatur depends on its synecdoche between the formal work of the text and the mental state of the author. This point is wholly different from the old truism that all literary work is, in essence, veiled autobiography. Quite the contrary, it notices an opposite tendency: the way modernist work offers itself as a functional replacement for the biographical self.

Readers of these tales, as I have argued, are in a peculiar predicament. If they recognize that the critics, reviewers, editors, and devotees in the stories are faulted for not reading the exemplary author's works, or for not reading them well, readers necessarily come to this conclusion either by deducing James's repudiation via his narrative technique or by inducing it from James's other writings, applying Jamesian ideas learned elsewhere, such as his notebooks or prefaces. Because James never presents "chapter and verse for the eminence," readers seem, however reluctantly, to be in similar circumstances to those of the readers represented in the text, their currency also being unsubstantiated authorial reputation. The epistemological difference that makes the difference between these two perspectives is the guarantee supplied by the Jamesian imprimatur. Only by taking the author's stance for granted can readers witness the ironic predicament that exemplary artistic consciousness faces with respect to oblivious literary institutions, which brings us to the third stipulation advanced in James's stories of literary life.

The third stipulation: public renown, when awarded, is awarded thoughtlessly, with indifference to the merit of the author's work. In James's stories of literary life, it is assumed that the distribution of renown to authors takes no account of the exemplary work. In James, this monstrous indifference is less the stupidity of the crowd than the mechanisms of the literary marketplace, "the whole loathsomely prurient and humbugging business," which claims to represent the reading public – "their conception, their representation of their public – its ineffable sneakiness and baseness."[38] The presumption that readers are only interested in the private lives of writers James offers as particularly damaging to literary lives.

Of the tales of literary life, each of which, in one way or another, concerns a literary death, only "John Delavoy" takes this death as a point of departure. As it begins, Delavoy is already dead. As with the other tales, James speculates about what the institutions of emerging literary markets have to offer literary and aesthetic projects. Unlike the worthy authors in "The Private Life" or "The Figure in the Carpet," who have already attained a measure of renown, or those in "The Death of the Lion" or "The Next Time," who clamor for it, John Delavoy dies unknown. He dies uncrowned by renown, untouched by the crowd, "the most unadvertised, unreported, uninterviewed, unphotographed, uncriticised of all originals."[39] With the person of the author out of the way, so to speak, this story of literary life gives us the chance to see what James might really have in mind for it.

The plot operates around a constitutive misunderstanding about the name John Delavoy and three seemingly incommensurate notions about what the author's name signifies, about what authors are for. On one side is Mr. Beston, the editor of "the celebrated *Cynosure*"; on the second is the anonymous narrator, a critic who idolizes John Delavoy; on the third is Miss Delavoy, the posthumous author's sister. For Beston, who claims to represent the interests of 10,000 subscribers and shareholders, an anonymous public "as vast as a conscript army," Delavoy is merely forage for a public hungry for personalities but certainly not for literary art.[40] For the critic, John Delavoy's lack of publicity – among both the reading public and literary insiders – makes his writings all the more exquisite. When Delavoy's last work appears to little fanfare, he is ecstatic: "The impression it made," he remembers, "was of the deepest – it remains the author's highest mark."[41] For Miss Delavoy – to Beston's consternation – her brother is not so much a sibling or an intimate, but an imprimatur. Asked to reminisce about her brother's personality rather than his work, she abjures, declaring the task impossible: "how can I speak of him at all? – how can I articulate? He *was* his work."[42]

Beston agrees to publish the critic's study of his literary idol, sight unseen, on the condition that he meet with Miss Delavoy. They meet and she approves of his "highly sensitive study."[43] At this point, however, we also learn of a pencil rendering she drew of her brother, the only representation of John Delavoy in existence, which Beston has already claimed "in the event of his publishing an article."[44] This drawing turns out to be the real reason for Beston's interest in both his article and Delavoy's posthumous reputation. Upon finally examining the critic's study, Beston inevitably rejects it. Miss Delavoy frantically tries to block Beston from publishing her drawing without the critic's essay, and, in confronting him, she becomes the mouthpiece for the third stipulation:

You advertise yourself with it because it's a very great literary figure because it wrote very great literary things that you wouldn't for the world allow to be intelligibly or critically named. So you bid for the still more striking tribute of an intimate picture – an unveiling of God knows what! – without even having the pluck or the logic to say on what ground it is that you go in for naming him at all.[45]

Her reproach uses the object pronoun *it* to denote both the drawing of John Delavoy and the *great literary figure* himself. As this objectification suggests, she understands John Delavoy as a commodity, too, but, unlike Beston, she claims to ground it in *great literary things*. Her outrage is directed not at marketing John Delavoy *per se* but at Beston's obscene need to possess the commodity while discounting its source of value.

For James and many modernists to come after, anxiety about the literary marketplace has less to do with the proliferation of middlebrow readers than with the proliferation of a liquid and ubiquitous, often feminized, commodity culture. James's stories of literary life document a somewhat mournful awareness that too often authors and texts are, like other commodities, put to indiscriminate ends. Mitigating against this awareness, these stories also attest to the insistent modernist belief that the uses of texts and authors are not necessarily beyond the influence of production. With the stipulations they advance, the stories model a literary condition in which fictional readers are faulted for not seeking authors in their works, and, consequently, invite actual readers to rectify this demonstrated shortcoming in their readings of James. In response to the threat of literary devaluation, the modernist text seeks to motivate demand for imprimaturs among readers.

WITHIN OR BEHIND OR BEYOND OR ABOVE

Perhaps no text better demonstrates the effects of the modernist tendency to engage readers in the production of imprimaturs than James Joyce's *Portrait of the Artist as a Young Man* (1916). The Joycean imprimatur – drawn from the reader's experience of Stephen Dedalus – elevates the Jamesian postulates of exemplary artistic consciousness into possibilities for a "new terminology" (in Stephen's words) for identity and agency. "Possibilities" is the right word, I believe, because both skepticism about this mission and the contingency of Stephen's role in it not only are well justified but also form a crucial interpretive modality.[46] Stephen, after all, never becomes an artist. We never learn what becomes of him outside of Dublin. More specifically, we never learn if he makes good on his preposterous valediction at the novel's end: "Welcome, O life! I go to encounter for the millionth time the reality of experience and to forge in the smithy of my soul the uncreated conscience of my race."[47]

What we do suspect when we read *Portrait* is that James Joyce himself may be a better fit for this aesthetic and political terminology than Stephen is. That is, *Portrait* posits this as possible (though certainly not ineluctable). Crucially, at the end of *Portrait*, it is Joyce's "exile" from Ireland and not Stephen's that is invoked:

Dublin 1904
Trieste 1914

This is also the detail that Pound found most indispensable: "It is the ten years spent on the book," he wrote, "the Dublin 1904, Trieste 1914, that counts."[48] Only when such deliberate clues that Joyce is the "truth" of Dedalus – that Stephen is an artist very much like the young Joyce – are read side-by-side with persistent clues that Stephen is an object of ironic ridicule can we discern how the two working in tandem serve to register *Portrait*'s political implications.

From Joyce's death in 1941 until the mid-1960s, much of the scholarship about *Portrait* was narrowly trained upon a critical debate about Stephen, around which inferences from Stephen to Joyce form a pervasive framework. A single question ruled this debate. Hugh Kenner phrased it most baldly: "How seriously are we to take Stephen?" Invoking the classic dichotomy first identified by Robert Scholes – is Stephen "an actual or even a potential artist" or is he "a posturing esthete"?[49] Is he, as Harry Levin claims in *James Joyce: A Critical Introduction*, a budding specimen of the eminent artistic personality or, as Kenner would have it in *Dublin's Joyce*, a priggish faker, an ironic send-up of artistic pretense?[50]

In Levin's account, *Portrait* is a typical *Künstlerroman*, based on a literal transcript of the first twenty tears of Joyce's life. Stephen is James Joyce himself in so-called thin incognito. The novel thus is akin to a controlled laboratory for examining the formation of "the personality of the artist, prolonging and brooding upon itself" in an inhospitable world.[51] In Kenner's account, it is a mock *Künstlerroman*, a deliberate study of the failed case, a "meticulous pastiche of [artistic] immaturity."[52] It executes what Kenner calls "the generic Joyce plot, the encounter with the alter ego" – an overt encounter between Stephen and his mythic avatars (the "fabulous artificer, [the] hawklike man") and a covert encounter between Joyce and his younger selves, most pointedly "the priggish, humorless Stephen of the last chapter," his "fake artist" alter ego. In this latter figure, Kenner speculates, "Joyce abandoned the original intention of writing the account of his own escape from Dublin [and] recast Stephen Dedalus as a figure who could not even detach himself from" the place.[53] Stephen, notice, still signifies Joyce himself, only in this interpretation, Stephen is Joyce through a glass darkly.

This dichotomy is false: the genuine Stephen and the ironic Stephen are two sides of the same coin, interpretations propped up in both cases by a particular recourse to Joyce the authorial coinage, the imprimatur. The imprimatur is implied in the logic of Kenner's initial question, how seriously are we to take Stephen? The question invokes authorial intentions only to conceal them in passive syntax; this literary critical grammar is endemic to the commentary of both camps. Readers like Levin, who insist on Stephen on his own terms, hear Joyce's authoritative voice in Stephen's; readers like Kenner, who refuse to take Stephen on his own terms, attempt to find Joyce's authoritative voice in their own aversion to Stephen. The inference from the particular reader's response to the authoritative response – the response presumably sanctioned by "Joyce" – depends upon the imprimatur-consecrated notion that Joyce's intelligence is embodied in his representation of Stephen or, more precisely, in Joyce's ironic distance from the representation. The inference of Joyce's authority takes place notwithstanding that Joyce spares Stephen (and us) his explicit, authorial judgment – moral, aesthetic, or otherwise.

The real "illusion of auctorial impartiality," then – to borrow one of Kenner's key phrases – is not reducible to the pages of Stephen's notebook or any other strictly formal matter but rather works as an effect of a particular reading practice, aligned with the implied perspective of Joyce himself. This practice distances the subject matter – Stephen, his aesthetic theory, his furtive literary efforts – from both reader and author. Readers in this camp insist that the very possibility of an ironic reading of Stephen depends on the amount of "intelligence Joyce postulates in his reader" – with the "unlikely case" being that the reader's intelligence is "comparable to his [Joyce's] own."[54] Readers who recognize Joyce's irony about Stephen as interpretive necessity pass something akin to a modernist intelligence test. Seemingly, for Kenner and other like-minded readers, the fundamental interpretive precondition is the notion that readers have the capacity to detect the author's intelligence in the text, a notion which promises the most literary sophistication to the reader who believes that he or she is most like the author. In effect, their readings return in the guise of the reader the impulse to authoritative narrative comment which modernists like Joyce so famously cut in the name of form.

Both camps, furthermore, draw heavily on an ideal of generation, aesthetic maturity – artists mature, they enter a major phase, or else they prove themselves pretenders to the vocation. And here it is worth remembering that the movement from immaturity to maturity rewritten in aesthetic registers is the major thematic axis of the novel. In a sense, whether these readers take Stephen seriously or not, they slip into the logic of his presentation – his framing, his "*Portrait*" – in order to read, interpret, and evaluate him.[55] If the Dedalus ethos is judged puerile (Stephen, his aesthetics, and his art are the stuff, in Kenner's words, of "so many permanent under-graduates"), then discerning its immaturity involves tacitly validating the supreme formulation of Stephen's aesthetic theory – that "the artist, like the God of the creation, remains within or behind or beyond or above his handiwork, invisible, refined out of existence, indifferent, paring his fingernails."[56]

The Kenner question – how seriously are we to take Stephen? – recoils from Stephen's pompous aesthetic mission. How seriously can we take Stephen, it asks, when he likens the artist to God in creation and, by implication, himself to that artist? Still, critics like Kenner, it seems to me, object more to the speaker than the sentiment. If we must have an author-god, they seem to say, let us have a legitimate author-god.[57] That is, let us have Joyce the Master. Again and again, we find both camps reading the handiwork (*Portrait*) for traces of the artist (Joyce). The possibility of ironic distance between Stephen and Joyce serves to reinforce the intransigence of this reading pattern; the certitude that Joyce is an exemplary artistic consciousness rests on the likely possibility that artistic consciousness as manifest in Stephen may be half-baked.

Unwilling or unable to see their own reading habits enmeshed in the broader aesthetic project of *Portrait*, both camps, above all, contribute vital conceptual glue to the imprimatur, enacting as if on cue the missing author named Joyce. *Portrait*'s aesthetic project is given only its most nascent enunciation in Stephen; the reader completes the task. Readers apprehend (to borrow a fundamental term from Stephen's aesthetic system) the aes-thetic form (the narrative itself) and guarantee it with the notion that Joyce himself is "within or behind or beyond or above" the form. Appre-hending authorship in the formal inventiveness of the narrative, the reader supplies the missing transcendental horizon of meaning which Stephen's quasi-theological aesthetics call for but which Stephen, as the subject of this narrative, cannot himself observe.

Stephen's ecstatic vision of the bird-girl, at the end of the novel's fourth chapter, may be the ultimate expression of his forming artistic identity. But, whether for irony or for example, the ultimate manifestation of lit-erary authority as such comes in the fifth, the chapter which begins and ends with Stephen taking leave – first, of his family's decrepit domicile (the pawn tickets, his martyred mother, his contemptuous father) and last, of a notebook ("27 April: Old father, old artificer, stand before me now ever in good stead") stamped with date and place of the novel's inception and completion.[58] Somewhere between these markers, exemplary artistic consciousness is "forged" – this word Stephen uses repeatedly to connote deliberate fabrication. That is, forging aesthetic consciousness is always a kind of forgery. As I have attempted to show, it is forged not in Stephen's lone literary product, but by the reader, who apprehends, vis-à-vis a tacit inference with Joyce, the contingency of Stephen's "mode of art" on his "mode of life": the very improbability of Stephen trying to become an artist, his "striving to forge out an esthetic philosophy" out of the meager raw materials of his own identity and his Dublin environment.[59]

For Stephen, art depends, before anything else, on the production of his own identity, a self-birth which is inescapably counterfeit because like the Jamesian cases it must posit its own originality: "When we come to the phenomena of artistic conception, artistic gestation, and artistic reproduction," he tells his classmate Lynch, "I require a new terminology and a new personal experience."[60] In the succession of conversations at the university in the fifth chapter, he formulates and reformulates this aesthetic terminology. Each time the formulation is paired with a gesture of political resistance or agency. With his fellow student Cranly, for example, he puts it like this:

I will not serve that in which I no longer believe whether it call itself my home, my fatherland, or my church; and I will try to express myself in some mode of life or art as freely as I can and as wholly as I can, using for my defense the only arms I allow myself to use – silence, exile, and cunning.[61]

For Stephen, it seems, artistic consciousness necessitates breaking with the prevailing registers of social and political identification. He tells Cranly that he will not serve that which he no longer believes, that is, he will not be subject to home, fatherland, and church. He refuses to play his role in traditional modes of life (family, poverty, Easter duty, Empire) in which scripts, not individual actors, determine both performances and outcomes, modes of life predicated on obedience and not, in the rule, individual assent. By refusing to serve these modes of life, he plans to "fly by [the] nets of language, nationality, and religion."[62]

The refusal owes something to romanticism's legacy of the flamboyant artist-hero, the "proud gesture of refusal" Stephen finds so compelling in the Count of Monte Cristo's "Madam, I never eat muscatel grapes."[63] Yet, to view it as an unqualified hang-over of romanticism overlooks Stephen's uneasiness with other systematic departures from traditional modes of life, which are rooted squarely in the romantic forms of identification. For Stephen, newly manufactured traditions, whether inventions of Irishness or universal brotherhood, are even less compelling than traditional scripts such as Catholicism, because they require the same indiscriminate identification as traditional modes without their intellectual depth or aesthetic weight.

Refusing to serve the traditional demands of language, nation, and religion does not mean that Stephen can will them away, or even that he desires to stop suffering their pull. When he meets the dean of studies, a transplanted English Jesuit, for instance, Stephen recognizes that even though he may surpass the dean in knowledge of the English language, the Englishman's "language, so familiar and so foreign, will always be . . . an acquired speech."[64] Stephen does not propose to refuse himself the use of the English language; he tries to refuse its demands on his identity and his movements. He seeks, instead, to press his language with all its baffling limitations – as well as his nation and his religion – into new domains governed by artistic consciousness. His refusal, then, is less romantic apostasy than heretical revision, a rewriting of traditional identities in new aesthetic vocabularies. Stephen apprehends Dublin through idiosyncratic filters of cosmopolitan reading habits. Walking from his parents' domicile to his university lectures, he superimposes on the scenes of his morning walk words and images drawn from the works of Hauptmann, Ibsen, Newman, Cavalcanti, and Ben Jonson as one flips transparent overlays in an anatomy text.[65]

However modestly, Stephen's act of apprehending artistic consciousness represents the political implications of his will to artistic identity. As an act of self-fashioning, it contrasts with the forms of social and political interpellation he refuses before and after, for it alone enables him to act as agent. Even before he leaves Ireland for "exile" on the continent, Stephen rewrites Ireland in the aesthetic terminology he has gathered, however improbably, from the literary history of Europe. Yet this modest cultural subversion exhausts the political possibilities of artistic self-fashioning if understood strictly within the narrative frame, that is, if understood in reference to Stephen Dedalus. The politics are rather thin; Stephen exhibits little interest in injustice to others, including his own family. He rejects modes of life only in so far as they are not conducive to his idiosyncratic definitions of art and self, his artistic self-fashioning, and his cult of apprehension. Moreover, Stephen's future as an artist is hardly a sure thing. Readers cannot take for granted, to begin with, that he represents a specimen of exemplary artistic consciousness, as they can with Henry James's artist-protagonists.

As evidenced in the *Portrait* debates, the imprimatur can make good on Stephen's dubious rhetoric – both in his sense of artistic exceptionalism and its promise to provide resistance to the full sociopolitical determinacy facing modern subjects. Stephen, like Henry James's critic-narrators, provides the sympathetic but suspect frame of reference, the ironic gap which gives readers space to admire the Joycean handiwork. In this sense, the beneficiaries of Stephen's unfulfilled political and aesthetic ambitions are *Portrait*'s ideal readers. They fulfill Stephen's project of artistic consciousness – the "disposition of sensible or intelligible matter for an aesthetic end," in Stephen's phrase[66] – by detecting the imprimatur of the literary modernist. This disposition of sensible or intelligible matter has readers apprehending artistic consciousness in the literary text, bringing conscious artistry and artistic consciousness into a combination that, seeming to be everywhere and nowhere at once, is neither fully determined nor entirely active and resistant.

MODERNIST AFTERLIFE, PROXIMATE POLITICS

The movement from Vereker to Dedalus marks the emergence of the imprimatur in defiance of literary professionalization, re-describing the traditional, romantic author-hero as a regulative principle of the flow of value to high literary work. The movement from Dedalus to the stories of literary life in the thirties marks increased cynicism about the valorization and political potential of authorial identity as such. Quite predictably, literary life continues to be a well-trod theme, but, repeatedly, the story of it comes unraveled in the thirties. Works such as Edward Upward's *Journey to the Border*, Christopher Isherwood's *Prater Violet*, and Evelyn Waugh's *Vile Bodies* reveal a more ambivalent take on authorial fashioning. Here, the rhetoric of exceptionalism is troubled, rather than guaranteed, by the workings of the imprimatur. In Upward, it is delusional, a coping strategy; in Isherwood, it is something to be shelved for more financially lucrative work in screenwriting; in Waugh, it is yet another means of securing an aimless, on-again, off-again marriage. Whereas in James, Vereker's genius was to be presumed genuine, and in Joyce, Stephen's was dubious yet somehow tenable, these would-be artists are jobbing tutors, screenwriters, and gossip columnists.

Rewritten twenty years on, the story of literary life in *Portrait* might look a lot like Edward Upward's neglected novel, *Journey to the Border* (1938). The novel owes much to *Portrait* as it is, both stylistically and thematically. Upward's Oxbridge-educated protagonist, a penurious, nameless private tutor, is coaxed into a day-trip to the horse-races by his upper-class employer. As is the case in *Portrait*, a series of provincial, mundane encounters inspires personal redefinition of seemingly world-historical proportions. Readers who find Dedalus' priggishness barely tolerable may find the tutor's snotty intellectualism deadly, but, again like *Portrait*, the novel's technical presentation mitigates against preposterousness, discouraging the reader from taking the tutor's case as merely a comedy of self-delusion.

By presenting the "foisting of human consciousness on to a non-human world" – to use Upward's phrase – without using first-person narrative and then spotlighting the tutor's capacities for perception and aesthetic embellishment, Upward suggests – again, in the narrative technique, as it were – that the tutor's consciousness is exceptional rather than solipsistic. All humans may foist consciousness on to the non-human world, but, for most, it passes unnoticed. The tutor, alone among the characters, approaches this process with aesthetic reflexivity; his "poetic dreams" improve upon objective reality, transforming it "into a coherent, a satisfying pattern." As the novel begins at least, the tutor bases his agency on a kind of aesthetic apprehension, which echoes *Portrait*. In his "poetic dreams," his subjective acuity, the tutor plots his escape from the determinism of his objectively meager circumstances.[67]

The following passage illustrates the way the act of perception conveys and then merges with the tutor's desires for political agency. The tutor apprehends the landscape from a moving automobile:

To the left the tableland ended in an abrupt invisible slope, defined only by the descending tops of a few fir trees. Beyond the slope stretched a huge plain of variegated green. Smooth isolated hills broke up the line of the horizon. The sun was brilliant. Travel, love, joy, creation – nothing would be impossible for the tutor. "All the worlds of nature and of art," he said to himself. What wouldn't he do, what sights, odours, feelings he would savour. Don't wait a moment longer. Oh, begin, begin.[68]

Moving from description to exhortation, the tutor's act of perception leads him to ecstatic self-transformation much in the vein of Stephen's "Welcome, O Life!" A landscape that seems unbounded because of topography leads to a form of desire that is, after all, also an illusionary perception, namely desire for identity unbounded by the various limitations of social and political positioning, a place beyond the left.

As I argued before, Dedalus' "I will not serve" goes beyond the preliminary wish for unconditioned, self-positing agency. Dedalus does not – or cannot – merely wave away political and social determinism. We leave Stephen at the end of *Portrait* planning to press second nature into aesthetic form, ready to rewrite traditional identities in new aesthetic terminologies, ready "to forge in the smithy of [his] soul the uncreated conscience of [his] race."[69] What's remarkable about *Journey to the Border*, given its debt to

Portrait, is that the tutor finally renounces the path of artistic consciousness altogether. Upward's tutor rejects the identity and example of the exemplary artist as a viable remedy to the coercive binds of society. By the end of *Journey to the Border,* the tutor concludes that poetic dreams – the aesthetic perceptions he claims to value most – are merely dreams of escape, "twisted fantasies" which are "unhealthy substitutes for practical action" with the so-called Internationalist Movement for Working-Class Power. At the novel's end, he leaves not to become an artist but to join the Party and struggle for a socialist future.

So why is struggling to be an artist politically viable for Dedalus but not for the tutor? What has changed between the moment of *Portrait* and the moment of *Journey to the Border,* some twenty years later? One change is that the protagonist has lost faith in the immediate political potential of artistic consciousness – its deferred promise does not serve the tutor's present as well as Stephen's. Each of the tutor's encounters makes a pressing, inexorably political demand upon him: his employer, the propertied reactionary; his employer's friend, the *faux-déclassé* liberal; his employer's daughter, the parlor socialist; and, most crucially, her fiancé, the fascist. Stephen, we recall, also encounters politicized types but easily dismisses them, because they demand indiscriminate obedience at the expense of aesthetic apprehension. In the tutor's case, aesthetic apprehension repeatedly obscures authoritarian political realities. The most trenchant example is the fascist fiancé, the fast-driving imperialist on leave from the Colonial Civil Service. He cuts a figure that the tutor initially admires, even emulates, but after the fiancé rallies the crowd at the race into fascist salutes and denunciations of International Jewry, the tutor begins to question the political efficacy of his own poetic dreams. What can poetic dreams do to stop the likes of the fascist?

Journey to the Border poses problems for artistic identity that presume that the times, not artistic consciousness, have changed. Whether Stephen's Dublin is more politically charged than the tutor's English countryside is beside the point – the issue is, instead, to borrow Perry Anderson's essential phrase, the "imaginative proximity of social revolution."[70] This rising structure of feeling records its effects in the overt narrative of *Journey to the Border* – the choice of political awakening over the modernist story of literary life – but underneath the skin, so to speak, the imprimatur retains its structuring function, regulating both the tutor's choices and the scene of reading where these choices are made. After all, the burden of the tutor's decision to join the Party rests upon the weight of his refusal to become an artist. In a sense, the very denial of artistic pretensions, offered as a monument to how bad the times have become, demonstrates that the imprimatur continues to play the regulative role. For this brand of revolutionary teleology, the denial of the artistic consciousness constitutes the ultimate Party sacrifice. At the same time as the politicized context seems to unmake a would-be literary life, Upward's implied relationship with the text ensures that the value of conscious artistry to the Party remains present, albeit off-stage, as part of a critical scene of reading. Though lacking, because the lack wants to be filled, the entailment between artistic consciousness and conscious artistry still ensures the significance of the tutor's journey. On second inspection, the tutor's predicament turns out not so differently from the one in *Portrait*, in which the artist's identity, deferred in the story itself, returns retroactively in the scene of reading.

A similar triangulation of conscious artistry, artistic consciousness, and politicized context emerges in Christopher Isherwood's *Prater Violet*. Isherwood's plot configures these tensions somewhat differently. Again, the political bogey rendering literary life suspect is fascism – albeit a fascism which calls for the demise of the cultured, civilized self without Upward's socialist rebirth. Once more, impending catastrophe is a *fait accompli*, characters describing its inevitability with eerie detachment. "Like all my friends," the narrator writes,

[I] believed a European war was coming soon. I believed it as one believes one will die . . . It was unreal because I couldn't imagine anything beyond it; I refused to imagine anything: just as a spectator refuses to imagine what is behind the scenery in a theatre. The outbreak of war, like the moment of death, crossed my perspective of the future like a wall; it marked the instant, total end of my imagined world.[71]

Here, we see the deeper significance of Anderson's phrase "imaginative proximity"; the devastation to come is represented as proximate to the total end of imagination. Another character likens this sense of coming terror to the beating of Poe's "Tell-Tale Heart": "It ticks every moment . . . Death comes nearer. Syphilis. Poverty. Consumption. Cancer discovered too late. My art no good, a failure, a damn flop. War. Poison gas. We are dying with our heads together in the oven."[72] Significantly, the individual artistic failure, the "damn flop," is placed alongside the other horrors. It sits, however, among such immense catastrophes uncomfortably, implying not symbolic equivalence between bad art and poverty, poison gas, and death, but rather the guilty futility of artistic work in such a framework. With the coming crisis, *my art – my imagined world – is no good* (in Auden's words, with the coming crisis, *poetry makes nothing happen*). If the coming crisis marks the end of conscious artistry, what should the conscientious artist do in the intervening time?

Intensifying the imagined proximity, Isherwood sets *Prater Violet* (published in 1945) in London in 1933, a year chosen explicitly for its political evocations; daily news from the continent – the Reichstag fire trial, for instance – exists just beyond the margins of the story. The narrator, the fictionalized Christopher Isherwood, shelves his novel-in-progress for the more financially lucrative work of screenwriting, helping Friedrich Bergmann, an Austrian-Jewish film-auteur, create light melodrama for Imperial Bulldog Pictures. While Christopher and Bergmann fumble to create *Prater Violet*, a saccharine, nostalgic movie about Imperial Vienna, news reports filter in through radios and newspapers about actual Nazi misdeeds in Austria where Bergmann has left his family. Against this backdrop of horrors, which threaten to implicate Bergmann personally, the conscious artistry Christopher sacrificed for money rather than political principle (like the tutor, he reads socialist newspapers, nods to union workers, etc.), put in hock to write a shamelessly commercial film, seems doubly debased. The terms in which Christopher initially casts this work – false, cheap, vulgar, hack work – coupled with the contemptuous scorn that the film's financiers feel for art – suggest a seemingly Jamesian predicament. Christopher, fallen from artistic grace, is "betraying [his] art" by selling out.[73] Understanding his task in these terms, Christopher, not surprisingly, finds the work blasé, and, fittingly, the only dialogue he can supply for the film's characters comes half-remembered from other movies. This changes. Under Bergmann's influence and, the least likely of all sources, an interpretation of the film itself, he begins reformulating his notion of the artistic self.

When Christopher faces a case of writer's block, Bergmann interprets the film for him so that it implicates his artistic pretensions. Its sentimental plot (pairing Toni, the poor flower-girl, and Rudolf, the disguised Prince of Borodania) conceals a "symbolic fable":

The dilemma of Rudolf is the dilemma of the would-be revolutionary writer . . . all over Europe. This writer is not to be confused with the true proletarian writer, such as we find in Russia. His economic background is bourgeois. He is accustomed to comfort, a nice home, the care of a devoted slave who is his mother and also his jailer. From the safety and comfort of his home, he permits himself the luxury of a romantic interest in the proletariat. He comes among the workers under false pretenses, and in disguise. He flirts with Toni, the girl of the working class. But it is only a damn lousy act, a heartless masquerade . . . Suddenly Rudolf's home collapses, security collapses. The investments which built his comfortable life are made worthless by inflation. His mother has to scrub door steps. The young artist prince, with all his fine ideas, has to face grim reality. The play becomes bitter earnest. His relation to the proletariat is romantic no longer. He now has to make a choice. He is declassed, and he must find a new class.[74]

Bergmann's interpretation proposes that the declassed artist (i.e., Christopher) has two choices, two narratives, two scripts.[75] Once the bottom drops out of the artist's world, the artist can choose either to continue courting the proletariat with new honesty or to continue abusing the proletariat with a renewed heartlessness.

The first narrative is based on the presumed continuity between authentic artistic consciousness and "the great liberal-revolutionary traditions of the nineteenth century." "If he is loyal to his artistic traditions," the real artist "will know where he belongs. He will know how to align himself. He will know . . . his real friends and his real enemies."[76] The second narrative aligns the destructive call of fascism with the bogus artist: the artist-faker who chooses this narrative "prefers to join the rank of the dilettante nihilists, the bohemian outlaws, who believe in nothing, except their own ego, who exist only to kill, to torture, to destroy, to make everyone as miserable as themselves."[77] These are, in fact, not choices at all but rather suppositions based on the notions that good art does political good; that bad art, which supports political mischief, is not art at all; and that the current moment is, in fact, revolutionary when such things are readily apprehended.

To make the first choice – the only choice, really – is to go on making art. The irony is, of course, that Bergmann's interpretation is, strictly within the narrative frame of reference, merely politically expedient, supplying Christopher with the instrumental impetus to go on with the screenplay. By pointing the "symbolic fable" at Christopher ("it represents your deepest fear," he tells him), not the proletariat, Bergmann, in effect, shows him how to interpret hack work as conscious artistry, by reading himself into the story. In this sense, Bergmann's fable imparts Christopher with an impossible frame of reference, the perspective of Christopher Isherwood, the novelist. It enables the fictional character to interpret the making of the film in a novelist's framework: the story of making the film is really a pretext for a story about making Christopher, more specifically, making him realize that "the young artist prince" faces up to "grim reality" when he helps Bergmann secure his family's transit from the fate of Nazi deathcamps to the sanctuary of Hollywood. Consequently, as the film becomes another story about artistic life for a would-be artist, the reference of the words *Prater Violet* changes, referring less to the film's sentimental plot and more to the experience of making the motion picture *Prater Violet*, the plot of Isherwood's novel.

Once the "symbolic fable" makes its appearance, the picture's sentimental plot becomes redundant, no longer a site of struggle between Christopher and Bergmann or between Bergmann and the production company. In fact,

Bergmann, later in the novel, in a fit of anger, proves all too ready to dismiss it as "heartless filth," a "wretched lying charade," using the same sort of terminology he assigns to the second choice in his fable:

To make such a picture at such a moment is definitely heartless. It definitely aids Dollfuss and Starhemberg, and Fey and all their gangsters. It covers up the dirty syphilitic sore with rose leaves, with the petals of this hypocritical revolutionary violet. It lies and declares that the pretty Danube is blue, when the water is red with blood. . . .[78]

A friend of Christopher's, ignorant of Christopher's role in its production, also understands the film in such terms: "besides being an insult to the intelligence of a five-year-old child," he says, it "is definitely counter-revolutionary," chiefly because it diverts people from their social and political miseries.[79] In the end, the film opens "with a great deal of publicity, and . . . very good notices," but Christopher chooses not to go see it.[80]

The film's latent political content, the narrative of Christopher's awakening aesthetic politics, comes to readers only via the purchase enabled by the imprimatur, the narrative's indexing with the implied mind of Christopher Isherwood the novelist. Christopher's (fictional) mother, who does attend the film, has a revealing response to it: "When we saw your name on the screen," she writes, "we both felt *very* proud, and applauded loudly. Richard [Christopher's brother] kept saying, 'Isn't that *just* like Christopher?'"[81] The messy process of cultural production comes out of the crucible of consumption as a name, as Christopher (Isherwood). What could be more loyal to the great liberal-revolutionary traditions of the nineteenth century than the fiction of liberation understood in strictly individualized terms?

The indexing between Christopher Isherwood the character and Christopher Isherwood the novelist is anything but perfunctory. The fictional Christopher Isherwood shows up repeatedly in Isherwood's work. Yet Isherwood's instinct for autobiography is itself a supreme fiction, introduced in ways coyly misleading. Sometimes he presents the novelist and autobiographer in league, and that *with him, everything starts with autobiography*. Other times the two are at odds: "it is not . . . an autobiography . . . Read it as a novel. I have used a novelist's licence in describing my incidents and drawing my characters."[82] Even much later in life, when Isherwood writes *Christopher and His Kind* as a corrective to *Lions and Shadows*, promising to make the next ten years of his memoir more "frank and factual," he detaches Christopher Isherwood from the narrator using the third person. To seek the true Isherwood in these works leaves one with a sense of tautology, shuttling from fictional representation to fictional representation. Does the fictionalized Isherwood carry the traces of the true Isherwood, or does the autobiographical subject begin as a figment of the novelist's license, too? Because Isherwood is, in a sense, always already fictionalized, we as readers are dealing above all with the *idea* of Isherwood. Consequently, we give epistemological preeminence to a third Isherwood, he who applies the license, the author of conscious artistry, he who alone organizes the difference between Christopher Isherwood and the idea of Christopher Isherwood.

Too often critics and scholars have unmasked real-life models for literary characters without scrutinizing the masquerade itself. The following passage, for instance, from Maurice Beebe's *Ivory Towers and Sacred Founts*, demonstrates the practice. As Beebe discusses two figures – the literary representation and the real-life analogue – he unwittingly confers a third, intervening figure, the author, with transcendental status. The story of literary life, Beebe writes,

> can be seen in much the same manner as the writer's letters, diaries, notebooks, prefaces, or memoirs – though, of course, the careful critic will not make a one-to-one equation between a work of art and an autobiography. [In fact, such fiction] is often more revealing than primary documents, for writers frequently tell more about their true selves and convictions under the guise of fiction than they will confess publicly.[83]

Here, we have, first, the would-be literary self-representation, the subject of the story of literary life; second, the real-life self presented in primary documents, letters, diaries, notebooks, prefaces, memoirs; and, third, the true self – something behind (within? beyond? above?) first and second, albeit peeking through occasionally – the posited actor who applies conscious artistry (in the first case) and unconscious deception (in the second) to self-concealment. As Beebe describes it, reading authorship is a one-way street: real-life connections implicate biography not interpretation. Narrative indexing between the "real-life" author and the fictional representation is incidental to reading. Yet, when the author's literary function is disavowed, the imprimatur's necessity is enacted. Following the lead of Joyce, Isherwood, other modernists, and longstanding critical habit, Beebe disavows overestimating the connections between, first, the literary representation and, second, the real-life analog, at the same time as he carefully positions, third, the author's true self within, behind, beyond, and above the text. The disavowal has the character of the classic disclaimer, coming straight from the legal department, fueling the very innuendo it repudiates. As with such disclaimers, the formulaic insistence that all resemblances may be merely coincidental provides the surest sign that they are necessary.

Evelyn Waugh is the master of this sort of disingenuous disclaimer. He attaches, for example, an author's note to *Put Out More Flags* – a work famous for skewering Isherwood and Auden for their wartime emigration to the USA – insisting, among other things, that "[n]o character is derived from any living man or woman." Waugh's use of disclaimers, back to his earliest work, illustrates the way modernist self-effacement works instead to insinuate authorship into the scene of reading.[84] According to Martin Stannard, the caricature in Waugh's first novel, *Decline and Fall* (1928), was so viciously transparent that his publisher, fearing litigation, required him to include a disclaimer.[85] Waugh's eventual concession twisted a compulsory disavowal into a stab at his publisher's prudery:

I hope that my publishers are wrong when they say that this is a shocking novelette. I did not mean it to be when I wrote it . . . In fact I have never met anyone at all like any of the characters . . . Please bear in mind throughout that IT IS MEANT TO BE FUNNY."[86]

Your excoriating roman-à-clef is, it seems, my light satire. The "Author's Note" in *Vile Bodies* (1930) continues in this vein of mischievous duplicity. This time, the disclaimer itself plays for comic effect:

All the characters and places mentioned, newspapers, hotels, night clubs, restaurants, motor cars, etc., are wholly imaginary and, of course, titles such as Prime Minister, Archbishop of Canterbury, Home Secretary, etc., are used without reference to present, past and future holders of the offices.[87]

Being pointlessly scrupulous subverts the conventions of the disclaimer, casting the real-life identity of "all the characters and places mentioned" in the drapery of an open secret.

The original typescript for *Vile Bodies* marks this paradoxical intent clearly:

BRIGHT YOUNG PEOPLE AND OTHERS KINDLY NOTE THAT ALL CHARACTERS ARE WHOLLY IMAGINARY (AND YOU ARE GETTING FAR TOO MUCH PUBLICITY ALREADY WHOEVER YOU ARE).[88]

Vile Bodies became a "runaway best-seller" and Waugh insured his celebrity as a novelist on the assumption that the Bright Young Things were *not* wholly imaginary.[89] Many "bought the book as an adjunct to their romantic absorption in gossip columns."[90] It was often used as an instruction book on the behavior of the irresponsible rich; one could take lessons in their slang ("too, too sick-making," etc.) and match Agatha Runcible, Lottie Crump,

Nina Blount, and Adam Fenwick-Symes with "real-life" counterparts in society columns. Waugh's own public persona, for instance, encouraged certain connections with Fenwick-Symes. Like Fenwick-Symes, Waugh worked for a newspaper while trying to secure his marriage. Following the appearance of *Decline and Fall* and his marriage, he began to appear in newspapers with some frequency, and he pointedly recognized their importance as organs of literary promotion.[91]

One way to account for reading *Vile Bodies* as part roman-à-clef, part instruction book, is that it misses the joke. To imitate the novel's exaggerated dialogue and fantastically profligate parties is to be captivated by the fashionable emptiness being exposed. How could one miss that *Vile Bodies* – with its bleak ending on the waste land of "the biggest battlefield in the history of the world" – was intended as, in Stannard's phrase, "a manifesto of disillusionment"?[92] How could one miss this purpose given that the one substantial intrusion of the narrator's voice in a novel composed mostly of dialogue is censorious?

(. . . Masked parties, Savage parties, Victorian parties, Greek parties, Wild West parties, Circus parties, parties where one had to dress as somebody else, almost naked parties in St. John's Wood, parties in flats and studios and houses and ships and hotels and night clubs, in windmills and swimming baths, tea parties at school where one ate muffins and meringues and tinned crab, parties at Oxford where one drank brown sherry and smoked Turkish cigarettes, dull dances in London and comic dances in Scotland and disgusting dances in Paris – all that succession of massed humanity . . . Those vile bodies . . .).[93]

Who is speaking here? With James, the figure of the unnamed critic gives a localized, albeit somewhat unstable, perspective for narration. With Joyce and Upward, the thinly disguised would-be writer and his halo of associations focalize the narrative perspective, and, with Isherwood, the figure of the thinly disguised would-be writer even lays claim to the first person singular. *This* parenthetical disembodied voice, however, is decidedly not the voice of Adam Fenwick-Symes, the fictionalized would-be writer. This alone sets him apart from the other author-protagonists we have seen.

Just as crucially, the intrusive narrator's voice is decidedly different from the voice of mock disclaimer in the author's note. Due to this disjuncture, we cannot simply accept the censorious narrator's stance as authority in parenthesis. The author's own willingness to promote the roman-à-clef, instruction book reading of the novel mitigates against the narrator's distaste for the subject matter. If one Waugh conveys a perspective of bitter reactionary antipathies, with a slippery passage from parties to massed humanity to vile bodies, then the other Waugh, whose success hinges on making fictional bodies recognizable to a mass readership, reverses the passage. One parodies its object of promotion; the other promotes its object of parody. This disjuncture between Waugh the publicist and Waugh the narrator further nuances the presumed distance between the fictionalized author, Fenwick-Symes, and the imprimatur.

In the fallen literary world Waugh describes, a would-be author is anointed a "brilliant young novelist" in the gossip columns with no literary output whatever (his novel manuscript is burned senselessly at customs).[94] Having failed as a novelist, he takes a job as a gossip columnist. In this vocation he achieves some success, inventing fads for a public which mindlessly takes up what he promotes. So, ironically, it is in his success as a publicist that Waugh most resembles Fenwick-Symes. Just as Fenwick-Symes' gossip writing entails the Bright Young Things actually taking up the preposterous fads he ascribes to them, so too, Waugh's imprimatur entails his presentation of the Bright Young Things being taken up as a definitive account of the object of his satire. Just as success undoes Fenwick-Symes when the real-life manifestation of Ginger, a character he invented in his columns, enters the picture, takes on his job as gossip columnist and marries his fiancée, so too, success undoes the narrative perspective, when "Waugh" becomes a synecdoche for the world, which, we are led to presume, he decries. In other words, the imprimatur secures a frame of reference that joins the naïve reading, fascinated with publicity, with the disillusioned reading, galled with publicity, by supporting a framework in which *Vile Bodies* works as parody *because of*, not despite, its own publicity. The imprimatur enables Waugh both to authorize his work as parody and, simultaneously, to embrace the object of this parody as means for self-promotion.

In *Vile Bodies*, Waugh joins other writers of the period in their cynical "discovery" that literary promotion can coexist with the various cultural forms of disillusionment which they have joined to high aesthetic form and purpose. The prevalence of the satirical roman-à-clef in the twenties and thirties is no coincidence, for it is a form that draws its appeal from the popular notoriety of its targets. In this regard, the artistic milieu – the social domain in which this work sought to make its mark – made for especially profitable subject matter, because it closes the circuit. Works such as *Vile Bodies* conformed to a recent precedent set by Ezra Pound's *Hugh Selwyn Mauberley* (1920), Aldous Huxley's *Crome Yellow* (1921) and *Point Counter Point* (1928), and Somerset Maugham's *Cakes and Ale* (1930). Wyndham Lewis's *Apes of God* (1930) and Anthony Powell's *Afternoon Men* (1931), appearing nearly at the same time as *Vile Bodies*, both set their sights squarely on Bloomsbury, while Richard Aldington's *Stepping Heavenward* (1931) targeted Tom and Vivienne Eliot.

At a glance, the satirical bent of such works seems starkly at odds with the deliberately autobiographical modes of Isherwood and Upward. Yet veiled autobiographies, such as *Lions and Shadows* and *Prater Violet*, were no less obvious when it came to poaching the notoriety of their contemporaries. In Isherwood's review of Stephen Spender's autobiographical *World within World*, itself a response to his own *Lions and Shadows*, Isherwood describes the pleasure one feels when a friend publishes such a work: "When one of your best and oldest friends tells you that he is writing his autobiography, you naturally feel excited. You know that you will appear in it, and you are curious to see what you'll look like."[95] Even here, in what purports to be a review of a memoir, there is the somewhat disingenuous circuit of self-referentiality. The pleasure Isherwood describes exists only for those writers whose identities have already become disembodied objects of renown and whose reputations are consequently pegged to the reputations of their fellow literary travellers. The manner in which Isherwood universalizes an inherently particularized experience points to the increasing instrumentality that writers like Waugh, Isherwood, and others found in using authors' names and signatures as imprimaturs and as mechanisms of celebrity. The larger issue here is that the two cultural economies become mutually revealing: the imprimatur moves beyond aesthetic economies, which are predicated on the idiosyncrasies of individual talent and styles, and sanctions the wide dissemination of elite cultural signatures in mass economies of value.

EXPERIMENTS IN MODERNIST *VANITAS*

In the early 1980s, *Le Monde* published a series of weekly interviews with leading European intellectuals. One interviewee, billed theatrically as *le philosophe masqué*, insisted on anonymity as a precondition for his appearance.[96] Deliberately subverting the featured interview's conventions, the unnamed author's condition of anonymity correlates cleverly with the subject advanced in the interview. If authors are not named do they function as authors? Is the identity of the unnamed author thinly masked, as the newspaper's editors would have it, bedecked like Christo's Reichstag in drapery that refuses to conceal? Or, does the author simply cease to exist once unnamed?

Along these lines, the interviewee proposed something akin to a thought experiment:

I shall propose a game: that of the "year without a name." For a year books would be published without their authors' names. The critics would have to cope with a mass of entirely anonymous books. But, now I come to think of it, it's possible they would have nothing to do: all the authors would wait until the following year before publishing their books.

Thought experiments pose impossible interventions in the world and then speculate about their consequences. The intervention proposed here – disrupting the literary marketplace by a year in which anonymity masks all authors – promises to contemplate the possibilities produced by founding a regime of authorial non-entity.

The promise is forestalled. The experiment gets only as far as confounded reviewers unable to make discriminations, tangled in a mess of indistinguishable texts, and then goes awry, when the interviewee remarks that the authors themselves would refuse to participate. Authors, he foresees, would prefer to cease to exist than serve a marketplace that refuses them their names. From the standpoint of those who see themselves as potential authors, authorial unnaming blocks the object of their desires – a literary marketplace that unnames authors turns the function of authorship upside down.

It is worth noting that the experiment does not run its course in the directions that Roland Barthes imagines in "Death of the Author." Comprehensive effacement of authorial identity does not give way to Barthian idealism: the etherizing ethics of unhierarchical intertextuality, readerly liberation, and the author-god dethroned. Authorship, once demystified, does not dissipate. The author, in this formulation, is stronger stuff, a property of literary systems at once historical, epiphenomenal, and inexorable. It is historical in that its appearances are rooted historically; it is epiphenomenal in that it is neither the nominal nor the officially sanctioned commodity of literary production but rather a side-effect; and it is inexorable in that, to use show-business lingo, it is "part of the act" – without it there is no act. Having authors *becomes* an inescapable requirement for regulating certain, historically circumscribed forms of cultural consumption. Though they are meaning-made, authors are, in other words, neither merely meaning-made bodies nor meaning-made things easily barred from literary systems. Instead, authors function like delivery vehicles for specific, historically registered parcels of meaning.[97]

The interview, the lead-piece in the Sunday supplement of *Le Monde* that week, is accompanied by an illustration evoking the uncanny protagonist of the 1933 film *The Invisible Man*, a filled-out suit, empty, professorial, Hamlet-like, contemplating a skull held in an outstretched glove.

Anonymity is modernist *vanitas*. We are assured by this illustration, the interview's eminent placing in the newspaper, and the text of the interview's header, that, though unnamed, the interviewee is "un grand nom" and a figure "de grand renom." It is somewhat different to read this interview among the interviews and essays of Michel Foucault's *Politics, Philosophy, Culture*, but, even contained in *Le Monde*, it already has Foucault's *name all over it*.[98]

If nothing else, its implicit critique of Barthes' "Death of the Author" leads "perspicacious readers" (the kind, recalling James's words, on whom nothing is lost) to Foucault's "What Is an Author?" *Le Monde*'s editors frame the interview in these terms at any rate, explaining it to their readers as an exercise in the detection of authorial identity. By the end of the interview, they write, the most perceptive readers will have no problem solving the mystery, unmasking the mysterious identity of the respondent. Effacing the authorial name, it seems, lays bare an even more resilient role for the author-function in the textual condition – that is, reading texts to detect the traces of authorship. On the face of it, Foucault's experiment with anonymity cannot come off, but is this not, after all, the point?

In "What is an Author?" Foucault writes that literary anonymity is "not tolerable" for readers, because they "accept it only in the guise of enigma."[99] Just as the *Le Monde* thought experiment suggests how anonymity is intolerable to authors, so too, Foucault's larger experiment with anonymity suggests how such anonymity is intolerable to readers. It demonstrates how high reading places its stakes in detecting authorship even, perhaps especially, with those works with shadowy authorship. If the text and its textual frames were wiped free of all ideolect marked by Foucault (the usual haunts, the pet subjects, phrases and words), the need to detect the author's name would become, quite paradoxically, more acute as a "classificatory function" (in Foucault's words).

Foucault's "What Is an Author?" – the most far-reaching theoretical consideration of this topic – redirects critical attention from the author outside the text, who appears exterior and antecedent to the work, to the author on the inside, so to speak. It is the author on the inside (the author's name, the implied author) who designates and guarantees a unified, self-identical work. This name, Foucault writes,

permits one to group together a certain number of texts, define them, differentiate them from and contrast them to others . . . The fact that several texts have been placed under the same name indicates that there has been established among them a relationship of homogeneity, filiation, authentication of some texts by the use of others, reciprocal explication, or concomitant utilization. The author's name serves to characterize a certain mode of being of discourse: the fact that the discourse has an author's name, that one can say "this was written by so-and-so" or "so-and-so is its author," shows that this discourse is not ordinary speech that merely comes and goes, not something . . . immediately consumable. On the contrary, it is . . . speech that must be received in a certain mode and that, in a given culture, must have a certain status.[100]

At issue in Foucault's description of the practice of classifying texts via authorship is the distance of the authorial figure. On the one hand, the author's purported individuality is empirically remote from the critical scene of reading. Where else is the author except in acts of reading where authorial causality is detected and attributed? On the other hand, as a concept, the author remains intact as, Foucault writes, "the principle of thrift in the proliferation of meaning."[101]

For all their categorical differences as epistemological functions, the coordinates of authorship (narration, implied authorship, real authorship, etc.) are not incommensurate frames of reference. If Foucault is buried in Paris, discussed in Berkeley, and open on my desk, where is the author? This particular category mistake – corpse, discourse, book – points to the global confusion of categories and registers that underwrite notions of subjectivity more generally, category mistakes which are commonplaces in the scene of reading. The author-function is rarely discrete – does the term "author" designate the literary producer, the biographical subject, the psycho-biographical subject, the lifework, the life and the work, the work, the object artifact, the oeuvre, the self, the transcendental ego, conscious-ness, creative faculties, the imagination, genius, general intention, reason, logos, cogito, ego, being, idea, thought, cognition, or mind? Keeping this repository of slippery, semi-distinct notions mystified is the privilege of literary discourse and bourgeois individuality, more broadly. For all their structural differences, keeping these coordinates radically apart proves intol-erable to readers, as Foucault suggests, and, what is more, there are a host of pragmatic incentives for promoting their measured proximity, stacked in a particular order, as the modernists discovered.

The author's *a priori* position as the absent cause for literary objects, the core of Foucault's analysis, supports the entire mode of discourse. When the author's name is connected to a work, it registers as an absent cause, and, as an absent cause, like Vereker's general intention, it is irreducible to either the interior or the exterior of the text. Seemingly, by indexing authorial self-consciousness "on the outside," the author's name signifies, willy-nilly, that the text itself is coherent and self-identical "on the inside." In Foucault's description, no intrinsic connection exists between authorial intentions (the self-conscious author, the authorial interior exterior) and textual coherence (the textual manifestation of the author, the textual exterior interior), but rather, a constitutive homology between notions of textual coherence and presumptions of authorial intentions produces the effect of authorship. Modernists, who embraced the disembodied and dispossessed mind of the author as the textual signified *sine qua non*, originate this mode of discourse, from which Foucault, despite his analysis, also recognizes that he cannot be extracted unharmed.

When the interviewer asks the anonymous Foucault to account for the condition of anonymity, Foucault claims to refuse the authorial name "[o]ut of nostalgia for a time when, being quite unknown, what [he] said had some chance of being heard," out of nostalgia, as it were, for a time when "the surface of contact [with readers] was unrippled."[102] Behind this desire for communicative transparency lies a distinctly modernist wish: the obliteration of authorial self by the author's work. In this formulation, work itself is understood in a particularly modernist way, as a presentation of mind. In the interview, Foucault expresses a desire that readers have unmediated contact with that which the text presents them, which turns out to be nothing less than his ideas presented as self-sustaining mental events. The register of Foucault's problem shifts into a modernist framework when the problem of describing the relationship between the author and the text is resolved by describing the author's mind in a textual site of embodiment.

In the context of modernism, as we have seen, author effects also come in the form of thought experiments about the absent cause of literary work. As Foucault suggests in the *Le Monde* interview, these experiments tend to leave authorship at once dispossessed and enhanced, resolved with authorial selfhood damned at the same time as the mark of the author is sacralized. In "Tradition and the Individual Talent," for instance, T. S. Eliot comments upon the author-function *avant la lettre* by means of his famous "finely filiated platinum" analogy. Splitting the "mature" artist into "the man who suffers" and "the mind which creates," Eliot, in effect, dispenses with the surface features of the romantic authorial ideal – specifically, that authors express their personal emotions through their art – while tacitly reinforcing the logic of this ideal – that authors are instruments of transcendent valuation. In the analogy, a shred of platinum (the artist's mind) catalyzes oxygen and sulfur dioxide (the ordinary mental states of all who suffer) into "sulphurous acid" (exquisite works-of-art). Though the catalytic agent, the pure substance of the artist's mind, passes through reaction unchanged and unabsorbed, its agency is nevertheless realized by enabling the process. At the same time as he removes personality (ordinary sufferings) from authorship, Eliot reifies the authorial mind, the shred of platinum, as an agent whose sole agency lies in making the production of the great works-of-art possible.[103]

Equating impersonalization with the disinterestedness of scientific method, Eliot argues – in a famous instance of modernist as scientist manqué – that the impersonalization of modernist aesthetics and literary production, more broadly, approaches "the condition of science." He means, in other words, that the practitioner's "personal emotions . . . provoked by particular events in his life" are immaterial in both fields.[104] Eliot's "impersonal theory of poetry" concerns, in fact, the role of authorial agency in modernism.[105] He does not impersonalize the content of poems in themselves *per se* but rather impersonalizes production for itself, "the relation of the poem to its author." Tellingly, his "mature" author is a thing not a person; the reification is evinced not only by his framing analogy, but also by his use of the relative pronoun "which" rather than "who" – *the man who suffers, the mind which creates*. Authorial agency, then, represents not so much a feature of superlative subjectivity but a signifying thing, a functional manifestation of the times. Dispossessed of the sufferings of his "private mind," having escaped personality, the mind of Eliot's mature author comes to signify the zeitgeist instead, representing the "mind of Europe – the mind of his own country."[106]

Eliot is reluctant to name the exact cause of this transformation; he only suggests how and where to recognize its signifying effects, namely, among preeminent monuments of culture, "all the works of art which preceded it": the author's significance "is the appreciation of his relation to dead poets and artists. You cannot value him alone; you must set him, for contrast and comparison, among the dead."[107] The conception of authorship – as the distinguishing imprimatur of exemplary artistic consciousness – enables the author's name to circulate as a type of rarefied commodity in the economies of great names that circulate in modernist critical prose and elsewhere.

Herbert Read's application of Eliot's catalyst metaphor in *The Politics of the Unpolitical* (1943) shows how this conception of authorship slips into political registers. Read revisits Shelley's infamous phrase, so often transmuted into High Modernist boilerplate: great writers are "the *unacknowledged* legislators of the world." They constitute "the expression of the mind of a whole people" (Eliot), "the antennae of the race" (Pound), "the consciousness of the race at any given time" (Leavis), and "our storehouse of our recorded values" (Richards). The reason the legislation has gone unacknowledged, Read writes, is because the artistic mind is not only "unchanged" in the process but also "unabsorbed" by it.[108] To use Eliotic language: dead writers are not acknowledged to be the true legislators of the world because they (that is, their suffering catalyzed into works-of-art) are really that which is legislated. In this manner, modernists like Eliot contrived an economy in which a sparse selection of literary names of the past becomes a means of conferring value on select modern works-of-art. In the guise of the imprimatur, the modernist plots a phantasmal escape through the imagined hazards of the literary present into transhistorical economies of valuation.

That the modernist's signature had become a supreme commodity itself was not lost on literary modernists. In *The Revenge for Love* (1937), Wyndham Lewis's satirical novel about British intellectuals and artists and the Spanish Civil War, the artist Victor Stamp – whose name itself conveys the signature – is literally disassociated from his signature. Specimens of Stamp's well-practiced, flamboyant autograph float through the text. Initially, Stamp treats his signature like a prized component of his artistic identity. Yet, he never has a chance to control the circulation of his autograph. First, he exhibits unsigned paintings with the People's Art League (an institution, no doubt, based on Roger Fry's Omega Workshops). These will not sell even at "deliberately low prices" because they lack the necessary mark of distinction. Later, Stamp is employed in the faking of Van Goghs in an art-counterfeiting factory. There, he produces his best work – a Van Gogh simulacrum better than the original – but when the factory's signature specialist comes in to forge Vincent's signature, Stamp decides to destroy the painting. In the novel's last chapter, Stamp becomes embroiled in a plan to run guns to Spanish communists, and a forgery of his signature mysteriously appears on a letter that will implicate him in the political intrigue. Stamp responds with measured indifference: "Use my name! Why not? It's all one to me. What's in a name?"[109] If Stamp's indifference and loss of control of his own signature radically questions the political potential of imprimaturs as means of artistic agency, it also signals the literary modernist's acquiescence to liquidity and ubiquity, to its use and exchange values. Like Lewis's novel, thirties author-novels such as *Vile Bodies, Journey to the Border*, and *Prater Violet*, which draw their own conclusions about the mass commodification of the artist's work, mark an increased sense of the emptiness of the construction of modernists' authorial identity in times of crisis.

Yet, the imprimatur, whether embraced, parodied, or renounced by individual authors, remains stubbornly entrenched in the scene of reading and suspended in the cultural superstructure. "What difference does it make who is speaking?"[110] Foucault's *Le Monde* experiment negates this question with which he ends the "What is an Author?" essay. The studied indifference of the question, Foucault writes, is "one of the fundamental ethical principles" of contemporary *écriture*. It is

"ethical" because this indifference is not really a trait characterizing the manner in which one speaks and writes, but rather a kind of immanent rule, taken up over and over again, never fully applied, not designating writing as something complete, but dominating it as a practice.[III]

As a prescriptive ethics, the poststructuralist attempt to free writing of authorship has obscured the ongoing functionality of the "immanent rule" that modernism stipulates, namely that *who is speaking*, because it can be dispossessed, disembodied, and made fungible, is everything.

CHAPTER 2

Adjectives

The anecdote about how Ezra Pound taught the young Ernest Hemingway to guard against over-populating his work with adjectives is well known. Hemingway refers to the lesson in *A Moveable Feast*. In the early 1920s, Pound

> was the man I liked and trusted the most as a critic . . . the man who believed in the *mot juste* – the one and only correct word to use – the man who taught me to distrust adjectives as I would later learn to distrust certain people in certain situations.[1]

Adjectives are cads, second- or even third-raters in the pecking order of syntax, crowding verbs, becoming dependent on nouns to which they add color, a characteristic, an attribute perhaps, but little else. From the beginning, Pound's critical prose is preoccupied with this brand of grammatical alarmism. One must keep a close eye on the proliferation of words, especially adjectives. In *The Spirit of Romance* (1910), for example, he writes: "the true poet is most easily distinguished from the false, when he trusts himself to the simplest expression, and when he writes without adjectives."[2] Without claiming that poets can abandon them altogether, Pound treats over-used adjectives as uncontrolled poetic contagion, deteriorating the distinctions that separate true from false poets.

In later work, Pound counts the imprecise use of adjectives among the many deleterious signs of "bad economics" – "with usura the line grows thick/with usura is no clear demarcation," et cetera – recommending the Chinese ideogram as a more exact alternative.[3] For Pound, the problem with adjectives stems from their liquidity and their oversupply. A red dawn may be "rosy-fingered" for Chapman's Homer, cloaked "in russet mantle" for Shakespeare, but, for Milton or Swinburne, the epithets are on loan, "an advance [which is] too often merely a high-sounding word and not a swift symbol of vanished beauty."[4] According to Pound, the ideogram for red is more precise than any English epithet, because its reference has been set to a fixed standard: it joins an abstraction to "the real shape of things," not metaphor, but "abbreviated pictures of ROSE-CHERRY-IRON RUST-FLAMINGO." An abstraction should consist of "something everyone KNOWS," something specific to a national culture. "If ideogram developed in England," he writes, "the writer would have possibly substituted the front side of a robin or something less exotic than a flamingo."[5] In the *Guide to Kulchur* (1938), the decisive statement of Pound's cultural project for better and worse, he argues that an entire national culture is proven – in the senses of demonstrated *and* secured – by the worth of its most minuscule details, in its adjectives, so to speak.[6]

Given the diagnosis, one wonders what Pound made of the frequent transformation of his own name into the adjective *Poundian*. In 1920, for example, in a review of "Homage to Sextus Propertius," a critic writes:

More and more as we read we become aware of the Poundian personality: that queer composite of harsh levity, spite, cocksureness, innuendo, pedantry, archaism, sensuality, real if sometimes perverse and unfortunate research and honest love of literature.[7]

By adding the adjective suffix *-ian*, the reviewer, in effect, uses *Pound* to diminish Pound's own work, offering the word as a shorthand for the bundle of cutting associations elaborated in the remainder of the sentence. With somewhat invidious effect, the adjective *Poundian* insinuates that Pound's work suffers because it derives from him. Here, calling Pound's work *Poundian* indicates that it does not stand on its own, that it must instead be buttressed with the objectionable presence of Pound's personality.

Even when not reflected back on the author named, the authorial adjective accommodates the purposes of critical excoriation quite well. As in:

[The writer] has adopted his subject's deliberately simple declarative style. The opening and closing of the book are archly Hemingwayesque; some parts of the 640 pages that come between are simply Hemingwayese.[8]

Or:

[The writer's] examination of Milton's verse keeps turning into Sitwellian claptrap.[9]

Or:

In this new short book he is more a Poundian than a critic.[10]

In all three examples, the authorial adjectives intimate that the writer under scrutiny is derivative. While *Hemingwayesque* may be preferable to *Hemingwayese* in the first example, the application, by pointing out

Hemingway's susceptibility to stylistic parody, degrades both parties compared. The second example uses the word *Sitwellian* less to elucidate the meaning of *clap-trap* than to compound its affront. Begging the question of whether or not the Sitwells' literary efforts are, in fact, a particular variety of claptrap, the statement engages one critical object (an examination of Milton's verse) by trafficking in another critical judgment surreptitiously (the Sitwells are prone to claptrap-ism). The third example enacts this dynamic of covert criticism as well. *Poundian*, in this case a substantive, *an admirer or disciple of Ezra Pound*, weighs both subject and object of the comparison, Pound's would-be critic and Pound himself, syllogistically:

This would-be critic is a Poundian, not a critic.
A Poundian is a kind of failed critic.
Ergo, Pound himself (that is, Pound in some aspect of his notoriously telegraphic and bombastic critical idiom) *is a kind of failed critic.*

In this fashion, authorial adjectives are nothing if not critically functional, even if not always employed for purposes of devaluation.

Because they work via implied comparisons, comparisons which, at least potentially, draw upon the entire reference of an author's name (and which yield an inventory of slippery, semi-distinct notions about author and text), authorial adjectives tend to handle authors as if they were critical balances and counterbalances. When a book reviewer writes

in the Beckett age, he [Shakespeare] can be the first to stare boldly into the meaningless abyss which is our universe

the sentence works like a weighing machine of names – and imprimaturs.[11] Its basis – that a reader recognize a particular idea for carrying Beckett's imprimatur – in fact, does the critical work it purports to take for granted; it posits characteristics of Beckett's writings. Joined to a specific characteristic, the author's name becomes a means of universalizing a continuous, ontological restatement of the author function. The adjectival *Beckett* (or Beckettian) promises to condense and digest the entire work of reading Beckett in a way that can pull Shakespeare out of history, inviting the past to scrutinize the present.

Although coining authorial adjectives is notoriously easy, applicable in theory to any author, only a limited number of instances have attracted notice in *The Oxford English Dictionary*. Most of these are the obvious choices, the ones that seem most invested with cultural currency, though some inclusions and omissions seem capricious. One finds in the second edition, among others, *Ibsenian* and *Ibsenite, Jamesian,*

Shavian, Wellsian, Galsworthian, Yeatsian, Firbankian, Sitwellian, Woolfian, Poundian, Lawrentian, Joycean, Waughian, Huxleyan, Hemingwayan, Leavisian, Audenesque, Orwellian; from outside the English-speaking world, *Proustian, Kafkaesque, Flaubertian*; prior to the twentieth century, *Wildean, Paterian, Ruskinian, Brontëan, Dickensian, Arnoldian, Wordsworthian, Byronic, Shelleyan, Blakean, Burnsian, Miltonic, Johnsonian, Shakespearean, Spenserian, Chaucerian, Petrarchan, Pindaric, Sapphic, Homeric.* As this partial catalogue reflects, the form was not applied to modernists exclusively. Nor was it applied by modernists exclusively. Yet, taken together, these entries comprise a makeshift register, an inventory of authorial names charged with the utmost degree of connotative aura, a situation homologous with a conception of literary value articulated in much of modernist literary criticism.[12]

The entries for these words are remarkably uniform. The definitions themselves do not convey differences between authors, nor do they convey the varied shades of critical utility, documented in the citations. The following hypothetical entry, redressing one of the more acute oversights, incorporates the typical features of an entry:

Eliotic

Eliotic, /ɛlˈiɔtɪk/, *a.* [f. the name Eliot (see below) + -ic.] Of, pertaining to, or characteristic of the American (later naturalized British) writer and poet T. S. (Thomas Stearns) Eliot (1888–1965), his work, or the human condition which it evokes; like, or of the style of, Eliot; resembling or influenced by the style of Eliot.

Like all adjectives, the adjective *Eliotic* denotes a quality of a noun, a named thing. Specifically, the quality differentiating the noun is T. S. Eliot. Yet such definitions do not help those untutored in the oeuvre of T. S. Eliot to understand the phrase *Eliotic modernism*. Like the entries for authorial adjectives in the *OED*, the definition of *Eliotic* verges on tautology. Only rarely – in the case of *Orwellian*, for example – do entries specify the qualities being conveyed with detail or reference to particular works. Entries such as these do not explain, for example, what sort of mannerisms are Poundian mannerisms, what flavors are Joycean flavors, what intrigues are Firbankian intrigues, what burble is Miltonic burble and so on. Like Pound's ideal literary language – where direct experience of flamingos helps one understand "red" – to understand fully the word *Runyonesque* one must have direct experience of Damon Runyon's slang and to understand fully the phrase *Eliotic modernism*, direct experience of *The Waste Land*. Otherwise, the premise of authorial adjectives works much as Pound conceived the ideogram, by fixing an abstraction to a notional concretion. Although the concretion is alleged to exist beyond discourse, paradoxically, only repeated encounters with discourse can bear this out. Only a reader who has expertise with the alleged concretion, a reader who has read the author in question, can discern what characteristics, qualities, or mannerisms the adjective signifies in a given context, whether *Poundian* in a given context means polymath literary borrowings; crackpot economic and linguistic theories; idiosyncratic translations; Italian fascism; telegraphic prose; impatient stylistic experiment; a den of literary protégés; epistles to American senators; zealous phallus worship; a penchant for Provençal songs, Cavalcanti, Gavin Douglas, Chinese ideograms, abbreviated modal verbs, or maple syrup; or an aversion to Jews, Milton, Roosevelt, Amy Lowell, or certain kinds of adjective usage.

From a Poundian point-of-view, then, *authorial* adjectives are the *right* kind of modifier, but to say this only scratches the surface of a deeper congeniality with interwar thinking about the value of authors. More broadly construed, the uses and abuses of authorial adjectives, however ironically, represent a distilled restatement of a logic prevalent in period essays, occasional and practical criticism. In the critical wings of modernism, as in the discourse of authorial adjectives, 1) authors' names are compared and weighed, until 2) they come to comprise makeshift registers, in which value is adjudicated relationally, that is, 3) they are couched in a mystified entreaty to the *things in themselves*, to the "originals." In concert, these three features regulate a literary ideology based on exhaustively maintained scarcity. Ironically, writers often so censorious about the de-creating consequences of capitalist valuation were actively involved in the promotion of an economy that was itself based upon a kind of fetishized commodity, the scarce supply of literary "originals." In this economy, a sparse selection of names of the past becomes an instrument for conferring value on selected works-of-art in the present; and the need "to avoid saying what has already been said as well as it can," as Eliot puts it in *After Strange Gods*, becomes a relentless injunction with seemingly unlimited applications . . . down to the adjectives.[13]

Eliot and Pound did not really invent this ideology; they were among its most influential ideologues, its most orthodox "economists," in the company of I. A. Richards, F. R. Leavis, Q. D. Leavis, and the *Scrutiny* writers. Their criticism represents a narrow, albeit highly influential, intervention in a much broader economy of names, which spans the range of contemporary critical responses to modernist authors. These include the critical work of journalists and editors, like Edmund Wilson, Gilbert Seldes,

Malcolm Cowley, J. Middleton Murry, R. A. Scott-James; literary notables and belletrists, like Richard Aldington, Virginia Woolf, E. M. Forster,
Robert Graves, and Laura Riding; as well as a host of other, somewhat
less-illustrious reviewers and academicians. The combined effect of their
activities creates what is, perhaps, the ultimate makeshift register, the closed
system of interdependent, inter-signified names which enables the name of
an individual author to circulate as elite currency. In the twenties and thirties, responding to modernism often meant trafficking in various authorial
names like so many emergent currencies; each critical approach, an arbitrage of names; each sustaining the system and its logic of valuation.

In 1929, James Joyce authorized C. K. Ogden to translate a large section of
"Anna Livia Plurabelle" into Basic English.

Anna was, Livia is, Plurabella's to be. Northmen's thing made southfolk's place but
howmulty plurators made eachone in person? Latin me that, my trinity scholard,
out of eure sanscreed into oure eryan! *Hircus Civis Eblanensis!* He had buckgoat
paps on him, soft ones for orphans. Ho, Lord! Twins of his bosom. Lord save us!
And ho! Hey? What all men. Hot? His tittering daughters of. Whawk?

becomes

Anna was, Livia is, Plurabella's to be. Our Norwegian Thing-seat was where Suffolk
Street is, but what number of places will make things into persons? Put that into
Latin, my Trinity Man, out of your Sanskrit into our Aryan. *Hircus Civis Eblanensis!*
He was kind as a he-goat, to young without mothers. O, Laws! Soft milk bags two.
O, Laws! O, Laws! Hey! What, all men? What? His laughing daughters of? What?

Basic English was, as the passage above makes clear, an invented, streamlined
version of English, described by its inventor as "the International Language
of 850 words in which everything may be said."[14] The selling point was its
simplified lexicon that fit, supplemented by simplified grammar and usage
notes, on a single small crib. It was designed by Ogden and I. A. Richards not
to replace "Complete English," but rather to provide non-native learners
with a fully functional propaedeutic – one, they hoped, which would lubri-
cate universal understanding and global exchange.[15] According to Ogden
and Richards, the 850 represented the condensed lexicon of "Complete
English," the basic commodities in constant lexical demand, encapsulating
the meaning of all other words.[16] Using a method that Ogden, a Bentham
enthusiast, called "panoptic conjugation," they removed all redundant
words: all complex words – that is, all words definable in ten words or

less – were replaced with their "more basic" definiens. The stripped-down grammar of Basic followed the same anti-discursive logic. The standard parts of speech were scrapped, replaced by 400 general things (abstractions), 200 picturable things, 100 general qualities (adjectives), 50 opposites (more adjectives in binary pairs), and 100 operators (verbs, conjunctions, prepositions).[17]

George Orwell's dystopian Newspeak in *Nineteen Eighty-Four* was doubtlessly a meditation on the darker implications of this utopia.[18] Syme the lexicographer tells Winston Smith that

the whole aim of Newspeak is to narrow the range of thought . . . In the end we shall make thoughtcrime literally impossible, because there will be no words in which to express it. Every concept that can ever be needed will be expressed by exactly *one* word, with its meaning rigidly defined and all its subsidiary meanings rubbed out and forgotten.[19]

One might suspect that Basic, however salutary its intent, was broadly ridiculed in a literary climate not especially given to language stripped of its literary pretensions or concerned with utilitarian ideals such as "technological efficiency" or "purely functional or operational phrases" for the transmission of meaning.[20] Such was not the case; quite the contrary, in fact. Along with Joyce and I. A. Richards, G. B. Shaw, T. S. Eliot, Ezra Pound, William Empson, Lawrence Durrell, and even Orwell, it seems, at one time or other, spoke in favor of Basic.[21] Utopian premises aside, Basic momentarily seemed, for Joyce and others, to be a potentially viable means for disseminating literary work both beyond the highbrow and abroad, a possible intermediary step between originals and either annotations or translations.

Pound's reaction, as usual, best glosses the compatibility between the lexical rationing of Basic and modernist critical projects. In an article written for *The New English Weekly* in 1935, he claims that Basic's benefits are threefold:

I. As a training and exercise, especially for excitable yeasty youngsters who want so eagerly to mean something that they can't take out time to think: What?
II. As a sieve. As a magnificent system for measuring extant works. As a jolly old means of weeding out bluffs, for weeding out fancy trimmings . . . If a novelist can survive translation into basic, there is something solid under his language . . .
III. dly, and this is our specific opportunity. The advantage of BASIC vocabulary limited to 850 words and their variants . . . for the diffusion of ideas is, or should be, obvious to any man of intelligence.[22]

In effect, the three points translate the Basic English program into a modernist's critical vocabulary of weights and measures. The points resemble the original Basic planks of education and dissemination superficially, but the emphasis has shifted, underscoring Basic's function as an instrument of authentication while ignoring its ambitions as a universal second language. The first point proposes Basic as a means to authenticate language-use, a way to train students to employ only words *charged* with the *utmost degree* of *meaning* and shape their aimless literary aspirations with chisels of Basic translations and propaganda.[23] Even in the third, most straightforward point – in which recognizing Basic as a potent medium of knowledge becomes an intelligence test – the rhetorical shift is evident. The second point, however, most alien to the Basic agenda, best expresses how the economics represented by a scaled down lexicon comes to implicate the literary uses of words and their authors.

For Pound, the relationship between the concepts of a bounded lexicon and a bounded register of authors' names is more than analogical: Basic promises the ultimate means to authenticate an author's words by, in effect, undoing them, by disenchanting the words from the superficial residue of authorship, so to speak. If "Anna Livia Plurabelle" remains Joycean in Basic form, then original words are proved to be more than prolix ornaments pointing immaterially to greater and greater numbers of words. What else is Pound's *solid* referent *under language* besides Joyce the authentic remainder, the remainder for the sake of which an author is admitted into the active register of *extant* names, the list of survivors for which literary value had been thus secured.[24]

The "harsh treatment . . . accorded a number of meritorious writers," Pound writes in *ABC of Reading,*

proceeds from a firm conviction that the only way to keep the best writing in circulation, or to "make the best poetry popular," is by drastic separation of the best from a great mass of writing that has been long considered of value, that has over-weighted all curricula, and that is to be blamed for the very pernicious current idea that a good book must be of necessity a dull one.[25]

It is the same ideology of scarcity, underwriting attempts to reduce, regulate, thin out, digest, and condense the names of authors in circulation, which leads writers like Pound to rail against the "superfluous word," call for vigilant accounting of proliferating adjectives, and endorse Basic English. Critics who have argued for a sea-change midway through Pound's career, from aestheticism to political activism, often miss this remarkable continuity in the modes of applied scarcity across the span of his critical work.[26]

Pound's aversion to the over-use of adjectives in his imagist phase is not merely an early fixation of Mauberley-like aesthetic dilettantism. On the contrary, it is rooted in a more comprehensive aversion to oversupply, which Pound shares with other early advocates of modernism and which forms much of the basis for their critical interventions in mass culture and society.

Pound's imagist polemic of 1913, "A Few Don'ts," for example, his most famous jeremiad against adjectives, is not only preoccupied with *le mot juste* but also with an economy of valuation that seemingly cannot resist finding broader applications. "Use no superfluous word," he writes,

no adjective which does not reveal something. Don't use such an expression as "dim lands *of peace*." It dulls the image. It mixes an abstraction with the concrete. It comes from the writer's not realizing that the natural object is always *the* adequate symbol.[27]

The same over-use which has worn out words also signifies the decay of influence:

Be influenced by as many great artists as you can, but have the decency to acknowledge the debt outright, or try to conceal it. Don't allow "influence" to mean merely that you mop up the particular decorative vocabulary of some one or two poets whom you happen to admire.[28]

Influence, for Pound, must be harnessed with restrictive caveats. Calling attention to the widespread circulation of devalued, second-hand goods fuels demand for originality. When Pound recommends reading lists of *great artists*, which he will with increasing frequency in the coming decades, each carefully accounted name represents a particular debt owed to specific authors, the few whom he calls the inventors and masters. In this way, the critical accounting of influence supports a system of literary value backed by the preeminence of a few authors. Consequently, a writer who carelessly spreads phrases like *dim lands of peace* does detriment to the system; he or she disseminates someone else's words without paying tribute to productive sources.

This kind of thinking, moving readily from adjectives to authors, is easily applied to non-literary forms and so lends itself to a broader scrutiny of the times. Thus, in the same passage, Pound complains of

[a] Turkish war correspondent . . . recently caught red-handed babbling in his dispatches of "dove-grey" hills, or else it was "pearl-pale," I can not remember.[29]

Once elaborated, the cautions Pound offers would-be modernists turn out to be less *ex cathedra* and more pragmatic than they have often been represented. It is, of course, a characteristically modernist form of pragmatism, one which, as Balachandra Rajan so aptly writes concerning Eliot's criticism, is "embedded in and nourished by the literary situation it endeavors to move forward . . . seeking to reconsider the canon in order to align it with contemporary interests."[30] More precisely stated, this form of criticism does not describe the features of the contemporary literary scene of the period so much as make the notion of a contemporary literary scene possible. When Pound writes that the poetry of the coming decades will be "austere, direct, free from emotional slither" and "will have fewer painted adjectives impeding the shock and stroke of it," it is less a prediction than a prescription indispensable to the survival of small-scale cultural production in an age of mechanical reproduction.[31]

The prescription of applied scarcity, nascent in even Pound's earliest critical writings, comes to a head in his didactic guidebooks of the thirties, his seminal pamphlet *How to Read* (1931), and books like *ABC of Reading* (1934) and *Guide to Kulchur* (1938). Its first substantial airing comes, quite tellingly, in the early twenties, with Pound's contribution to the inaugural volume of Eliot's *Criterion* in 1923. The piece, "On Criticism in General," presents his version of *The Criterion's* mission – beating out Eliot's official editorial statement by one issue. It pins the future of the journal's literary mission on a well-pruned readership willing to implement the aesthetic *risorgimento*. With quasi-militaristic language and dispatch, he casts aside half the journal's readership as unfit for duty and calls to action "the half-thousand exiles and proscripts who are ready to risk the coup" to re-organize their reading habits "in some stricter fashion."[32] To this end, he unveils a formal system of categories, a heuristic designed to assist the army's campaign of singling out the authors worth reading. Anticipating his attraction to Basic ten years later, he explains the heuristic as a critical sieve, a means of *augmenting value* by way of *reducing number*. Retained and tweaked throughout the thirties, this heuristic distills Pound's longstanding literary critical preoccupations, redressing the need he highlighted ten years before in *The Spirit of Romance* for a means to adjudicate the present literary scene by means of the literary past, "a literary scholarship, which will weigh Theocritus and Yeats with one balance, and which will judge dull dead men as inexorably as dull writers of today."[33]

Outwardly, Pound's heuristic consists of five classes of authors ranked by degrees of originality and innovation:

A. The "predecessors," inventors, discoverers of fragments which are later used in masterwork; Arnaut Daniel and the better Troubadours, the hypothetical ballad writers who went before Homer, etc.
B. The "greats," the "masters."

C. The diluters, those who follow either small discoverers or great writers and who produce something less, something more flabby, in the wake of the real.

D. (and this class contains the bulk of all writing). The men who do more or less good style of a period. Of these, the delightful anthologies, the song books, the matters of taste, for you prefer Wyatt to Donne, Donne to Herrick, Drummond of Hawthornden to Brown who wrote "Led by the blind and halit by a bairn," or vice versa, in response to a purely personal sympathy. And these people . . . add but a slight personal flavour, a slight variant, to their own pages, without affecting the main form of the story.

E. One might add a fifth class: the starters of crazes . . . whose wave of fashion flows over writing for a few decades or even centuries, and then subsides, leaving the solid things where they were.[34]

Pound later added a sixth class: the "writers of belle-lettres," the "men who didn't really invent anything, but who specialized in some part of writing, who couldn't be considered as 'great men' or as authors who were trying to give a complete presentation of life, or of their epoch" – though the addition appears only for the sake of completeness.[35] To put the heuristic to proper use, Pound instructs readers, they must train themselves solely on the first two classes, on identifying the so-called *inventors* and *masters*, those responsible for innovations and those responsible for perfecting them. Thus, inventors and masters not only merit the majority of one's critical attention but also become one's critical instruments: "If a man have these two in his memory, he can fairly well 'place' or estimate any example of the latter classes . . . he won't be sold a pup by some dealer in false antiquities."[36] It is telling that Pound equates the capacity to discern the first two classes of authors from the remainder with the ability to detect inferior goods in the marketplace. For him, inventors and masters are, in effect, benchmarks, standards of critical measurement. The connection with the marketplace is crucial for this mode of literary criticism both in its manifest rhetoric and its less conspicuous yet consummate veneration of scarce goods. A reader who has an operative sense of the two categories, Pound writes, can cut through empty literary orthodoxy (the "half-knowing and half-thinking critics") crowding the great writers and present readers like a "mass of dead matter" in marketplace proportions of "one barrel of sawdust to each half-bunch of grapes."[37]

The heuristic relating author to author has the avowed purpose of guiding readers into a well-regulated economy of words as they "examine works where language is efficiently used."[38] Evoking his appraisal of Basic, Pound's *system for measuring extant works* links a few words, a few authors, a few works, and a few readers as mutually defined and mutually dependent commodities, things that seemingly find their inherent correspondences in shared scarcity.[39] The heuristic and its instructions, at the heart of "How to Read" and the *ABC of Reading*, represent literally, as the titles intimate, the basic rules for compiling reading lists for all "those who might like to learn," from the most inexperienced student to the professor hardened with "empiric professional knowledge."[40] Pound's heuristic purports to enable readers to see for themselves, to construe their own closefisted catalogues of inventors and masters, to figure for themselves, in Eliot's phrase, the "balance-sheet of English literature."[41] Pound repeatedly incites readers to call the bluff ("YOU WILL NEVER KNOW either why I chose them [some authors over others], or why they were worth choosing, or why you approve or disprove my choice, until you go to the TEXTS, the originals"), but whether different readers will arrive at different balances is beside the point.[42] Here, the precise names canonized are less significant than the act of instituting originality, mastery, and scarcity as operative principles in the use of words and the circulation of authors' names.

The most familiar version of this form of literary economics comes from Eliot in "Tradition and the Individual Talent." According to his account of elite literary production, the master is compelled "to write not merely with his own generation in his bones, but with a feeling that the whole of the literature of Europe from Homer and within it the whole of the literature of his own country has a simultaneous order and composes a simultaneous order."[43] The most superlative living authors, in other words, have an innate sympathy with the economy of names. This defining capacity, which seems to defy knowledge or intention, takes in the economy of extant names and reconfigures it to account for it own emergent currency. When a new work appears, it alters the order of

all the works of art which preceded it. The existing monuments form an ideal order among themselves, which is modified by the introduction of the new (the really new) work of art among them. The existing order is complete before the new work arrives; for order to persist after the supervention of novelty, the *whole* existing order must be, if ever so slightly, altered; and so the relations, proportions, values of each work of art towards the whole are readjusted.[44]

Eliot's existing monuments are structurally related to Pound's countless "exhibits"; E. M. Forster's British Museum reading room; F. R. Leavis's Eliot, Pound, Hopkins, Austen, George Eliot, James, Conrad, and D. H. Lawrence; Edmund Wilson's Yeats, Eliot, Joyce, Stein, Rimbaud, Valéry, and Proust; F. O. Matthiessen's Emerson, Whitman, James, and Eliot; and countless subsequent works of literary criticism in and through which the limited register circulates. And, where is this economy best exemplified – brought into being, so to speak – other than in the specific, ahistorical brand of literary economics elucidated and promoted by Pound, Eliot, and fellow economists?

F. R. Leavis, among the earliest, most studious readers of Eliot and Pound in this context, describes their critical instigations as a bid for "stock-taking . . . that has long been overdue . . . into the state of literary culture."[45] In *How to Teach Reading* (1932), responding to Pound's *How to Read*, he attempts to straighten out the accounts:

> It is assumed, of course, that he [the modern reader] is familiar with the classics, major and minor – and they are, in conventional acceptance, many – of his own tongue. Then there are *the* Classics. Homer, Aeschylus, Sophocles, Euripides, Theocritus, Virgil, Ovid, Catullus, Lucretius, Petronius, Apuleius and the rest . . . [I]t is the current "culture"-values that must be taken seriously: Joyce, Proust, Lawrence, Eliot, W. H. Auden (now that E. E. Cummings has gone out), Faulkner (succeeding to Hemingway), Valéry, Gide, Eluard, St.-J. Perse and a wide varying fringe. Apart from the *chic* contemporary names, one knows, of course, French literature in general and certain high currency-values in particular: Rimbaud, Laforgue, Corbière, Baudelaire . . . And the Russians are not yet forgotten. Then there is Dante, whom one hasn't merely read, as one has Goethe and Lucretius (for one has, of course, read Santayana's *Three Philosophical Poets*) . . . The list is long.[46]

Tongue in cheek, he describes the system of names inside which "the cultivated modern must pretend to be at home," demonstrating in the process the familiar ease with which modernists apply economic notions of currencies, commodities, and markets to literary culture. Names, ideas, whole national literatures go up or down in value; following the market becomes a full-time business. The joke is, of course, that the over-long list Leavis exhibits registers the influences of his own private reading, his various modernist informants, Pound, Eliot, Santayana, and Edmund Wilson. Ironically, for Leavis, like Pound and Eliot before him, the problem at hand – that is, the one facing the supposed "minority" for whom culture is more than dissipating distraction – remains over-accumulation. The extant names must be constantly thinned out, not so much to make them manageable as for the sake of preserving the list's elite cultural purchase.

As Eliot suggests in "Tradition and the Individual Talent," the principles of originality, mastery, and scarcity hold out in themselves the possibility that critical equilibrium may be found while sifting through, to use Leavis's metaphor, the contemporary scene. The principles encourage readers to apply themselves to the literary works of the living, the works which, *pace* Eliot, they have been charged to perceive in "simultaneous existence" and "simultaneous order" with those of the dead.[47] Hugh Kenner, for example, completes Pound's critical work *in absentia*, when, as if on cue, he borrows his heuristic and applies it to the still nascent modernist canon in *The Poetry of Ezra Pound* (1951). Kenner's application is, in a sense, the truth of Pound's heuristic, because it follows Pound's script, placing Pound on top, making him (once again) the recipient of his meticulously fashioned identity, poetic impresario, *il miglior fabbro*, latter-day Arnaut Daniel:

(a) *The inventors.* In our time, pre-eminently Pound.
(b) *The masters.* Eliot and Joyce.
(c) *The diluters.* Auden, Spender, the Sitwells, "the thirties".
(d) *Workers in "the style of the period."* To be filled in *ad lib.* W. C. Williams? Hemingway?
(e) *Belle Lettres.* Ford Madox Ford, perhaps.
(f) *Starters of crazes.* Gertrude Stein.[48]

For Kenner, in effect, Pound's program for a well-regulated economy of names yields but three for further consideration: Pound, Eliot, and Joyce. Here, as Kenner inscribes Pound within Pound's own notion, Pound's seemingly disinterested program to economize words and names, to level literary present and past, to place Theocritus and Yeats in a single balance, reveals itself to be one of modernism's most canny specimens of self-promotional propaganda.

Without a doubt, this deliberate overemphasis on too few authors made modernism appealing to those eager to amass cultural capital, including, among others, certain members of academia. It also, beyond any doubt, buttresses charges of modernism's fundamental cultural elitism. Yet, do Pound, Eliot, Leavis, and critical company in this regard interact with authorial names any differently in kind from other readers, or is the difference a question of amplitude? If their dependence on an ideology of originality, mastery, and scarcity is culturally oppositional (either elitist or resistant, depending on one's cultural politics), it nevertheless draws upon, and perhaps amplifies, prevalent, preexisting systems of value. The question at hand is whether or not the economy of names promoted by modernist literary economics is different in kind from the names circulating in the economy at large. The names of at least two of Kenner's three, James Joyce and T. S. Eliot, circulated in both economies; they conveyed broader associations and increasing renown throughout the twenties of an order coexisting with and even preceding their conceptual significance for modernist literary criticism.

THE SYMPTOM OF ELIOT

"It is hardly necessary at this time of day to point out the importance of Mr. Eliot as a symptom."[49] So writes a reviewer in early 1929 in *The Oxford Magazine* in a notice of Eliot's *For Lancelot Andrewes*. The context for this statement was the growing coherence of Eliot's political and religious conservatism and growing coherence of Eliot as a signifier. By the end of the twenties, readers had become accustomed to taking "Eliot" as a signifier for a number of social and cultural conditions; now, the reviewer observes, Eliot the symptom was undergoing significant changes. Eliot's conversion to Anglicanism, for example, which took place less than two years earlier, had been a keenly watched public display, and seemed to be undertaken as such, an act intimately related to his decision in the same year to become a British subject. As Leonard Woolf put it, it seemed that Eliot was "becoming an Anglican in a desperate effort to show that even in religion he is not an American."[50] More crucial than Eliot's citizenship, however, is the sense explicit in Woolf's remark that, for Eliot, becoming British and Anglican was a kind of performance, a display for which a broader interpretation was not just appropriate but also inevitable. From prominent acquaintances such as Woolf to anonymous undergraduate reviewers, the characteristic way T. S. Eliot was taken in his own time was as a kind of ominous cultural signifier, a symptom of the general state of cultural affairs. Between Eliot's somewhat unpropitious literary arrival with *Prufrock and Other Observations* in 1917 and the raising of the literary, political, and religious tricolor with *For Lancelot Andrewes* in 1928, finding out *the importance of Mr. Eliot the symptom* became a full-scale project for occasional reviewers, comparable only perhaps to the related phenomena with respect to *D. H. Lawrence* and *James Joyce*.

During these ten or so years, Eliot's name represented more than a coterie concern, more than a fringe avocation in bohemian quarters and among the literary intelligentsia. But, who knew of Eliot, one might ask, if fewer than 15,000 copies of *The Waste Land* (with and without his appended notes) made rounds in 1922 and 1923 in England and the United States between *The Criterion*, *The Dial*, the Boni and Liveright, and the Hogarth editions? In some ways, *who was reading Eliot* is the wrong yardstick to measure the circulation of Eliot's name. As a cultural signifier, Eliot's name represented more than the sum of those intimate with his works. In Lawrence Rainey's provocative formulation, modernism's success depended largely on the promotion of the author's reputation among non-readers, and "the not-reading that was practiced by the editors of the *Dial* [is] itself a trenchant 'reading' of *The Waste Land*'s place in the structural logic and development of literary modernism."[51]

Two examples will suffice to indicate the extent and nature of Eliot's celebrity following the publication of *The Waste Land* and the awarding of the Dial Prize. First, the following testimonial, with which the editors of *Vogue* nominated him to their "The Hall of Fame" in 1924: Eliot "has, metaphorically," they write, "the highest brow of any man alive"; second, the inaugural issue of *Time* magazine in 1923, then as now fashioning itself as an omniscient intermediary between highbrow and lowbrow. It published a spurious notice for *The Waste Land*, entitled "Shantih, Shantih, Shantih: Has the Reader Any Rights Before the Bar of Literature?" The case for the prosecution, it seems, consists solely of the coda of *The Waste Land*, the last eight lines, which, tweezed from the poem and any explanation, are offered as an open and shut case for condemnation. "There is a new kind of literature abroad in the land," *Time*'s writers remark, "whose only fault is that no one can understand it." In *Time*, highbrow inaccessibility is a fault; in *Vogue*, it is a virtue; but, in both cases, it is inaccessibility which solicits wider notice.

To track the circulation of Eliot's name we cannot confine our consideration to the name that circulates on the spines of books; owning the book and reading it, as publicists know, is only a temporary stopover in the greater circulation of the author's name. The reach of the name *James Joyce* during this period may best illustrate this point. Because of the troubled publication history of Joyce's work, there was an inescapable imbalance between those who knew of Joyce and those who knew Joyce's texts first hand. In the October 1922 *Dial*, the issue preceding the *Waste Land* number, the editors puff Eliot's coming attraction with a comparison to *Ulysses*, which comes out of this context: "It is not improbable that the appearance of *The Waste Land* will rank with that of *Ulysses* in the degree of interest it will call forth."[52] Why was this judged to be effective publicity? After all, who at this time in the United States or England was reading a complete copy of Joyce's *Ulysses*? Owning it was not only banned in both countries (until 1933 and 1936, respectively) but also prohibitively expensive.[53] Yes, copies were obtainable, through French diplomatic post, borrowed, smuggled-in copies, but even eager would-be readers like F. R. Leavis did not have access to them. Leavis tried to circumvent the ban in 1926, by appealing unsuccessfully to the Home Office for a dispensation "for purposes of illustration and comment in his course 'Modern Problems in Criticism.'"[54] It is Leavis's keen desire to have a copy of *Ulysses* and not the copy itself (or the contents thereof) that marks the reach of *James Joyce* the signifier.

In Michael Arlen's *The Green Hat* (1924), a novel which sold over 185,000 copies, Iris Storm picks up a copy of Joyce's *Ulysses* from a floor "so littered with books that you might hardly take a step without stumbling over one."[55] Looking at it "vaguely," she then drops it "absently on the floor amongst the others."[56] The modernist's name works as a signifier *because of, not despite*, a degree of inaccessibility – not despite Storm's indifference to Joyce among the wrecks of an exploded library but because of Joyce's naming in Arlen's much more widely disseminated work. Consequently, the sum of limited printings, editions, and other opportunities readers had to access Eliot's works do not represent an accurate gauge of the extent of Eliot's renown. The very rationale of the limited edition as a business model, the middle term in what Rainey calls modernism's "tripartite production program – journal, limited edition and public or commercial edition," starts from this assumption.[57] Signed, illustrated, finely papered and wrapped, gold-edged, printed in off-set colors, these luxury commodities were designed to be scarce, to be more heard of than come across, and to redound their excess aura to the authorial name.

The prominent position of the limited edition in modernist publishing practice, exemplified by small presses with names like Cuala, Hogarth, Contact, Hours, Three Mountains, and Black Sun, indicates that modernists were quite savvy when it came to using scarcity as an iconoclastic instrument of self-promotion and valuation.[58] The editors of *Dial*, in fact, associate their realization of Eliot's value with the awareness that their copy of *Prufock and Other Observations* had been filched: "When Prufrock in paper covers first appeared, to become immediately one of the rarest of rare books (somebody stole ours as early as 1919) Mr Eliot was already redoubtable."[59] In their case, apparently, not owning a copy of Eliot's poems serves as an acute marker of ascendant demand for Eliot. Indeed, it is this sense of demand, stoked by word-of-mouth, table-talk, letters, occasional reviewing, sample passages, documented by trips to London to buy books and magazines, and missing copies of *The Waste Land*, expertly torn from *The Dial* in the collections of the Bodleian library at Oxford and no doubt elsewhere, that records the pull of Eliot the signifier.

The references to Oxford and the *Oxford Magazine* above are by no means capricious; undergraduates at Oxford and Cambridge (like their counterparts at Harvard, Princeton, and Yale, whom Malcolm Cowley describes in *Exile's Return*) were among the first keyed into the Eliot phenomenon and among the first to register the demand for modernism as a potent vehicle for reputation, provocation, and desire. In *Memoirs of an Aesthete*, Harold Acton takes credit for introducing Eliot to Oxford in the early twenties during his infamous undergraduate career, writing that he "did more than anyone else to celebrate the achievements of Eliot [at Oxford]."[60] In an extraordinary passage, Acton locates Eliot at the center of a dilating bacchanalia of modern experiences, collegiate memories cross-indexed with homosexualized exoticism, white jazz, and the degeneration of the West:

George Gershwin's "Rhapsody in Blue" accompanied every rough and tumble on the sofa. The strumming wistful hesitations, the almost one finger tinkling about on the piano, picking a tentative way towards the opening carefree chord-crashes of Paul Whiteman's Boanergetic band, with every brilliantined head wobbling and bobbing up and down and loose double-jointed limbs jerked out in dislo-cated paroxysms of rhythmic abandon; the languid negroid nostalgia alternating with the Jewish; the passages of purely mechanical virtuosity developing into the triumphant sex-cries of robots – all this wham-slam whine-drone expressed a des-perate modernity entirely un-European which yet voiced the emotion of "April is the cruellest month." It excited the nerves . . . [and] cast a twentieth-century spell which dove-tailed into the divagations of Picasso, Mr. Prufrock and Gertrude Stein.[61]

As the passage suggests, from certain privileged viewpoints, such as that of the Oxford aesthete, modernity appears as an undifferentiated mine of signifiers loaded with covert prestige: cocktails, jazz, homosex, machines, racial others, cubism, and T. S. Eliot.

The specific pairing of Prufrock and cubism seemed to convey such undercurrents at Oxford even before Acton came up. In 1919, for example, *The Isis*, an undergraduate journal, printed a short poem, entitled "The Sad Story of the Young Man from M-rt-n":

> "I will wear Cubist
> Trousers,"
> He said.
> "I will make Oxford beautiful.
> I will make the High
> Hectic,
> And the Corn
> Crimson," he said.
>
> "I *will* wear Cubist Trousers."
> However, the Philistines
> (Who were not
> Beautiful)
> Beset him.

"We will not have Cubist
Trousers," they said.
"It is not nice to wear Cubist
Trousers,"
They said.
"They are affected.
Let us de-
Bag him."
And they de-
Bagged him.

This is what always happens at
    Oxford
When one tries
To be Decorative.

We *will* wear Cubist trousers.[62]

Certainly, the poem (and accompanying illustrations, see Figures 2a–c) draws on the longstanding Oxbridge discourse of dandy–aesthetes and equally longstanding folklore about the animosity between the dandy–aesthetes and the philistine–hearties, antedating even Matthew Arnold's days at Oriel College.[63] Eliot's insertion into this folklore, recommended by a number of clues, resonates with his name's suggestion of oppositional culture and its accompanying covert prestige.

Eliot himself, of course, spent time at Merton College (i.e., M-rt-n) as a postgraduate during the war years, 1914 and 1915. It is the charge of cubism, however – *cubist trousers*, more specifically – that seals the connection between this minor verse and Prufrock. In 1916, Arthur Waugh reviewed Pound's *Catholic Anthology*, which included "The Love Song of J. Alfred Prufrock," and leveled this somewhat peculiar charge: "This strange little volume bears upon its cover a geometrical device, suggesting that the material within holds the same relation to the art of poetry as the work of the Cubist school holds to the art of painting and design."[64] Waugh's sense of cubism holds the same relation to actual cubism (and to Dorothy Shakespear's vorticist cover art, for that matter) as his Eliot holds to Eliot's actual poetry; both of which count as little more than cultural patricide. Cubist verse, writes Waugh,

proceeds to the convenient assumption that everything which seemed wise and true to the father must be false and foolish to the son. Yet if the fruits of emancipation are to be recognized in the unmetrical, incoherent banalities of these literary "Cubists," the state of Poetry is indeed threatened with anarchy which will end in something worse even than "red ruin and the breaking up of laws."[65]

Figure 2a, 2b, 2c "The Sad Story of the Young Gentleman from M-rt-n."

Inscribed within this paternalistic narrative, the so-called literary cubists are represented as presumptuous upstarts, condemned at once for ordinariness, presuming their intelligibility, and for obscurity, suggesting the opposite. Above all, Waugh bristles at the following lines from "Prufrock":

> I grow old . . . I grow old . . .
> I shall wear the bottom of my trousers rolled.
> Shall I part my hair behind? Do I dare to eat a peach?
> I shall wear white flannel trousers, and walk upon the beach.
> I have heard the mermaids singing, each to each.
> I do not think that they will sing to me.[66]

Such lines stand for the nadir of the cubist "school of literary licence," the banality of its "premature decrepitude."[67] Lumping poet and poem together with the cultural pathology they diagnose, he cannot distinguish Eliot from Eliotic subject matter – that is, the premature decrepitude of Prufrock's superannuated fixations on trouser rolls and other prosaic matters – from Eliot's literary framework. This inability to distinguish poet from work leads Waugh to a startlingly brutal recommendation: as drunken slaves were exhibited in Rome, Eliot and his fellow literary cubists should be displayed as abject lessons so that aspiring poets will be made "ashamed at the ignominious folly of [their] gesticulations" and decide "never to be tempted into such a pitiable condition themselves."[68]

The idea of *cubist trousers*, returning to the *Isis* poem, if not a direct reference to Waugh's assessment of Eliot's "Prufrock," participates in the same cultural idiom. Not surprisingly, Ezra Pound's reply to Waugh's review, "Drunken Helots and Mr. Eliot," published in *The Egoist* in 1917, rehearses the same synthesis. According to Pound, Waugh's vehement opposition only serves to bear out Eliot's reputation:

[I]f . . . genius manifests itself, at once some elderly gentleman has a flux of bile from his liver; at once from the throne or the easy Cowperian sofa, or from the gutter, or from the oeconomical press room there bursts a torrent of elderly words, splenetic, irrelevant, they form themselves instinctively into large phrases denouncing the inordinate product . . . This particular kind of *rabbia* might almost be taken as the test of a work of art.[69]

As in the *Isis* poem, Pound's reply, somewhat impishly, turns vehement opposition on its head. Note again the unrelenting insistences that over-abundance is antithetical to value. In Eliot, he suggests, the overabundance of critical scorn undoes itself, becoming a sign of Eliot's intrinsic value. Eliot becomes "Mr. Heliot," a name transforming Waugh's rhetoric into a youthful and riotous array of covertly prestigious associations, for, Pound writes, is it not better to be in the company of helots, who "have a new music, a new refinement, a new method of turning old phrases into new by their aptness," than among "an aristocracy made up of, possibly, Tennyson, Southey, and Wordsworth, the flunky, the dull, and the duller"? [70]

Mr. Heliot, the representation of Eliot as a licentious poetic rebel, appears repeatedly in the undergraduate youth culture of the twenties. *The Oxford Broom*, Acton's short-lived literary journal publishing three issues in 1922 and 1923, reflects the continued influence of this particular conception of Eliot on undergraduate writing. An unsigned editorial, "Poetical Bread: A Note and Recipe," bemoans that "the world has become prosaic through a superflux of dainties." Once again, a stiff dose of Prufrock's trousers is the preferred remedy:

When the average poet of to-day hears "time's wingéd chariot hurrying near," he has not the sufficient faith . . . to say how he is affected. He will dare not express himself about it with the candid honesty of Mr. T. S. Eliot:
"I grow old . . . I grow old . . .
I shall wear the bottoms of my trousers rolled."[71]

Mr. Heliot was a phenomenon among Cambridge undergraduates as well – where Eliot's connection has been more frequently acknowledged vis-à-vis the English faculty. Just as at Oxford, so too at Cambridge, new undergraduate literary magazines, bannered with raffishly modernist titles like *Venture* and *Experiment*, were launched under these signs.[72]

Muriel Bradbrook describes the significance of Eliot among her undergraduate set at Cambridge in the late twenties:

Once I heard Sir Herbert Grierson read aloud the poetry which, as a young man, he had recited to himself ecstatically as he walked Edinburgh's New Town; and for those moments, listening, I could feel that Swinburne might be a great poet. What Swinburne was to Grierson, Eliot was to us.[73]

Each generation, his or her youth culture. The schism of taste cannot be bridged. Only for the briefest moment can Bradbrook imagine Grierson's Swinburne as a great poet and then only by analogy with her Eliot and her own youth: "Bliss was it in that dawn to be alive."[74] No small part of Bradbrook's "new world" involves experiencing Eliot as a near contemporary, being "able to go into a bookshop and buy a new volume entitled *Ash Wednesday*," an act of unembarrassed star-worship, which she recalls as a direct challenge to, of all things, the anonymous practical criticism protocols she experienced weekly in Richards' lectures.[75]

In fact, practical criticism protocols, Richards' research into undergraduate literary responses that culminated in the prescriptive hermeneutics

of *Practical Criticism: A Study in Literary Judgment* (1929), constituted a
selective refinement of a critical stance already available in Eliot's undergraduate prestige, which valued "Eliot" for his capacity as a contemporary
cultural symptom. In *Lions and Shadows*, Christopher Isherwood, also a
Cambridge undergraduate in the late twenties, describes this intervention
and transformation:

> [Richards] was our guide, our evangelist, who revealed to us, in a succession of
> astounding lightning flashes, the entire expanse of the Modern World. Up to this
> moment, we had been . . . romantic conservatives, devil-worshippers, votaries of
> "Beauty" and "Vice," Manicheans, would-be Kropotkin anarchists, who refused
> to read T. S. Eliot (because of his vogue amongst the Poshocracy) . . . Now, in a
> moment all was changed. Poets, ordered Mr. Richards, were to reflect aspects of
> the World-Picture.[76]

Until they encounter Richards, their tastes are shades of Malcolm Cowley's
"theory of convolutions": Isherwood and his friends (of the second con-
volution) choose *not* to read Eliot in order to "go beyond" (in Cowley's
phrase) "the Poshocracy" (of the first), who idolize Eliot largely because
still other students have not yet heard of him.[77] The change Richards occasions for Isherwood breaks these convolutions; Richards returns Isherwood
to T. S. Eliot, the poet of the Modern World, as a means of permanent
valuation, as a means to the *Weltanschauung*.

PARODY, PLAGIARISM, PROTOCOLS

In the newly restructured Cambridge English Faculty of the 1920s, Eliot
was one of the chief figures of contention. Younger faculty members came
out for and against Eliot publicly, in lectures, Cambridge publications,
and national journals. By contrast, Eliot found fewer proponents in the
English Faculty at Oxford, although he found equally vehement antago-
nists, such as C. S. Lewis and J. R. R. Tolkien, willing to go to lengths to
denounce heliotic undergraduate enthusiasms.[78] At Cambridge, the case
was different. Eliot's name "was as a red rag to a bull" for many members
of the faculty, but students like Bradbrook had lecturers like Leavis who
gave Eliot and other contemporary poets equal footing.[79] Leavis stood out,
according to Bradbrook, for the very reason that he repeatedly cited Eliot in
lectures (as well as Walter de la Mare, Edmund Blunden, Edward Thomas,
Ronald Bottrall, and William Empson).[80] Richards was also popular.[81]
Like Leavis, he made no secret of his debts to Eliot and to contemporary
authors more generally. In lecture, his "revolutionary method" of practical criticism deliberately concealed the authorship of his poetic specimens,

but he was inclined nevertheless to treat specimens as contemporaneous moderns through modernized spelling and modernizing omissions made "in the interests of the experiment."[82]

On the other side of the Eliot divide, opposing Richards and Leavis, was F. L. Lucas, a fellow at King's College and one of Eliot's most vociferous and prolific denigrators. The mouthpiece, according to Leavis's biographer, for "a large sector of anti-Eliot opinion" at Cambridge, he took umbrage at two related things: Eliot's use of erudite pastiche and his popularity among undergraduates, those least tutored in erudition and thus least equipped to judge as bogus Eliot's erudition.[83] Bogus erudition is, Lucas writes, a "particularly easy way to win the applause of the blasé and the young, of the coteries and eccentricities." Above all, the combination of sham erudition and popularity in the Junior Common Room and other degenerate quarters indicated to Lucas that Eliot was a poet manqué, a "toad" bedecked in "borrowed jewels."[84] As Leavis's biographer has astutely observed, Lucas tended to review Eliot as if he were evaluating unsatisfactory tutorial assignments.[85] His review of *The Waste Land*, for example: "Mr. Eliot has shown that he can at the moment write real blank verse; but that is all. For the rest he has quoted a great deal, he has parodied and imitated. But the parodies are cheap and the imitations inferior."[86] Inadequate work, Mr. Eliot – smacks of plagiarism.

Leavis and Richards defended Eliot's name both from such professorial condescension and from the undergraduate associations which elicited it. Beyond all other consideration, they sought to defend his name from association with the charge of plagiarism, the undergraduate crime *par excellence*. In an essay published in the *New Statesman* in 1926, one he considered important enough to include as an appendix to *Principles of Literary Criticism*, Richards argues that both phenomena – the quantity of "enthusiastic bewilderment" (read *undergraduate* "enthusiastic bewilderment") and the "irritation" (read *donnish* "irritation") Eliot elicits – are side-effects of Eliot's particular brand of genius:

We too readily forget that, unless something is very wrong with our civilisation, we should be producing three equal poets at least for every poet of high rank in our great-great-grandfathers' day. Something must indeed be wrong; and since Mr. Eliot is one of the very few poets that current conditions have not overcome, the difficulties which he has faced and the cognate difficulties which his readers encounter, repay study.[87]

Richards re-orients Eliot's association with the present, making it a correspondence with an advanced age rather than spurious youth: by all rights, he suggests, the moderns should have three times as many high-ranking poets as the romantics. The "cognate difficulties" of Eliot with his literary career and Eliot's readers with his poetry follow from problems in modern civilization.

In 1929, responding to an anonymous rant against *For Lancelot Andrewes* in the *New Statesman and Nation*, Leavis published a defense of Eliot in the *Cambridge Review* quite similar to Richards', albeit one even more rhetorically bracing. The *New Statesman and Nation* piece had all the traces of the F. L. Lucas brand of condescension, and Leavis judged him the likely culprit.[88] Fittingly, Leavis called his defense "T. S. Eliot – A Reply to the Condescending." For a critic of Leavis's professional purpose, condescension, especially when trained on his literary and critical avatar, was an impermissible critical mode. He locates its cause accurately in the distinctly uncritical prejudices elicited by Eliot's "great reputation among the young."[89] In this regard, condescension is a misguided by-product of Eliot's notoriety, a "snobism attendant, inevitably, upon the vogue that Mr Eliot enjoys, and suffers from." The "argument" against Eliot, which "tends to recur when the consciously adult, especially in the academic world, speak and write of Mr. Eliot," is less an argument than an assumption that the tastes of the younger coming generation are defective *tout ensemble*. All those "who practise and criticise the most recent fashions in literature" are supposed to be simply doe-eyed, star struck by the very idea of Eliot, the masterly autodidact, performing erudition with critical purpose.[90]

As "one who still counts himself among the young," Leavis takes it as a duty to contravene an assumption so intentionally hostile to the contemporary scene. Thus, in the studied rhetoric of modernist bookkeeping, Leavis uses Lucas' intemperate condescension as "a fair opportunity to acknowledge his debt [to Eliot] and define its nature." He writes:

we recognize in Mr Eliot a poet of profound originality, and of especial significance to all who are concerned with the future of English poetry. To describe him as "practising the more recent fashions" is misleading, and betrays ignorance and prejudice . . . [T]here is no other poetry in the least like Mr. Eliot's: he is an originator, and if he has his mimics, he could be confused with them only by the malicious or the incompetent.[91]

Eliot's *a priori* singularity, present in Richards' review, becomes even more strident here. Much of the *Scrutiny* writing to follow by Leavis and others continues in this vein specifically, thinning the herd of modernist poetasters by denouncing imitators of Eliot and the kinds of modernist tagalongs Leavis came to associate with *Sitwellism*.[92] The passage is a deliberate reversal of the charges Lucas levels at Eliot. Eliot represents such profound originality for Leavis that anyone who mistakes his peerless originality ("most modern of the moderns," "more truly traditional than the 'traditionalists'") for mere copies defines his or her failure as a critic. Eliot becomes the *locus classicus* for an emergent critical preoccupation with originality, a response which restates unruly undergraduate responses to Eliot (discussed above) in more respectable, more institutionally friendly terms. The lines from "Prufrock" ("I grow old . . . I grow old . . . / I shall wear the bottoms of my trousers rolled") remain the reference point of choice. In *New Bearings on English Poetry* (1932), he admits that these lines "must have been difficult to take seriously in 1917" but, in retrospect, sees this defiance of "the traditional canon of seriousness" as "an important event in the history of English poetry" as it follows "a complete break with the nineteenth-century tradition, and a new start."[93] The very preoccupation with originality was, as Leavis's notes in *New Bearings* suggest, itself a dialectical response to a broader cross-section of undergraduate reading practices, as mediated by Richards' practical criticism methods and examples.[94]

In 1929, the same year as Leavis's dust-up with Lucas and Eliot's political, religious, and aesthetic coming-out, Richards published *Practical Criticism*, collating the results of his famous experiments. Each week, Richards sent auditors home with an anonymous, unmarked batch of poems, asking them, under conditions of anonymity, to "comment freely in writing upon them."[95] These comments, called "protocols," once collected and analyzed, formed the subject matter for his subsequent lectures on literary misinterpretation and eventually, after he processed hundreds of protocols, the core of the book *Practical Criticism* itself. The subject group were mostly Cambridge undergraduates, although a small number of graduates, colleagues (including F. R. Leavis and Mansfield Forbes), and non-academics (including T. S. Eliot) also took part.[96] The book, writes Richards, "is the record of a piece of field-work in comparative ideology," a scientific foray into "the vast *corpus* of problems, assumptions, adumbrations, fictions, prejudices, tenets; the sphere of random beliefs and hopeful guesses."[97] In short, it is a foray into the mind of the Cambridge English student as it is transfixed by a certain kind of literary object.

Given the aggregation of documents and authors from which *Practical Criticism* is drawn, Richards' dedication is revealing: "to my collaborators whether their work appears in these pages or not."[98] The authors of the protocols and the authors of the poems provide the source of the first half of the text, and they represent the subjects for the correctives he proposes in the second. Both groups of absent collaborators share – and to certain extent, suffer from – a state of forced anonymity, which, Richards avers, is indispensable for narrowing the variables of the experiment, encouraging candor and eliminating interference from ostensibly irrelevant external factors and third parties. Anonymity is, for Richards, the means of isolating his object of study: the moment of communication, or lack thereof, between reader and poem. As such, it is temporary, a means to defer judgment, attributions, prejudices until – but only until – the poem is given a close reading. An appendix, necessitated by copyright "obligations," reveals the "particulars as to the authorship and date of the poems," but readers are told not to peek. "For obvious reasons," he warns, "the interest of these pages will be enhanced if the reader remains unaware of the authorship of the poems until his own opinions of them have been formed and tested by comparison with the many other opinions here given."[99] Readers will get the most out of the text, he suggests, if they take the test; if they simulate the experimental conditions themselves. In other editions, the attributions are appended at the back in mirror-image like solutions to a puzzle.[100]

Critics, noting Richards' debt to Eliot's theory of impersonality, on the one hand, and his influence on Leavisite and New Criticism, on the other, have often, and quite rightly, seen Richards' methods as a decisive component in the canonization of modernism in the academy. Still, what has been less understood is exactly why practical criticism found its ideal critical object in modernism. Richards' methodology depends upon a particular mode of detection, one which complicates received narratives about practical criticism's hermeneutic being constitutionally sympathetic to modernism's supposed impersonality, its aesthetics, or its preliminary canon. In his analysis and selection of protocols in *Practical Criticism*, Richards enshrines a particular sequence of literary detection in which originality is at once recursively attributed and conferred through the practice of interpretation. Contrary to received wisdom, authorship has a defined place in this sequence, one which Richards clearly acknowledges.

Of the three hundred or so protocols that Richards includes, a fairly large number attempt to attribute authorship in one way or another. With wide-ranging degrees of certitude, writers attempt to adduce authorship in their protocols: a given poem is

a combination of author A and author B, a disreputable offspring of C (misunderstood); it has a quite D-ic weight of statement, a strong E-esque vein, a taste of life as F knew it; it can be held on par with a similar one by G; it commences like an airy H rhyme for young and old, it ends with the tone of I, it could well have been written by a drunk devotee of J; did K write it?; it is, fairly obviously, by L; it has a smack of M; it is in the manner of N and O; it is linked somehow to P; Q expressed the same message; it made me think it was by R; it must be from S but cannot be placed exactly, influenced by T, worthy of U, rather like V but better, reminds me of W or W's remark in one of his poems; it *suggests X, is reminiscent of Y, is somewhat suggestive of Z*; it has *an expression which is AA-ian or a style which is BB-ian*; it is *either an imitation of CC, or CC in one of his worst moments*, it possesses *the language of degree of feeling of a DD or an EE.*

All are flat wrong, but, seeing them together, one gets the sense of a pattern, students grasping at associations, driven to associate anonymous poems with authorial names, adjectives, and qualities but lacking the requisite breadth of reading and attendant catalogue of literary names and associations to do so. The scatter-shot approach of protocol 1.19 is typical of the lot: "The passage is reminiscent of the whole effort and accomplishment of the greatest poets, and in a secondary way of passages in Shakespeare, Shelley, Wordsworth, Browning, etc."[101] Yet, even under the impossibly encompassing blanket of 1.19 – the kind of vague reading Richards later describes as putty "bespattering the bull's-eye" – the protocol-writer resorts, however inappropriately, to hierarchical greatness as a means of attribution.[102] The protocol-writer is faulted for imprecision but not the activity itself.

Significantly, Richards does not count the drive to attribute authorship *per se* among his ten impediments to criticism. All the same, he lodges erroneous attribution under one or more of the ten depending on the way the protocol botches attribution in each case. Because it is so difficult to pull off, Richards is generally suspicious of those protocols proceeding from alleged resemblances, comparisons, and attributions. In fact, he claims that "only the closest most sensitive reading" can yield successful detection; many such failures originate in irrelevant personal associations, which run roughshod over the "liberty" and "autonomy" of the poem:

Superficial resemblances as may be picked up in cursory reading prove nothing unless we can trace them deeper . . . Direct comparisons based upon the supposition that poems . . . in the same class (cloud poems, immortal-beauty poems, graveyard poems, sonnets, and so forth . . .) must be alike, can only serve to exhibit stupid reading. As with other associations, the quality of the link (the depth of its grounds in the inner nature and the structure of associated things) is the measure of its relevance.[103]

Thus, the rare case in which attribution is not botched is a reading practice that Richards can hardly discount. Indeed, he writes, when the protocol connects the anonymous poem with "another poem by the same author," the association is "likely to be relevant" – not faint praise from Richards at all. He judges three attributions as relevant.

When a text such as *Practical Criticism*, documenting so many examples of error yet carrying the general proviso that "value cannot be demonstrated except through the communication of what is valuable," presents its exemplary cases, readers are meant to take notice.[104] Richards lets his few exemplary cases (Russo counts "about 30") stand on their own, using them, he says, to "round the discussion off," as if their mere presentation counters all the deleterious effects of the others.[105] Two protocols in *Practical Criticism* get the attribution correct, protocol 8.5 and protocol 8.7; one, protocol 5.81, draws authorial associations reasonable enough for Richards to judge the connections relevant:

8.5
It runs an appalling risk of sentimentality and yet seems to have escaped all offensiveness: a considerable achievement. It is poignant, but not, I think, of very great value. The accent is familiar. D. H. L.?[106]

8.7
The striking thing is, that the poet (D. H. Lawrence? or American?) knows quite well that it is so, and does not try to make capital of sentiment. The simplicity and accuracy with which he records his feeling – and the justness of the expression, not pitching the thing up at all – somehow alters [*sic*] the focus; what might have been merely sentimental becomes valuable – the strength of the underlying feeling becoming apparent through the sincerity and truthfulness of the expression.[107]

5.81
This is a studied orgasm from a "Shakespeare – R. Brooke" complex, as piece 7 from a "Marvell – Wordsworth – Drinkwater, etc. stark-simplicity" complex. Hollow at first reading, resoundingly hollow at second. A sort of thermos vacuum, "the very thing" for a dignified picnic in this sort of Two-Seater sonnet.[108]

The three protocols introduce the name of the author to achieve precise effects. In each case, it is used as a specific means of description via critical paraphrase. While 8.5 and 8.7 sniff out traces of the authentic D. H. Lawrence in "The Piano," a poem, in fact, written by Lawrence, 5.81 uses authors as conceptual abstractions to delimit pseudo-literary emotional states ("complexes") in poems by other authors, Edna St. Vincent Millay (poem 5) and J. D. C. Pellew (poem 7) respectively. Richards, it seems, can countenance authorial attribution, even when not precisely accurate, if it is grounded in what he recognizes as "detailed observation of the matter and manner of the poem." In other words, protocol 5.81, unlike protocol 1.19, recognizes the signs of an insincere selection, and the authors it invokes become instruments to ward off the supposed derivative expression. The protocol writer has, echoing Pound, outfoxed the dealer in false artifacts.

Numbers 8.5 and 8.7 merit commendation because they also pass the test – not merely for being keyed into Lawrentian qualities nor for confirming the poem's authenticity of expression, but rather, because they proceed from the assumption that Lawrentian qualities are synonymous with a particular brand of authentic expression.

Following suggestions left in some of Leavis's remarks and contextual and stylistic clues, MacKillop believes that Leavis and Mansfield Forbes authored these and other exemplary protocols.[109] Ironically, the same combination of imprimaturs, hierarchical associations, and unveiled anonymity that wins Richards' approval in *Practical Criticism* is in effect in the systematic attribution of the most "superior" protocols to Richards' most "superior" auditors. Still, as MacKillop observes, the conceptual kinship between these three protocols and the mission of Leavisite criticism cannot be missed:

It was certainly the mission of Leavis as literary critic to try to ensure that a writer's originating style was not eclipsed by derivative mixtures . . . This critic's endeavour was to protect Wordsworth from the Wordsworthian, to beware the stylistic packages that form when an adhesiveness in one style cannot resist an appealing surface shape in another. Leavis was much concerned with authenticity. He liked to set examination questions challenging candidates to distinguish Shakespeare from the Shakespeare-ish (something slightly different from the Shakespearean).[110]

Distinguishing Shakespeare from Shakespeare-ish or Shakespearean, like ranking the originality of sentiment in Richards' packets of poems, is an illusory test. The examiner, who is never blind to the distinctions he wishes to test, never confirms them. No amount of surveying will convince Richards to alter his posited hierarchy of value (i.e., his predetermined howlers, middling, and brilliant poems). So, the test-taker "passes" only when he or she has learned to second-guess the test-maker successfully: when he or she has learned that, for Leavis, for example, the merely Shakespearean is less like Shakespeare than Shakespeare himself, and that Shakespeare himself is likely to be the least Shakespearean of all. In the end, Leavis as well as Richards habituate their students and readers to an operative, highly influential notion of predetermined originality, which posits that *a poet of profound authorial originality* such as Eliot can never be merely Eliotic. To estrange an author from the associations invoked by the author's name is to mystify originality in a way that at once refers to and yet at the same time is irreducible to the author's definitive qualities; thus originality becomes a subject of citation rather than discursive exposition, and literary value can be only adjudicated by means of comparisons.

If we take as axiomatic John Harwood's observation that modernism, "in any of the reified versions now deployed in academic debate, did not exist in 1909, or 1922 [but] is an academic invention . . . retrospectively imposed on the works and doctrines it supposedly illuminates," we must also recognize that these works and doctrines, *now understood* as modernist, played a historical role in this process.[111] The "historical" modernism had an active stake in producing the conditions for what effectively became its own reification – in becoming, in other words, "High Modernism." For all its convenience and utility, a more inclusive rubric such as *modernisms*, preferred following Peter Nichols' decisive work and recent developments such as the annual New Modernisms conferences of the Modernist Studies Association, tends to obscure this process.[112] The modes of literary criticism fostered and elaborated around the historical modernists – inaugurated by Pound and Eliot, elaborated and carried through by Richards, Leavis, and others *during the interwar period* – entrenched many of the inured, "modernist" assumptions underlying the practice of literary studies subsequently instituted in British and American universities after the Second World War. Once these assumptions – in particular, the supposed impersonality of critical method and the supposed autonomy of the objects of literary discourse – are viewed in light of work of the literary ideologues who occasioned them, they disclose a profound point of overlap between modernism and mass culture, two systems of cultural value long alleged to be at odds, the point of overlap being where the elite promotion of authorial originality meets with the mass phenomenon of celebrity.

Modernism's supposed antagonism towards mass culture and mass culture's supposed indifference to modernism have long been features of – some would say the chief impediments to – the academic invention of modernism. Modernism's cultural antagonism meets popular indifference, which in turn provokes further antagonisms. The scenes of confrontation are compulsively rehearsed. Modernist cultural producers are said to scorn mass audiences, their preferred cultural forms, their seeming indifference; consumers of popular culture are said to take little notice; and on and on. No doubt, the idea of a mass of venal consumers with slavishly homogenized tastes for popular culture is as misleading as the idea of a hermetic cadre of modernist producers immune to the exigencies of the mass marketplace and the ubiquity of its commodities. Increasingly scholars have begun to trouble this narrative. Works such as Andreas Huyssen's *After the Great Divide*, Michael C. Fitzgerald's *Making Modernism*, Joyce Piell

Wexler's *Who Paid for Modernism?*, Lawrence Rainey's *Institutions of Modernism*, Jennifer Wicke's *Advertising Fictions*, many of the essays collected in Kevin Dettmar and Stephen Watt's *Marketing Modernisms*, as well as numerous single author studies, have gone a long way towards complicating criticism's overinvestment in what is, finally, one of modernism's own favorite mythologies about aesthetic agency. As much of this criticism argues, modernism – for all its seeming distaste for consumer culture and capitalism more broadly – made selective use of popular forms and had its own popular ambitions.[113]

Nevertheless, for good materialist reasons, certain core elements of the antagonistic explanation cannot be simply discarded. Beneath the circular narrative replayed above lies two problematics, one concerning elite production, the other, popular consumption. During a historical period when the institutions and techniques of mass consumption became culturally preeminent, modernist production was decidedly – if not deliberately – small-scale, seemingly disinterested in the mode and means of consumption. For all the explanatory deficiencies of a monolithic narrative of antagonism, the difference in scale between modernist production and popular cultural consumption remains an unavoidable framework, helping to account for the anxious freighting of mass culture in modernist artistic culture. These and other explanatory difficulties give rise to a misleading tendency to explain high culture almost exclusively as a phenomenon of production while simultaneously treating mass culture almost exclusively as a phenomenon of consumption.

One need not wade too far into the discourses of mass culture before noticing that, in contrast to modernism's literary economists, the producers of mass culture, wherever they may be, are, as a rule, fetishists of consumption. (Before even stepping into a McDonald's, customers are well-versed in how to line up at the register, how to order, how products will look on trays at the counter and on trays at their seats, how unwrapping them will sound, how holding them will feel, and, when mealtime is over, where they will stow their empty trays and throw their waste.) Like advertising, critical discourse about mass culture tends to focus on the habits of consumption, deliberately oblivious to the forces of production at work behind the curtains. If producers of mass culture are to be believed they hardly exist; as Lord Northcliffe, the founder of the *Daily Mail*, famously put it, they simply give readers, audiences, and consumers "what they want." As early as 1932, the American critic Gilbert Seldes – the same Seldes who was the managing editor of *The Dial* when it brought out *The Waste Land* – rebuked Old-World advertisers for their neglect of consumers, enjoining them to join their stateside counterparts in aiming their strategies squarely on consumption.[114] Later, he urged advertisers to enlist the services of professional critics, formerly at the service of the highbrow, to perfect their methods. "I am a professional in the most important branch of the advertising business," he wrote in 1954, "which is, of course, the receiving end. I have read more ads and listened to more commercials than any copy writer has composed."[115] Any given person with access to newspapers, radio, and television has consumed exponentially more advertising than any given copy writer has produced; Seldes' point is that the critic, alone among the rank and file, brings professional credentials to the experience.

As Seldes' appeal to advertisers seems to intuit, cultural criticism in all forms ministers to consumption. Rather than fetishizing the act of consumption in itself for itself, however, the literary economics of "highbrow" modernist criticism serves to promote consumption only by exalting aesthetic production. Thus it cultivates taste for a rarefied commodity, which is not only difficult to consume but even difficult to obtain. The effort required to access modernist texts makes consumption a secondary event to hearing about production. As this notion of production is mystified, it becomes generative, subject to copious elaboration, presented in sites "upstream" and "downstream" with respect to the producer. With reference to Eliot's *The Waste Land*, for example, "upstream" sites include the work of composition, editing, and collaboration, whereas "downstream" sites include efforts to place the poem, various editions, the *Dial* Prize, and the kind of public sites we have examined here, the criticism, reviewing, commentary, promotion, enthusiastic bewilderment and irritation which the modernist work occasions. Whatever the orientation to the source, these discursive modes do not, *pace* Seldes, take up the search for places and means of consumption – potential uses, audiences, or readers. Nevertheless, despite the apparent distaste for the open literary marketplace, they enact nothing if not a decidedly capitalist response to the proliferation of cultural material. It is a response which, in order to bolster value, seeks to maintain the meticulous scarcity of commodities; it is, that is to say, the response of the monopolist.[116]

In the domain of mass culture, only celebrities provide an analogous case. The same way modernists and modernism's literary economists fetishize authorship, celebrities and their publicists fetishize the production of self. The rhetoric of both insists on alleged indifference to consumption, studied insensitivity to existing tastes of consumers, readers, audiences, and publics. Yet, both presume a notion of production that cannot be confined to a single productive source but that instead measures production in

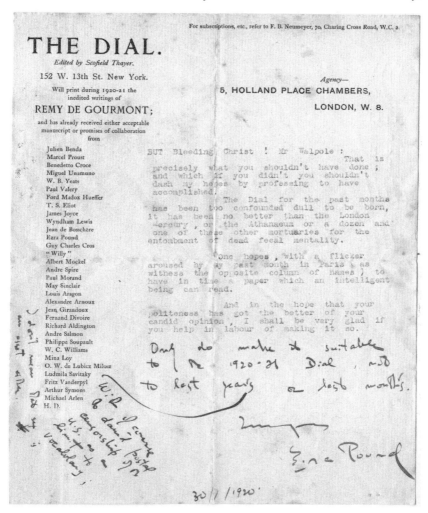

Figure 3a   Pound's letterhead, circa 1920.

terms of both the circulation and the relative valuation of its commodities. In both cases, these are its brand names. The differences between one and the other should be measured in scale, not technique or ambition. In 1920, when Pound worked as the London correspondent for *The Dial*, he fashioned a letterhead that includes a long list of names, including himself, Joyce, Eliot, H. D., Wyndham Lewis, Ford Madox Hueffer,

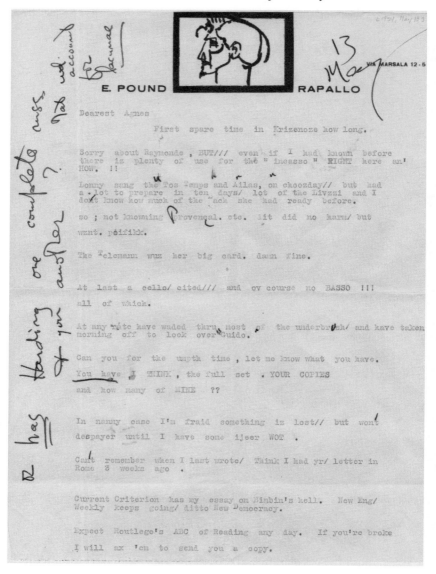

Figure 3b   Pound's letterhead, circa 1930.

Mina Loy, Proust, Rémy de Gourmont and twenty-four other prominent modernists. From these names, the letterhead states, *The Dial* has received "either acceptable manuscript or promises of collaboration" (see Figure 3a).[117] On 30 July, Pound used this stationery to tell Hugh Walpole off: if Walpole wanted to see his submission published in *The Dial*, Pound wrote, he had better revise it to make more suitable company for the column of illustrious names billed opposite. By the early 1930s, Pound achieved the same effects with a letterhead consisting only of a logotype of his own head by Henri Gaudier-Brzeska (see Figure 3b).[118]

CHAPTER 3

Collaborative work

"Somewhere, silently and without fuss or desire for réclame there is quite apt to be a man or a woman who will turn out the masterpiece that puts to shame all the intriguers or politicians."[1] Robert McAlmon – once one of modernism's fellow-travelers, now all but out-of-print – wrote this. That these words are nowhere to be found in any available editions of the work in which they originally appeared – *Being Geniuses Together* (1938), McAlmon's chef-d'oeuvre – raises some uncomfortable questions about the sentiment, the myth of the singular artist, the solitary genius. How will the hidden masterpieces prevail without fussing, without réclame, without trespassing intriguers and politicians? The omission is strategic. It is the first substantial cut in Kay Boyle's bowdlerized version of *Being Geniuses Together*, first appearing in 1968, ten years after McAlmon's death. Having systematically pruned, edited, and reshaped McAlmon's original, adding an introduction, photographs, footnotes, and twelve chapters about her own expatriate experiences, Boyle has good reason to suppress McAlmon's formula for posthumous reputation. It jars with her wholesale reframing of his text as a *posthumous collaboration*, to adopt Malcolm Cowley's peculiar yet apt phrase.[2] Introducing the new edition, Boyle even justifies the tampering for the sake of fuss and réclame:

It is my hope that the present edition will do more than provide a deeply sympathetic portrait of a writer and publisher who deserves to be remembered for his unique qualities, but it will as well help to accord to Robert McAlmon his rightful and outstanding place in the history of the literary revolution of the early nineteen-twenties.[3]

One works for texts and authors like this only if their claims to authority are easily trespassed. In the sense that Boyle fussily imposes her own imprimatur in order to rehabilitate McAlmon's reputation, her cuts and additions are, in fact, so many acts of modernist bad faith. Enter Authorship to deliver Publicity.[4]

Save for an extant literary imprimatur, McAlmon had all the right modernist credentials – not least the habit of undertaking work for other modernists behind the scenes. The Zelig-like American tops any list of most connected moderns: he wrote for little magazines; ran one in New York with William Carlos Williams; socialized with the "crowd" in expatriate Paris; spent loads of Bryher's money; dutifully served as Joyce's drinking companion, money lender, and typist; and, most significantly, perhaps, published the Contact Editions, deluxe first editions of Hemingway, Pound, Stein, Mina Loy, William Carlos Williams, H. D., Edith Sitwell, Mary Butts, and other luminaries. McAlmon's suppressed sentence, if restored, appears to deny such activity its due as a necessity of modernist literary production and instead takes the romantic hang-over at face value, solitary genius defined in opposition to the cruelties of publicity. Because McAlmon is blind to the inevitabilities of collaborative work, it as if he is made to submit to it in full, the price being that, quite literally, his will to Authorship is unwritten by Collaboration. For canny, career modernists, the need for collaborative work was never a blind spot. It was rather territory visited frequently but cautiously, entered into for various ends and above all for purposes of promotion. Moreover, it was also work that they sharply and recursively differentiated from authorship. As McAlmon's posthumous encounter with Boyle suggests, from the modernist point of view, the insistently productive and material need for publication, publicity, and celebrity runs counter to the modernist's most cherished of mythologies, the self-positing work.

Consequently, there is built-in incentive to alienate this work, to embody collaborative work in the alien and often female bodies of *intriguers* and *politicians*. As the vexed bibliographic history of *Being Geniuses Together* already intimates, again and again, gender informs these labors in ways that are at once familiar and strange. Often, accounts of working relationships between modernist contemporaries fall into such feminized patterns by default, presupposing inequitable power relations between the narrative subjects, hinging on suggestions of sacrifice, service, and subordination rather than models of equality or mutual gain. The following sentiments in Sylvia Beach's *Shakespeare and Company* are paradigmatic:

Ulysses was to be as Joyce wished, in every respect . . . I wouldn't advise "real" publishers to follow my example, nor authors to follow Joyce's. It would be the death of publishing. My case was different. It seemed natural to me that the efforts and sacrifices on my part should be proportionate to the greatness of the work I was publishing.[5]

Beach's account of working with Joyce is itself fully inscribed within modernist bad faith about the collaborative ontology of literary production. Thus, in order to begin discussing the role of collaborative work in the history of modernism, we should keep in mind two cultural materialist points of emphasis. First, modernist collaborative work exists – that is to say, representations of collaborative work have left traces of their propagandistic and polemical uses and implications in the bibliographic history of modernism. Second, the patterns of subordinating collaborative work to singular authorship form one of the crucial framing narratives in this history, enabling a few of the so-called "High" Modernists (James Joyce, T. S. Eliot, Ezra Pound, Virginia Woolf) to position themselves as singular literary paradigms.

One of the many potent contradictions of modernism is that, despite relentlessly advancing the cult of the singular artist – McAlmon's solitary genius – modernism's existence is repeatedly marked by the need for the unpaid work of others, others who were frequently women, a point to which I will return in a moment. Materially speaking, and as awkward as it may sound aired publicly, modernist cultural formations are predicated on dependency. And the very nature of this dependency troubles the brand of aesthetic self-sufficiency long understood to be the dominant message of modernist form. This conclusion is one of the crucial, if somewhat indirect, lessons of Lawrence Rainey's *Institutions of Modernism*. Over and over, Rainey's case studies in modernist promotional and publication history document that the production of the most celebrated modernist work is leveraged on the less esteemed work of financing, publishing, and publicity. Nevertheless, this "downstream" work (to return to a phrase introduced in the previous chapter), though less prestigious, was no secret: it was tightly and formatively bound to modernism's "upstream" cultural projects. So much so, in fact, that it is fair to say this: modernism's specific prerogative of collaborative work was, *pace* Rainey, its most formidable institution besides its particular take on authorship.

The services that modernists, would-be modernists, and their allies rendered to each other and each other's causes were the most effective means they had to foster, in Rainey's words, "a social reality, a configuration of agents and practices that converge in the production, marketing, and publicization of an idiom, a shareable language in the family of twentieth-century tongues."[6] Such institutions were, above all, not of mortar and bricks but institutions in a linguistic sense, familiar, iterated practices in a speech community, a "social and discursive space."[7] While these labors have never been wholly hidden from view, they have never been on display in modernism's canonical *masterpieces* either. Swept to one side of "upstream" cultural projects, arch literary compositions, books-in-print, and collected works, they have been nevertheless enshrined in the bibliographic record. Prominently documented in the host of bibliographic endeavors modernists undertook in the period in addition to high literary labor, modernism's collaborative work is documented in its limited editions, its small magazines, its little reviews, its introductions, its editing, and its anthologies.

Stories of collaborative work, moreover, play a prominent role in modernist memoirs, autobiographies, and biographies. The secondary documents of *intriguers and politicians* (illustrated with photographs by Bernice Abbott and Man Ray and with drawings and paintings by Augustus John and Wyndham Lewis) have historically carried much of the load of modernist publicity. Such texts include Boyle's and McAlmon's *Being Geniuses Together*, Beach's *Shakespeare and Company* (1956), Margaret Anderson's *My Thirty Years' War* (1930), and scores of similar accounts.[8] In these contexts, collaborative work moves beyond the ontological limbo of mere hearsay and biographical ephemera. Told and retold, the anecdotes, which form their raw materials, assume their own bibliographic reality, a reality which, if apocryphal, exists in the same troubled conceptual proximity to canonical texts as an apocrypha ought. Not surprisingly, the anecdotes themselves, which supply many of modernism's framing narratives of sacrifice, service, and subordination, rehearse stories about weakening the authority of modernist collaboration and casting the would-be literary collaborator in what is at best an apocryphal role. And, moving from memoir to biography to monograph to book-jacket blurb as if passing through porous media, these anecdotes unceremoniously lose the purchase of their original narrative contexts and become rooted in the lore of single authorship. Prototypical accounts of modernist collaborative work tend to be subordinated among the more substantial modernist genres, a process which devaluates the work of collaboration a second time. Would-be collaborators of Joyce become little more than chestnuts of Joyceana. In many ways, the best place to begin understanding the commonplaces about these labors is with some of this anecdotal evidence, which gives the subornation of collaborative work a suitably subordinate and unauthorized literary vehicle.

Take for example one of McAlmon's anecdotes. He reports that in 1921, after imprudently boasting of his skills as a typist to Joyce, he was saddled with the chore of retyping the "Penelope" episode of *Ulysses*. He quickly finds himself confronted with the strenuous tasks of deciphering "minute and hen-scrawly" handwriting, copious additions, and color-coded alterations.⁹ Although he begins fastidiously, his diligence quickly deteriorates:

> For about three pages I was painstaking and actually re-typed one page to get the insertions in the right place. After that I thought, "Molly might just as well think this or that a page or two later, or not at all," and made the insertions wherever I happened to be typing.¹⁰

Following an editorial principle that "Molly's thoughts were irregular in several ways at best," he wonders irreverently whether Joyce will notice these unsanctioned changes to what he calls, with some skepticism, "the mystic arrangement of Molly's thought." Some years later, he chances to ask Joyce, who claims not only to have noticed McAlmon's alterations but also to have agreed with McAlmon's principle for making them.¹¹

Familiar patterns emerge here. One notices straightaway, for instance, the mannered inequities. McAlmon's account lacks even a perfunctory sign that he and Joyce share footing as friends and fellow writers. The difference in their statures has been fully internalized in the narrative; subordination frames both the terms of their friendship and their working relationship. It is taken for granted that one helps the master modernist. One expects neither compensation nor reciprocity. Yet, like Bartleby the scrivener, McAlmon seems also to have seditiously turned iniquitous conditions to his advantage. Questioning Joyce's ultimate authority over the text, the would-be bondsman dictates the terms to the would-be master. However banally, the account seems momentarily to give McAlmon a hand in the authorship of "Penelope." Is McAlmon inviting us to be suspicious of Joyce's magisterial powers of authorship? At the very cusp of proposing himself as Joyce's silent partner, McAlmon turns back, reconfirming Joyce's powers and undermining his role in a collaboration, revealing that Joyce anticipated his trespassing emendations and even sanctioned them all along.

We find the same pattern in another anecdote set eight years later involving Harry and Caresse Crosby. The Crosbys eagerly solicit a manuscript from Joyce for their Black Sun Press. "We yearned," writes Caresse, "for a piece of the rich Irish cake then baking on the Paris fire."¹² On the condition that he is allowed proof-sheets and corrections, Joyce obliges, giving them the three sections of his "Work in Progress," which become *Tales Told of Shem and Shaun*. After Joyce sends back the first proofs marked "like a bookie's score card," the three begin an arduous course of corrections and re-corrections:

> "Now, Mr. and Mrs. Crosby," Joyce said, "I wonder if you understand why I made that change." . . .

"No, why?" we chorused, and there ensued one of the most intricate and erudite twenty minutes of explanation that it has ever been my luck to hear, but unfortunately I hardly understood a word, his references were far too eso-teric . . . [A]fterward we both regretted that we did not have a dictaphone behind the lamp so that later we could have studied all that escaped us. Joyce stayed three hours . . . and by eight he hadn't got through with a page and a half.[13]

Months later, with the pages finally set up on the press, the Crosbys' printer discovers that he miscalculated the layout: the last two lines "fall *en pleine page.*" The printer sees Caresse and demands that they "beg" Joyce for supplementary material. She will hear nothing of it; the Crosbys and their printer do not tamper with genius: "I laughed scornfully at the little man, what a ludicrous idea, when a great writer has composed each line of his prose as carefully as a sonnet you don't ask him to inflate a masterpiece to help out the printer!" The printer petitions Joyce anyway, who turns out only too happy to have one more shot at the text: it was only fear of Caresse Crosby, he tells the printer, that prevented him from bringing extra material on his own.[14]

Like the McAlmon anecdote, this story – from another key modernist memoir, Caresse Crosby's *Passionate Years* (1953) – promotes modernism's bad faith about collaborative work.[15] Again, there are mannered inequities and protagonists who recognize their role in being taken for granted, sub-ordination as self-definition. The threat reappears, however slight, that collaboration could undermine the author's authority over the work. If the Crosbys pressure Joyce into publishing more, do they have a hand in the authorship? Again, the suspicions raised about the author's magisterial powers are immediately placated: Joyce miraculously anticipates, validates, even authorizes the cause of what would be his undoing. As in the McAlmon anecdote, an improbable reassertion of Joyce's authorial authority rules the day. In fact, though Crosby's slavish devotion contrasts somewhat with McAlmon's jaded skepticism, there is no appreciable difference in the tra-jectory of their responses to Joyce's authorship. Apparently, a woman and man can play the role of the willing subordinate with the same outcome: collaborative work turns out merely to underwrite the exceptional status of singular authorship. We only begin to see the way gender informs this pattern of work when we consider that the anecdotal role of martyred publisher and publicist was played overwhelmingly by women, first by Anderson, perhaps to greatest effect by Beach. Through sheer reiteration, their anecdotes, stressing that singular, overwhelmingly male artists are both eminently deserving and beyond compare, encourage the systematic devaluation of collaborative work as a recognized element in the production of modernist texts.

Where apocryphal, elusive, subordinated collaborative work represents low literary labor, the high literary labor of the solitary genius is under-written by solid bodies of authoritative texts. In free-standing editions, so-called books-in-print, we have the modernist's most cherished *solid objects* (to borrow Douglas Mao's title and something of his argument). These impossible objects of modernist desire emphatically demonstrate Mao's claim that "the intertwined stories of the object and of production under modernism cannot be understood adequately apart from each other."[16] What better than the modernist book to draw us into "intertwined stories of the object and of production under modernism," into the archly mod-ernist tension Mao describes as modernism's "urgent validation of produc-tion and . . . admiration for an object world beyond the manipulation of consciousness."[17] Getting somewhat short shrift in Mao's argument is that such intertwined stories are more often than not stories of books, that is, stories of the production of authorized, free-standing durable literary goods with an attendant axis of exploitation (to return to a phrase from my introduction). From scarce hard-bound, limited editions to readily procured cheap editions and anthologies, extant books-in-print are mod-ernism's objects of desire *par excellence*.[18]

The reputations of women modernists (with certain significant excep-tions – Virginia Woolf, Edith Sitwell, Gertrude Stein, perhaps Marianne Moore) have long suffered by dwelling among the forms of low literary labor in memoirs and biographies; by and large, women modernists lacked access to the production of durable literary goods as vehicles of reputation. Roger Conover describes the situation aptly in reference to Mina Loy in his edition of her work, *The Lost Lunar Baedeker*, the culmination of a series of posthumous attempts "to establish a text for an elusive body of work":[19]

Loy's name is most often found in a string of names . . . She makes colorful appear-ances in dozens of biographies: in those of Djuna Barnes, Constantin Brancusi, Ernest Hemingway, James Joyce, Wyndham Lewis, Marianne Moore, Ezra Pound, Gertrude Stein, Wallace Stevens, Alfred Stieglitz, and William Carlos Williams, for example. In memoir after modernist memoir, she has been granted a forceful personality, a cerebral bearing, a perfect complexion, and a sexual body. But not a voice.[20]

This is where Conover locates his point of intervention: "restor[ing] a great poet's lost voice" means not so much rediscovering but rather inventing for the first time an extant edition of her work, an edition which never was:

Loy the oeuvre as solid object. Accordingly, he extracts her "misplaced" work from near apocryphal sources, from McAlmon's rare Contact Edition, *Lunar Baedeker* (1923), from short-lived periodicals such as *The Trend*, *Rogue, Others, Contact*, and *The Dial*, and from unpublished manuscripts.[21]

Without the solidity of an authoritative edition, all-too-rare scenes of reading Loy also take on an apocryphal quality; her readers become a storied, underground cadre, "the determination required to *find* her poems, let alone the perspicacity required to *read* them, [serving] as a qualifying experience."[22] Loy's texts circulate "like a secret handshake."[23] Until they become durable, well-circulated goods, she is but a codicil on long lists of more famous acquaintances, and even the testimonials Conover musters ("Basil Bunting, Eliot, Pound, Stein, and Williams praised her work" and "conceded" debts to her) impute reputation by this means of apocryphal association. According to this logic, customary modernist chronology is reversed; reputation is predicated on the multiplication of available texts. Like Djuna Barnes, H. D., and many other "rediscovered" modernists, Loy's ascendant reputation depends on finding durable goods – that is, raising a modernist textual apparatus – where there were only apocryphal accounts, replacing the wrecks and lesser labors of an "anti-career" with products of high literary labor as modeled, authorized, and perfected by more (contemporaneously) successful contemporaries.[24]

The key ingredient of modernist reputation is not merely the demonstration of high literary labor through extant literary texts, but the capacity to frame this work in reference to the contrastingly lesser work of certain contemporaries. There are numerous apocryphal figures who exist without association with their own works, but all canonical figures have both solid bodies of authoritative texts and apocrypha (consisting of the work of contemporaries), and, in this, an integrated textual apparatus recursively defining their authority over working relationships with contemporaries. This allowed certain authors the capacity to extend the reach of their imprimaturs through (the work of) their contemporaries. Like literary collaboration itself, the notion of literary contemporariness was particularly vexing for authors keenly invested in promoting unrivaled, detached originality. The subordination of collaborative work thus served as a controlling mechanism for ordering networks of literary relationships vis-à-vis hierarchy and self-promotion.

Among the institutions through which modernists represented and subordinated literary working relationships with their contemporaries, three stand out because they purposefully join collaborative work to high literary labor: introducing, editing, and anthologizing. All three are amply

documented in modernist bibliographies: modernists wrote introductions
to each other's work, they edited each other's work, they anthologized each
other's work. Each form of labor promotes a constellation of imprimaturs,
reputations, and modes of collaboration that either explicitly or implicitly
subordinate apocryphal narratives of working relationships under hieratic
signs of singular literary production. These three signify the sanctioned
"High" Modernist take on collaborative work, because they articulate working relationships by means of authorial imprimaturs and because they make
these relationships durable goods, which, as Loy's editor reminds us, is at
the crux of modernist desires for reputation. Each method recommends a
specific, straightforward application as a set of generic formulas, providing
us with opportunities to examine the kinds of collaborative work modernists sanctioned bibliographically, and thus three lenses through which
this chapter and the next will focus. Each presents possibilities to gauge how
men and women modernists fared with these institutions. Do Eliot's male
contemporaries make out differently in his introductions than his female
contemporaries? How does the would-be editorial relationship between
Pound and Eliot compare with the would-be editorial relationship between
Pound and Marianne Moore? How do the promotional strategies of Pound's
anthologies – or, for that matter, Edward Marsh's – compare with the promotional strategies of Edith Sitwell's?

The matter of modernist anthologies, which involves fixing an imprimatur against groups of contemporaries to represent literary brands (to
adopt Robert Graves' prescient term), will provide the basis of chapter
four. Unlike anthologizing *among* contemporaries, the work of editing
and introducing operates *between* contemporaries, fixing one established
singular artist/solitary genius to another would-be singular artist/solitary
genius. As I argued in chapter two, modernist careerists like Ezra Pound and
T. S. Eliot had a stake in offering their literary durable goods as the embodiment of representative distinction: it was their means to economize and
thus monopolize the plentitude of the literary firmament. This task, I claim,
represents one of the chief functions of their criticism, one of the sanctioned
forms of "downstream" work organizing the modernist field of cultural production. There is, as I have already suggested here, a two-tiered system of
literary labor. Sanctioned forms (criticism, reviewing, introducing, editing,
anthologizing, even blurb-writing) have an open, often avowedly masculinist relationship to elite durable goods, whereas the forms of apocrypha documented in modernist memoirs are systematically devalued and feminized.
Both carry a crucial message about the role that singular artists perform
in the context of their own publicity and the frameworks of their own

careers. Keeping the functions – indeed, the very materiality of modernist apocrypha – not far from view, in what follows, I examine two instances of modernists working collaboratively above the table, arguing that Eliot's introductions and Pound's editing serve to enact their claims to representative distinction by assertively pressing the prerogative of the imprimatur on the necessarily collaborative work of publicity.

As genres, modernist introductions and editions utilize distinctive techniques of form and habits of content, which are, in a sense, inescapably collaborative, directly or indirectly coming to bear on the authors and works being introduced and edited. Each promotes a specific brand of imprimatur-derived revaluation – which we could term finding and framing, respectively – that presupposes a privileged relationship between the introducers or editors and the authors and works being introduced or edited. Each also suggests an emblematic usage for us to keep in the non-foreshortened background, a means to describe the institutionalized power dynamics in modernist literary networks that enshrines doing things with imprimaturs like finding and framing contemporaries in the history of texts. Insofar as these labors have as often helped to enhance the reputations of practitioners like Eliot and Pound – who write the introductions and act as editors – as they have done work for the reputations of their nominal subjects, we need to pay careful attention to the prerogatives of who is speaking.

WORTH INTRODUCING

A recent commentator, describing Katherine Mansfield's passage from the literary backwaters of New Zealand to the London literary scene, writes that Mansfield

> felt herself . . . doubly disadvantaged, as a woman writer and as a colonial, and it is fascinating, if rather disturbing . . . to see the ways in which from the beginning of her career she searched for male mentors who would perform the double function of protecting her from sexual exploitation (a real danger for a young woman entering a male professional world . . .) and of promoting her work. A succession of rather ineffectual young men were supplanted in this role by A. R. Orage, the powerful editor of the *New Age* magazine, who promoted Mansfield's work assiduously while, apparently, nicknaming her "the marmoset" behind her back and dubbing her "vulgar and enterprising." Would a young man in a similar position be censured in quite this way?[25]

Mansfield's reputation, it seems, depends on a particular introductory narrative, acquiescence to the interventions of powerful male others in male-dominated institutions, a process of submission to the powerbrokers of modernism, as it were, which threatened to corrupt every order of her social identity, her sexuality (predatory professional writers on one side, ineffectual amateurs on the other), her species (signifying "marmozet"), and her class (*vulgar* and enterprising social climber). Would a man in a position similar to Mansfield's be so thoroughly subordinated?

To the extent that the male modernist was insinuated in the prevalent narratives of literary publicity and promotion, the answer, quite often, was yes. One thinks, for example, of T. S. Eliot's comments in 1920 about the inevitability of adopting an attitude of paternalistic condescension to slightly younger writers, many of whom he thinks "borrowed a good deal from [his] poetry": "[M]en five years younger than I seem to me much younger, and if they become my friends I feel a sort of paternal responsibility . . . Osbert and his brother [Sacheverell Sitwell], [Richard] Aldington, [Aldous] Huxley, Herbert Read, and several americans [*sic*] whom I know by correspondence, all seem children almost."[26] And, for another aspiring young poet, "an odd American Jew here named [Maxwell] Bodenheim," Eliot will not go even this far:

I told him my history here, and left him to consider whether an American Jew, of only a common school education and no university degree, with no money, no connections, and no social polish or experience, could make a living in London. Of course I did not say all this; but I made him see that getting recognized in English letters is like breaking open a safe – for an American, and that only about three had ever done it.[27]

These private responses to contemporaries contrast sharply with the official announcement of the first *Dial* Prize, awarded to Eliot for, among other things, his literary altruism, his "service to letters."[28]

Having broken into the English literary scene, Eliot styles himself off the record as the scene's gatekeeper. In this capacity, he exhibits no benevolent notions about literary success having anything to do with intrinsic literary merit, professionalism, or fair play. Bodenheim's gifts, he readily admits to his correspondent, are superior to writers under his charge, but "what is one to do!"[29] The making of literary reputation presumes certain class markers that, to Eliot's mind, no Jew can hope to attain. For Eliot in 1920, class, race, and gender privilege are essential preconditions to literary reputation, but, as his attitude to the Sitwell brothers, Richard Aldington and other would-be male protégés indicates, taking an active interest in another writer's career requires something more. Above all, it requires that aspirant writers represent his literary subordinates, that they have arrived later and less splendidly than he has.

Duplicitous, double-edged literary altruism was endemic to the promotional system among the ranks and across gender lines of literary modernism. It is hardly unusual to find minor and major keys of insults, gossip, back-stabbing, and derision in letters between modernists who purport to be allies, particularly in the private narratives concerning publication and promotion – the return of the repressed, perhaps, for the sacrifices of institutionalized benevolence. Joyce, for example, parodies both Pound and Eliot in letters to Harriet Shaw Weaver.[30] Edith Sitwell, writing to Allanah Harper to thank her for a favorable review, includes a gratuitous dig at Nancy Cunard, her one-time collaborator on the *Wheels* anthologies: "If I may say so, I regret that you are mentioning Nancy Cunard, because I think she can be hardly regarded as a serious poet. Her work at its best is a bad parody of Mr. Eliot . . . It is rather a shame that a great poet like Mr. Eliot should have his work dogged by this kind of thing."[31] Edwin Muir trades letters with Eliot at Faber and Faber in the mid-fifties about Djuna Barnes' *Antiphon* manuscript. Adopting nothing of the obligatory awe rendered by Joyce's "collaborators," Muir recommends substantial revisions, and then patronizingly claims to regret his suggestions because Barnes "is living now what seems to be a lonely comfortless life in a street and house which would cast most people . . . into hopeless depression."[32] Later, mixing motives of literary *noblesse oblige* with critical amateurism, Muir refuses a reader fee: "I don't care whether I get one or not, and should prefer to think that I did what I did out of love of the work. I should prefer to leave it at that."[33]

These examples do not merely illustrate undercurrents of habitual debasement and condescension among modernists; they also advise us how derision and its inflections of gender are underwritten by comparing extant literary prestige. If we judge Orage's insults about Mansfield as two-faced, Eliot's intimidation of Bodenheim as bigoted, Joyce's parody of Pound and Eliot as good-natured, Sitwell's sabotage of Cunard as conniving, Muir's treatment of Barnes as patronizing, and so on, these assessments follow from the claims that literary reputation continues to make on the present. With Bodenheim having no contemporary reputation to speak of, it is easy to imagine it being derailed by Eliot: the reputations of Pound and Eliot seem more than able to withstand Joyce's missiles; whereas the reputations of Orage and Muir – subsequently eclipsed by those of their alleged protégées, Barnes and Mansfield – now seem to be misogynistically obstructionist; and Sitwell's use of her reputation only seems petty, counterproductive, reactionary. Public narratives featuring seemingly unselfish acts of literary altruism, the reputed *services to Letters*, are frequently, in fact, just as rooted in the hostile, subordinating institutions of literary publicity as the most private strains of resentful literary gossip; most such interventions for other writers are, in other words, foremost acts of self-documentation and promotion. To the extent that both women and men writers were willing subjects to these institutions, we should ask: first, did the institutions treat them differently, and, second, did they implicate their literary careers differently?

One way to investigate this problem is to compare the way modernists introduced each other's works. As I mentioned earlier, introductions link working relationships between authors to the documentary transmission of the literary work; unlike apocryphal stories originating in private narratives, conversation, letters, and other apocryphal matter, which only become public *after* the figures involved became well known, introductions always already make working relationships between authors public domain. Do female modernists, then, get introduced any differently from male modernists? The passive construction is intentional, for my hypothesis is that literary reputation is in the introducing rather than in the being introduced. Introducing, particularly when it involves modernist contemporaries, reflexively subordinates literary reputations. Before one even opens the book, the mere presence of an introduction by another author announces a working relationship, which hierarchizes their comparative statures. With an introduction, another author sets up shop in the book's front-matter, effectively, the default position of framing and enunciation. What is the pretext for the introduction? Is it a service to letters or a service to something less disinterested? In either case, the questions are posed by the introducer not the introduced. It is no accident that Pound places the impresarios above geniuses in his ladders of literary value, for discovering the next new thing trumps being the next big thing.

When it came to introducing books by other writers, Eliot was among the most prolific modernists. Between 1924 and 1965, the poet whose entire corpus consists of less than four thousand lines of verse published almost fifty introductions, prefaces, forewords, critical notes, and similar documents, thereby interposing his name into the pages of works by almost fifty other writers, onto the spines of their books, into their bibliographic records. Speaking quantitatively, Eliot's abundant introduction writing after *The Waste Land* contrasts sharply with his scarce "literary" output. The latter follows, at least in part, from the archly modernist preoccupation with undersupply, stoking demand by under-stocking the literary marketplace, but what can we make of the former? Eliot introductions, it seems, remained in high demand *despite* his willingness to supply them for a copious and eclectic assortment of causes, texts, and authors, including his mother Charlotte's closet drama, *Savonarola* (1926), Kai Friis Møller's *En Engelsk Bog* (1948), and Stanislaus Joyce's *My Brother's Keeper* (1958). The plenitude of these labors in fact suggests that, unlike his more solidly "literary" work, the value of an Eliot introduction draws on sources other than its intrinsic potential for scarcity or difficulty. Simply put, while the introduction was certainly another vehicle for literary reputation, it was never a means to secure it – at least, not for Eliot. Affixed at one time or another to works by Ezra Pound, Djuna Barnes, Marianne Moore, James Joyce, Wyndham Lewis, Christopher Isherwood, G. Wilson Knight, and David Jones, to name some of the contemporaries and near contemporaries Eliot introduced, Eliot introductions were prized assets, partly prized for the highbrow cachet of Eliot's name, partly prized for his specific knack for credible prologizing, for his ability to make obvious propaganda seem suitably critical and disinterested.

In a letter to Margaret Anderson, Eliot's celebrated associate, Pound, mocks his own deficiencies at this kind of work:

I must get out of the big stick habit, and begin to put my prose stuff into some sort of permanent form, not merely into saying things which everybody will believe in three years and take as a matter of course in ten.

I. E. articles which can be reduced to "Joyce is a writer, GODDAMN your eyes, Joyce is a writer, I tell you Joyce etc. etc. Lewis can paint, Gaudier knows a stone from a milk-pudding. WIPE your feet!!!!!"[34]

Perhaps the failings Pound parodies help account for the general absence of his introductions to works by contemporaries. Eliot avoided these pit-falls by carefully crafting disinterestedness. Eliot's introductory idiom, carefully apportioning praise with doses of criticism, eschews Pound's brand of hyperbolic enthusiasm, which Pound himself recognized as verging on self-parody. Eliot avoids the hyperbolic tendency to sound like obvious propaganda by shading his introductions in uniform tones of what his colleagues at Faber called Faberese, a tone of knowing superiority which serves to position Eliot so far above and beyond the "uninstructed reader" that finally his position of enunciation supersedes the author's own.[35] In his introductions, this impossible vantage point leads Eliot to particular total-izing claims about the literary careers and reputations of contemporaries, as in his introduction to Pound's *Selected Poems*: "In the work of any major poet who does not repeat himself, the earlier part is necessary for under-standing the later, and the later for understanding the earlier."[36] Elsewhere, he describes this totalizing view as the simultaneity of literary "promise" and literary "achievement":

I cannot admit any easy distinction between *promise* and *achievement*; for the admission of promise is a recognition of something already there; and every real achievement, in spite of the brevity of life, should be a promise of something further.[37]

Given the impossible conceptual purchase of these claims, when Eliot begins his introduction to Barnes' *Nightwood* (1937) with oddly self-deprecating rhetoric, seemingly designed to discredit the very act of introduction-writing, the effects are necessarily duplicitous: "When the question is raised, of writing an introduction to a book of a creative order, I always feel that the few books worth introducing are exactly those which it is an impertinence to introduce." To introduce *Nightwood*, he claims, is to commit such an impertinence. *Nightwood* is worth introducing, precisely because it undermines his authority to introduce.

The logic of this perplexing sentiment takes for granted the introduction's implicit subordination of *the author being introduced* to *the author doing the introducing*. The need for introductions conveys a kind of literary inadequacy, a lack of self-sufficiency. As I mentioned above, the very ordering of documents in an introduced book implies which name carries more repute and which name needs more introduction. What confirms Eliot's excess of reputation more assuredly – that his name has reputation to spare, so to speak – than his lending its excess to other names? Here, Eliot styles the disruption of this process – or, more precisely, his second thoughts about it – as the ultimate compliment to Barnes and therein the ultimate form of introduction. By questioning his right to introduce Barnes' work, Eliot suggests, he indicates that her work is on a par with his, which, after all, needs no introduction.

To paraphrase: *Nightwood* is worth introducing, because it *ought not* to need introduction, and now only introducing it will rectify the imbalance of reputation. The last resort of promotion is often the presumption of neglect, that authors and texts have been unfairly denied their due. The "impertinence" Eliot describes may come from the bind he is in: if he introduces Barnes, he exposes the injustices of a literary system overvaluing certain names and undervaluing others; if he does not, he validates it. His rhetoric gives him a deeply ambiguous way out. It enables him to make use of his credentials by professing unworthiness of them. Insofar as his decision to question his literary reputation functions as the ultimate means of conferring literary repute, professing unworthiness again lets Eliot make the work of making use of literary reputation sound like the disinterested detection of intrinsic merit. To re-inflect Eliot's word somewhat, the *impertinence* here may be that part of the work of introducing involves buttressing one's own reputation, documenting one's stance and stature with respect to the author being introduced.

"I have already committed two such impertinences," Eliot's *Nightwood* introduction continues; "this is the third, and if it is not the last no one will be more surprised than myself." The other two texts are most likely Ezra Pound's *Selected Poems* (1928) and Marianne Moore's *Selected Poems* (1935). The other introductions Eliot wrote before *Nightwood* include one for *Savonarola*, his mother's dramatic poem. However unlikely, it is tempting to imagine Eliot offering his mother's *Savonarola* along with Moore's *Selected Poems* and Barnes' *Nightwood* as his three impertinences, three works by women authors making Great Tom genuflect about his literary renown. Yet the interplay of gender in Eliot's introductions is more rooted in the process of representing literary relationships than merely the notion that women writers occasion anxiety about reputation. *Pace* Sandra Gilbert and Susan Gubar's argument in the first volume of *No Man's Land*, anxiety about the rising literary reputations of women writers, as we see in the Barnes introduction, can itself serve to reinforce reputation, helping shore up the introducer's position of enunciation and bring about more introductory work. Eliot's willingness to count certain contemporary women writers among the most exemplary authors he introduces suggests less about Eliot's commitments to gender equality than it does about the coding of subordination as a dominant dynamic of introduction-writing and the functionality of this dynamic for consolidating the reputation of a male introducer. For Eliot, introductions are positions of enunciation and consolidation, from which he can model normative claims about working literary relationships among readers, texts, and authors using the specific form of literary working relationship that his introduction embodies. More important for him, he can at very low risk overtly focus attention on the book and author at issue, while covertly reflecting attention back on his own reputation.

With remarkable consistency, Eliot avoids overtly staking his reputation on the books he introduces. Instead, as demonstrated in the *Nightwood* introduction, he places these books along a continuum of value that offers the inability to impress them with his imprimatur as the ultimate signature of value. The best works stand alone; the ones he introduces implicitly do not, though some like *Nightwood* may get close. His introduction to *Savonarola*, his mother's "somewhat bloodless" long poem, marks one of the lowest risks.[38] No doubt, the *Savonarola* introduction, the second Eliot wrote, helped bring his mother's work into print. It is also the introduction most obviously related to a "personal" connection with its author. Mitigating against the issue of nepotism, he formulates a kind of patronizingly un-reflexive authority; the texts for which introductions are apposite are, recall, somehow also undeserving of the poet-critic's attentions. No reader – not even one schooled in Eliot's convoluted idiom of apportioning praise – would mistake his distant critical essay for ringing endorsement. Never mentioning his mother by name, he diverts attention from the charge of being too interested in his mother's work. Whereas Charlotte Eliot herself dedicates the text "to my children," her son only refers to his mother twice, each time as the nondescript "author of *Savonarola*."[39] (More space is dedicated to a footnote citing a "humble" paper he wrote for "that extraordinary philosopher Josiah Royce."[40]) The criticism also adopts the guise of disinterest, making the case for the "documentary value" of historical fiction: "a work of historical fiction is much more a document on its own time than on the time portrayed."[41] Apparently, the chief interest in such work lies in its value as a historical symptom, in its naïf representation of the cultural enthusiasms of the age that renders "a state of mind contemporary with the author."[42] The ease with which Eliot erases the gap between interest and disinterest speaks to the power of the introduction as a generic formation based on a privileged position of enunciation vis-à-vis other authors.

His preface to Simone Weil's *Need for Roots* (1952) makes the impossible standard at work here explicit: the most successful introductions, he claims, should achieve "permanent association" with the texts they introduce. So closely are the two works allied, publishing them separately becomes unthinkable; they become, in effect, "permanently" enshrined together, a single entity in the bibliographic record. Eliot's axiology always seems to settle for no less than "permanence," a concept closely connected with his brand of ahistorical historicism, the sense of the simultaneous *pastness and presentness of the past* articulated most famously in the seminal essay "Tradition and the Individual Talent" in 1918.[43] Eliot's approach does not so much involve supplying readers with a "permanent" interpretation of texts as much as it involves promoting a "permanently" privileged relationship between the personalities of author and introducer, a relationship which evidences a discrete point of productive exchange between two literary personalities, a *working* relationship.

Despite forswearing "permanent association" with Weil, Eliot actively encourages such ambitions in other introductions. These efforts are at their programmatic best in the "postscripts" and "retrospects" written for new editions, which purport to reconsider previously written introductory material. In his 1948 postscript to the 1928 introduction to Pound's *Selected Poems*, for example, he states that the

introduction, written over twenty years ago, still seems to me to serve its purpose better than would a new introduction to the same selection of poems. The contemporary of the author of the later *Cantos* cannot alter the introduction written when he was a contemporary of the author of *Lustra* and *Hugh Selwyn Mauberley*.[44]

Here, we see Eliot applying the notion of "permanent association" to himself, or else to the earlier self of his curiously detached, third-person formulation, "the contemporary of the author of *Lustra* and *Hugh Selwyn Mauberley*." Tellingly, he disassociates himself, circa 1948, from the earlier Eliot, circa 1916, 1920, and 1928 (the respective publication dates for *Lustra*, *Mauberley*, and *Selected Poems*), in order to associate the earlier Eliot more thoroughly with Pound's earlier work.

Likewise, his "Note to Second Edition" of Barnes' *Nightwood*, without demonstrating quite the same degree of self-fragmentation, treats his initial introductory imprimatur as inviolable historical material. As in the Pound postscript, he calls attention to the otherness of his earlier self. Between editions, it seems, Eliot's identity has become estranged from its earlier manifestation; he now detects some "evidences of . . . immaturity" in the original, written in his late forties, only a year after the appearance of the first of the *Four Quartets*, hardly puerile juvenilia like "King Bolo and His Big Black Kween." In both postscripts, he draws attention to potential items for revision or retraction, only to state adamant unwillingness to revise or retract. If revising and retracting are not permissible – or, as Eliot asserts, not possible – such statements are only meant to signal that the originals are irretrievable, the working relationship elapsed, the personalities extinct, and impossible to extract from the contexts for which they were elaborated. The gesture of the postscript serves to confirm the "cold" relationship between Eliot and the authors in question, and, at the same time, disavow any claims for them as relationships between living, biographical entities. The relationships now endure "objectively" as inactive, static monuments, literary associations persisting solely as books-in-print, as they must to acquire "permanence."

In "Tradition and the Individual Talent," Eliot writes that "the existing monuments form an ideal order among themselves . . . modified by

the introduction of the new (the really new) work of art among them."
For him, these monuments not only possess agency but also act as functional substitutes for their producers. "Someone said," he writes, "'the dead
writers are remote from us because we *know* so much more than they did'.
Precisely, and they are that which we know."[45] This idea stays with Eliot.
In *Notes towards the Definition of Culture*, he ascribes the development of
individual identity to "the people whom we meet in the course of our lives,"
clarifying parenthetically that by "people" he includes "the authors whose
books we read, and characters in works of fiction and history."[46] These
conceptions of permanent relationships between authors are on display in
Eliot's full-blown introductions. For the works Eliot finds most exemplary,
his introductions tend both to represent the material being introduced as
functional replacements for authors and to treat his encounters with these
books as quasi-social relationships. In his introduction to *Nightwood*, for
example, he writes:

I can justify this preface only in the following way. One is liable to expect other
people to see, on their first reading of a book, all that one has come to perceive in
the course of a developing intimacy with it. I have read *Nightwood* a number of
times, in manuscript, in proof, and after publication . . . [I]t took me, with this
book, some time to come to an appreciation of its meaning as a whole.[47]

Here, Eliot rehearses the program for "permanent association." Eliot the
introducer, having figured out a means to textual intimacy, supplies readers
with his own model for imitation. "What one can do for other readers," he
writes, "is to trace the most significant phases of one's own appreciation.
For it took me, with this book, some time to come to an appreciation
of its meaning as a whole."[48] And the novel takes over Djuna Barnes'
agency in his narrative; his relationship with *Nightwood* stands in for his
working relationship with Barnes. Readers who read *Nightwood* following
this example in turn simulate his role in an implied working relationship
between two authors.

   His introductions leave to speculation the task of filling in the details of
this relationship; readers are guided only by Eliot's intimations of full access
to all phases of writing, editing, and publication. Condensing and objec-
tifying the role of Barnes and others in the editorial work of *Nightwood*,
a series of discrete, narrated encounters between Eliot and the text effectively submerges their work in his work. First, he feels "the opening movement slow and dragging," "the doctor alone [O'Connor] . . . gave the
book vitality," and "the final chapter to be superfluous." On subsequent re-
readings, the encounter becomes more nuanced, other characters become

more prominent, O'Connor takes on a "more profound importance," and the final chapter seems more "essential, both dramatically and musically."[49] The supreme fiction of Eliot as a preferred reader, slowly coming to terms with an always already finished product, subsumes a more arduous and unruly apocryphal narrative: a troubled prepublication history, seemingly endless shuttling of drafts, manuscripts, and proofs; heated discussions with Emily Coleman, Coleman's editorial pruning, rejection slips from two publishing houses, the intercession of Edwin Muir, reluctant then enthusiastic acceptance from Eliot at Faber, more editorial give-and-take, the "hierarchical" blue and red pencils of Eliot and fellow Faber editor Frank Morley (respectively), more editorial input from Coleman, et cetera.[50] Barnes' publishing difficulties, the well-documented interventions of Muir, Eliot, and Morley, and, most decisively, the heavy editorial hand of Coleman are nowhere and everywhere in Eliot's so-called "approach . . . for the new reader."[51] In her diary, Coleman longs for a time when "the story of Coleman and Barnes over the ms. of Nightwood . . . will become a saga, a unique thing in literature."[52] If Eliot's introduction helped to undercut (or, in truth, simply postpone) Coleman's desires for "permanent association" with Barnes' work, it did so in ways more immediately instrumental to furthering his own claims for reputation than, say, had he merely substituted his story with Barnes "over the ms." for Coleman's. Unlike Coleman's story, his story is both embedded in and constructed from the mutually conferring apparatus of literary celebrity, the missing ingredient which separates the unheard call for literary justice in Coleman's diary entry, a source of potential authorial embarrassment, from the authorized words of Eliot's introduction, which Barnes keenly desired.

As the language framing his account of reading *Nightwood* suggests, Eliot not only treats literary objects as functional human substitutes, but also genders and sexualizes his "developing intimacy" with them. While this dynamic follows partly from his overzealous attempt to obscure *Nightwood*'s specifically lesbian content, as Cheryl J. Plumb argues, it also follows from the promotional logic of Eliot's mode of introduction-writing. From his privileged position of enunciation, his role as preferred reader, Eliot claims to offer readers his own experience rather than an interpretation *per se*. He offers them a script to imitate, a quasi-romance plot between reader and literary object – overcoming indifference, habituated attraction, and mutual fulfillment – implicated by his privileged access to Barnes' work. This plot is possible only because Eliot's position of enunciation implicitly subordinates the novel and its potential readers; he alone among interested parties is able to position himself outside the plot he describes. He alone is able to occupy an unmarked, disengaged position, where he can see that *Nightwood* "demands something that the ordinary reader is not prepared to give," that it "is so good a novel only sensibilities trained on poetry can wholly appreciate it."[53] That Eliot's sensibilities exceed these demands goes without saying, demonstrated by his ability to identify these deficiencies and possibilities in others.

It is worth noting that this dynamic does not emerge from any practices Eliot specially reserves for introducing works by female authors; the works of male authors are subject to the same regulative logic of patriarchal subordination. What is remarkable about this dynamic is that the subordination is most acute with the authors and books Eliot judges most exemplary, the ones he recommends with the least reservation. If an author qualifies, Eliot hands out "permanent association" even-handedly, no matter the author's gender. A comparison between Eliot's original introductions to Barnes' *Nightwood* and Pound's *Selected Poems* bears this out. Like the Barnes introduction, he begins the Pound introduction by intimating an active, familiar stake in the editorial fulfillment of the text. *Selected Poems*, Eliot begins, is not to be confused with Pound's *Personae*, the edition of shorter poems Pound "recently made for publication in New York": "I made a few suggestions for omissions and inclusions in a similar collection to be published in London; and out of discussions of such matters with Pound arose the spectre of an introduction by myself."[54] Eliot omits some crucial connective tissue from his account. Why wouldn't *Personae* work in England? Was the problem personal, promotional, or business-related (as Eliot mentions in a footnote, Pound had published a collection with the same title in London under the Elkin Mathews imprint in 1909)? Was Eliot with his "suggestions for omissions and inclusions" the obstacle, or was he merely assisting Pound (with a copyright issue)? Who proposed the introduction, Pound or Eliot, and to what end?

While Eliot's hints of a working relationship with Pound are somewhat more pronounced than they are with Barnes, they are still only hints; again, as with Barnes, details are less crucial than suggesting the preexistence of a working relationship. Eliot's intimations of charitable critical disagreements off-stage set the stage. Whereas Pound planned *Personae* to "consist of all of his work in verse up to his *Cantos*, which he chooses to keep in print," Eliot envisions *Selected Poems* differently, as a historical sampler of Pound's "continuous development, down to *Hugh Selwyn Mauberley*, the last stage of importance before the *Cantos*."[55] From Eliot's standpoint, then, Pound's present view of his past work does not have adequate purchase on the scope of his oeuvre. Even though he acknowledges that Pound is at the top of his game (*The Cantos* being "by far his most important achievement"), he claims that the work of the latter-day Pound suffers from not having enough readers who have "followed the author's poetry from the beginning":

The volumes previously published represent each a particular aspect or period of his work; and even when they fall into the right hands, are not always read in the right order. My point is that Pound's work is . . . much more varied than is generally supposed . . . This book [*Selected Poems*] would be, were it nothing else, a text-book in modern versification.[56]

Eliot's point (Pound's body of work as poetic monument) is put for comparison and contrast against more present-centered views allied with Pound himself (past work selected by the standard of the best, most recent work). Pound's implied willingness to submit to Eliot – his understood acquiescence to Eliot's idea of his works *worth keeping in print* – in effect comprises Eliot's qualification to provide "a convenient Introduction to Pound's work." As with *Nightwood*, the relationship between the authors – specifically, the relationship as a contentious, negotiated working project – is reified, reinscribed in Eliot's narrative of himself reading *Selected Poems* as stages in Pound's poetic development. Becoming the impossible readerly ideal, he can claim to have recognized Pound's corpus as corpus from the beginning, revisit the experience in *Selected Poems*, and model it as an introduction to the same volume. He thus unpacks then re-packs Pound's literary reputation, as if dismantling and reassembling nesting Matrioshka dolls, each encapsulated part returning an image of the whole.

The most well-disposed Eliot introductions make this gesture, even those, like his Barnes introduction, which preface single works. His foreword to Wyndham Lewis's *One-Way Song* (prefaced edition, 1960), for example, first makes the case that "the poem cannot be fully understood without some knowledge of Wyndham Lewis's prose work," proposing a hefty reading list for the neophyte. Later, taking another related, yet quite different tack, he states that readers who successfully navigate *One-Way Song* will then have a handy "introduction to the rest of his work."[57] For Eliot, each single work is partial, situated within the broader development of a larger body of work, yet – and also, precisely for this reason – each work entails the simultaneous fulfillment and anticipation of all past and future developments. His introduction to *Introducing James Joyce* (1942), for example, his posthumous anthology of Joyce's writings edited for Faber, follows the same trajectory: the early works, *Dubliners* and *A Portrait of the Artist as a Young Man*, present the justification of the later ones, *Ulysses* and *Finnegans Wake*. On the one hand, he claims to select passages according to a "principle of selection" that makes "the reader aware of continuity of development between one book and the next"; on the other, he claims to select "passages as nearly as possible complete in themselves."[58] That the dual aims of representing textual self-sufficiency and representing textual interdependency do not chafe reveals much about the particular logic of promotion in the Eliot introductions. To promote exemplary works by contemporaries, he finds it necessary to posit near critical omniscience, translating the act of "closely and continuously" following a contemporary's literary career into his current mastery of the author's body of work. When Eliot does not offer this sort of critical positioning for a near contemporary, or even questions it, it means he is offering mixed or even tepid praise.

Eliot's introductions to Harold Monro's *Collected Poems* (1933) and Harry Crosby's *Transit of Venus* (1931) fall into this category. In the Monro introduction, he once again invokes an impossibly personalized purchase on literary permanence, calling it here the "historical point of view":

The historical point of view, especially when we are concerned with our immediate predecessors and contemporaries, is largely impersonal; that is to say, it tends to emphasise what a man has in common with others, in subject matter, in style and technique, in his social background and assumptions. It also judges men according to what is taken to be their influence, or their importance in the main current. Such an attitude is bound to be unfair to the reputation of such a poet as Monro.[59]

Eliot, remember, invoked history in much the same terms when introducing his mother ten years earlier.[60] Middling writing of a given period lacks individuating factors; it is less "authored" than a consequence of origins in the humble commonalities of the "main current." Being able to recognize the "historical point of view" – or, in Eliot's case, actually inhabiting it – posits a second form of introductory omniscience. It allows readers such as Eliot impossible knowledge about which works have the defect of impermanence, which works possess values that are merely "historical." Significantly, Eliot does not class Monro in this category: "He does not express the spirit of an age; he expresses the spirit of one man, but that so faithfully that his poetry will remain as one variety of the infinite number of possible expressions of tortured human consciousness."[61] That said, Eliot is not sure where else to place Monro; after all, technical originality is the poet's main "business," and on that score, Eliot writes, "he was not an innovator."[62]

According to Eliot, given the role of Monro's Poetry Bookshop in the "confraternity of poets, [and] the publication and dissemination" of the Georgian poets, in particular, he is to be commended for the extent to which he resisted their influence at all.[63] Most of this group's output was, in a damning word, "static":

[I]t failed to show any interesting development in the mind and experience of the author. Monro, with his amiable, but uncritical capacity for admiring other people's verse, gives me the impression of having tried, in some of his earlier work, but probably unconsciously, to be more like other writers than he really was . . . Had Monro been a poet who could have worked out his own method in isolation, and ignored the attempts of his contemporaries, he might earlier have found a more personal idiom. It was part of the irony of the situation that, being essentially a different kind of poet, with different things to say, from any of his earlier or younger contemporaries, he was yet actively and passionately interested in "poetry."[64]

Tellingly, Eliot cannot distinguish Monro from his Georgian contemporaries nor can he detect Monro's opposition to *the spirit of his age, until* he reads ("re-reads") his body of work: "His originality, in all but his latest work, is not immediately apparent from any one poem; it was not indeed until re-reading the whole of his published work that I recognized how distinctly, in his whole work, the vision is the personal vision of Harold Monro."[65] With Barnes, Pound, Joyce, and company, the recognition was more immediate. For them, originality in the single work entails originality in the entirety of published works, both sites being readily apparent to Eliot narrating the act of re-reading. Unlike the most exemplary cases, Monro's logic of development cannot be discerned in his individual work, and, as Eliot explains it, this is a symptomatic defect – a lesser defect than being "merely historical" like the Georgians to be sure, but a defect nonetheless. Consequently, Eliot qualifies his assessment of Monro's reputation, professing his inability to identify specific lines of poetry or individual poems that unconditionally support claims to distinction. He writes: "There is no one poem, no few poems, which I could point to and say this will give you the essence of Monro."[66] For the most exemplary authors, Eliot concedes no such shortages, nor does he offer qualifications. His final words on Monro are rife with both: "I think his poetry, as a whole, is more nearly the real right thing than any of the poetry of a somewhat older generation than mine except Mr. Yeats's."[67]

The Monro introduction suggests Eliot's most favorable stance to the "somewhat older" literary generation, a group he is unwilling to label predecessors. Eliot's little-known introduction to *Transit of Venus*, Harry Crosby's posthumous collection of poems, suggests an equivalent stance for the somewhat younger generation, the generation which he was unwilling to label successors.[68] Accordingly, his introductory point-of-view remains provisional, exhibiting neither the will to "permanent association" nor the "historical point of view." Again he refuses to assess individual poems ("we do not pick out single poems for enjoyment: if any of it is worth reading, then it all is") and attaches even more equivocal provisos to Crosby's corpus than he does to Monro's:

> I am far from asserting . . . that I understand in the least what Crosby was up to, or that I am sure I should like it if I did. I doubt whether anyone himself engaged in the pursuit of poetry can "like," any more than he can "understand," the work of his contemporaries; if it is wholly unrelated to one's own efforts it is irrelevant, and if it has some relation it is merely disturbing . . . What I do like, in a serious sense, is the fact that Crosby was definitely going his own way, whether I like the way or not. And in spite of occasional conventional phrases – so conventional as perhaps to be deliberate – I am more interested in his work because of its imperfections, its particular way of being imperfect.[69]

Was there ever an introduction less taken with the work it purports to introduce? A more debased use of originality? More equivocating blurb-writing? Verging on indifference, Eliot's detachment is nevertheless couched in the first-person singular. A self-consciously private, imperfect reaction offered almost off the record (only 50 copies were published), it contrasts sharply with the Faberese, the official, impersonalized omniscience, in which Eliot often cast his readerly engagement, used especially, as in the case of the Barnes introduction, to convey profound attachment to a work. The implications of Eliot calling Crosby a contemporary turn out to be even more equivocal than commenting that his work is most fetching in its imperfections.

"I doubt whether we can ever understand the poetry of a contemporary," he writes, "especially if we are engaged in writing ourselves."[70] He uses the idea of being a contemporary of Crosby to opt out of any relationship with him, just as he uses being Monro's contemporary to excuse his mistaken sense of Monro's affinity with the Georgians. Poets cannot like, understand, or even relate to the work of their contemporaries . . . unless, of course, that contemporary happens to be Marianne Moore. In Eliot's 1935 introduction to Moore's *Selected Poems*, he recycles the sentiments about contemporaneity occasioned four years earlier by Crosby's *Transit of Venus*, advancing a familiar position:

> We know very little about the value of the work of our contemporaries, almost as little as we know about our own. It may have merits which exist only for contemporary sensibility; it may have concealed virtues which will only become apparent with time. How it will rank when we are all dead authors ourselves we cannot say with any precision. If one is to talk about one's contemporaries at all, therefore, it is important to make up our minds as to what we can affirm with confidence, and as to what must be a matter of doubting conjecture. The last thing,

certainly, that we are likely to know about them is their "greatness," or their relative distinction or triviality in relation to the standard of "greatness." For in greatness are involved moral and social relations, relations which can only be perceived from a remoter perspective, and which may be said even to be created in the process of history . . . But the *genuineness* of poetry is something which we have some warrant for believing that a small number, but only a small number, of contemporary readers can recognize.[71]

Since the Crosby introduction, the explanatory register has changed. Eliot counterbalances his often repeated doubts about liking, understanding, or relating to works by contemporaries with two certainties: first, little can be said about *the greatness of work of contemporaries* until *we are all dead authors ourselves*; and, second, some things can be said about *the genuineness of poetry* by the right sort of contemporary readers. Both certainties lead us straight to Eliot, the second getting us there more quickly. Significantly, he does not mention the scarcity of genuine poetry when it comes to his contemporaries but the scarcity of readers capable of recognizing its *genuineness*, capable of detecting which texts "avoid saying what has already been said as well as it can" by means of the *historical point of* view.[72] It is certain Eliot took for granted that the value of *genuine* poetry depended on scarcity, but here he deliberately elides that point to invoke the preeminence of the right reader, to promote his own role in the introductory narrative. Not surprisingly, the Moore introduction follows the Barnes-Pound-Lewis mode rather than the Monro-Crosby mode: engaging individual poems by Moore and perceiving in them in miniature, as it were, the arc of Moore's career. If "Miss Moore has no immediate poetic derivations," if "Miss Moore's poems form part of the small body of durable poetry written in our life," Eliot is also willing to cite specific lines to shore up these claims.[73]

As I mentioned, Eliot's first certainty leads us to Eliot just as surely as his second. This passage – a cunning passage, to be sure – occurs once we realize that he treats himself and the contemporaries he admires most as if both were already dead. His curious phrase "we are all dead authors ourselves" (*we cannot say with any precision* how anybody will rank when *we are all dead authors ourselves*) gives full expression to the idea that literary celebrity is authorial self-fashioning *in extremis*. Eliot claims that the living cannot know the "relative distinction or triviality in relation to the standard of 'greatness'" but then betrays his true sentiment by counting himself among the dead authors who will continue to speak. He is squarely in obituary mode in his introduction to Joyce, written shortly after Joyce's death. Its doubly omniscient insistence on inviting readers to perceive the *achievement* of individual works in Joyce's complete oeuvre and to perceive the *promise* of the oeuvre in individual works may be chalked up to postmortem revaluation. But, Eliot longs for the same approach in his introductions to Pound, Barnes, Lewis, and Moore, written during these authors' lifetimes.

In his introduction to Pound's *Selected Poems*, in which he refers to the specter-like character of introductions, he writes of a "final Pound," a figure synthesizing the early "antiquarian" Pound's archeological mastery of versification and the late "modern" Pound's revolution of technique.[74] The Moore introduction, which allegedly forswears the "remoter perspective," the view which puts the dead, great authors in relation, assesses her accomplishments by scaling them against his lifetime: "Miss Moore is . . . one of those few who have done the language some service in my lifetime."[75] The obituary mode does not enter into his introductions to Monro and Crosby, despite both being recently deceased when Eliot is writing, and he makes no claims about reconciling the would-be promises of their individual works with total literary achievements. Simply put, he will not play dead for their reputations. Because Eliot practices a form of authorial self-fashioning that is, in a sense, already posthumous, he is freed from having contiguous stakes in the work he is introducing. At the same time, the pose allows him to render literary judgments as if he himself had long achieved a kind of detached, textually embodied permanence. Editing becomes a phallomorphic exteriorization of impossible literary authority, an inflated, authoritarian exaggeration supplying a model of literary working relationships that can be subsequently and readily averred as posturing.

PHALLOMORPHOSIS

When it comes to this sort of modernist self-fashioning nothing for sheer odious brio really touches Ezra Pound likening himself to an engorged penis. Its very odiousness provides Gilbert and Gubar with rhetorical setup in the second volume of their *No Man's Land*:

"Make it new," Ezra Pound famously exhorted his contemporaries as he struggled to fashion a modernist aesthetic for a modern world. The statement would appear gender-free, but elsewhere the "Sage Homme" who acted as midwife to *The Waste Land* strikingly sexualized his definitions of what was new and who could make it. Explaining in his translator's postscript to Rémy de Gourmont's *Natural Philosophy of Love* (1931) [*sic*] that "the brain itself [is] only a sort of great clot of genital fluid," Pound went on to conceptualize originality as "the phallus or spermatozoid charging, head-on, the female chaos," adding in a confessional aside, "Even oneself has felt it, driving any new idea into the great passive vulva of London."[76]

Pound's modernist career is condensed to three telegraphic anecdotes: "make it new," midwifery of *The Waste Land*, self-fashioning as a prick.[77] If Pound's *make it new* dictum is emblematic for the modernist cultural project as a whole, then, Gilbert and Gubar suggest, his masculinist idea of cultural work – *from the wreckage of Europe, ego scriptor, charging, head-on into the female chaos* – is damningly synecdochal, returning *in the guise of the new* more of the same old gender thematics.[78]

And yet, what of the middle, appositional anecdote? The inclusion of Pound's "midwifery" of Eliot's *Waste Land* in this account reminds us of the feminization of what is perhaps still Pound's most famous association, his role as a nurturing collaborator. Between the allegedly "gender-free" signifier of the first anecdote and the flagrantly masculinist signified of the third – signs underdetermined and overdetermined by gender respectively – Pound's allegedly feminized role as editor represents an ironically resonant counterpoint, one which suggests that the third anecdote not only reveals the concealed truth of the first but also unmasks the preposterous impersonation of the second. As Gilbert and Gubar suggest, all three associations – Pound's motive to make it new, his relationship with Eliot, his desire to plow through the feminine chaos – are, without question, both gendered and sexualized; the question I want to raise here is whether these anecdotes, in fact, ever described incongruous projects? The problem lies with the initial framing assumption, for the motive to *make it new* was always already more than strictly a call for aesthetic liberation. It was first and foremost a specific model of self-promotion, rooted in propaganda for Pound's earlier work, his imagist anthologies, and his efforts for other writers. As he writes in 1934: "Let it stand that from 1912 onward for a decade and more I was instrumental in forcing into print, and *secondarily* in commenting on, certain work now recognized as valid by all competent readers, the dates of various reviews, anthologies, etc., are ascertainable."[79] In fact, on closer inspection, each anecdote indexes a specific parable of literary promotion linking Pound to literary work by himself and others, imagist anthologies, *The Waste Land*, his oeuvre at large. This side of the matter even creeps into Gilbert and Gubar's account, when they invoke Pound's "confessional aside" about feeling like a simulated prick thrusting the *new into the great passive vulva* of the London literary scene.[80] Should this kind of hyperbolic self-fashioning ever be taken at face value?

Pound was not oblivious to the value of playing the insufferable American prick as ironic self-deprecation. The vulgar American was one of his most longstanding "personae," a role he reproduces in numerous memoirs, offending Harriet Shaw Weaver's drinking sensibilities in Beach's

Shakespeare and Company, breaking Gertrude Stein's chair in Hemingway's
Moveable Feast, invading T. E. Lawrence's Oxford rooms in Robert Graves'
"These are Your Gods, O Israel," and consuming tremendous piles of pastry
in Ford Madox Ford's *English Review* reminiscences.[81] Significantly, this was
also the first popular image of Pound's literary celebrity. *Punch* caricatures
him twice along these lines. First as "Ezekiel Ton":

Mr. Welkin Mark [i.e., Elkin Mathews] . . . begs to announce that he has secured
for the English market the palpitating works of the new Montana (U.S.A) poet,
Mr. Ezekiel Ton . . . Mr. Ton, who has left America to reside for a while in London
and impress his personality on English editors, publishers and readers, is by far
the newest poet going, whatever other advertisements may say. He has succeeded,
where all others have failed, in evolving a blend of the imagery of the unfettered
West, the vocabulary of Wardour Street, and the sinister abandon of Borgiac Italy.[82]

Later as "Boaz Bobb":

A new poet is about to swim into our ken in the person of Boaz Bobb, a son
of the Arkansas soil, who has long been a resident of London studying Icelandic
literature for the purposes of a new saga on the Wild West. Those persons who
have been privileged to see Mr. Bobb's lyrics in MS. say that they can remember
nothing like them for their simplicity and candour. Mr. Bobb, with the delightful
lack of restraint and false shame that is so marked a characteristic of the age, takes
the reader into his confidence with complete unreserve, even when he runs the risk
of suffering in reputation from so doing. The title of the little volume is *Naked
and Unashamed*. It will be printed on hand-made paper, with the widest margins
of recent times.[83]

Letters to Dorothy Shakespear suggest that Pound found the representation
congenial; he even signs some letters as "Boaz." The conceptual distance
between the public image of the loud, swollen-headed American and his
self-fashioning as a lewd, invasive hard-on in 1921 was essentially nil. Shortly
after Pound was caricatured as Boaz Bobb and Ezekiel Ton, Henri Gaudier-
Brzeska was sculpting a large bust of him known as the Hieratic Head, a
half-ton marble block chiseled in the shape of a giant penis (see Figure 4).[84]
Without a suitable venue, it was planted on Violet Hunt's lawn in Campden
Hill remaining there awkwardly "for many years":

No one could afford a pedestal, so it stood on the grass, a prey to mud, moss,
snails, and the lawn-mower. Ezra would sometimes go and clean it up, borrowing
a brush from Violet's elderly maid, who on being asked Mr Pound's whereabouts
would reply that he could be found "a-scrubbin' his MONUMENT."[85]

This unflattering image of Pound on hands and knees polishing *his
MONUMENT* is as crucial to his literary persona as the archness of his

OF ALL BOOKSELLERS

GAUDIER-BRZESKA

A MEMOIR

BY

EZRA POUND

WITH 4 PORTRAITS & 34 ILLUSTRATIONS
REPRODUCTIONS OF SCULPTURE AND
DRAWINGS BY THE ARTIST

Crown 4to. 12s. 6d. net

LONDON : JOHN LANE, THE BODLEY HEAD, W.
NEW YORK : JOHN LANE COMPANY   MCMXVI

Figure 4 The Hieratic Head.

jarringly phallic likeness placed like a jar in Tennessee in one of the fenced gardens of a London residential street.

Wayne Koestenbaum writes that, with the ascendancy of women writers in the nineteenth century, "it was no longer feasible to equate pen and penis" because literary men were "unable to assert that creativity was incompatible with female anatomy, men began to see authorship as a feminine process that they must steal back."[86] With Pound, it seems, this was not quite the case. By the twentieth century, male literary authority no longer went without saying, but, for Pound, acting like a prick served as an ironic cover for the loss, a means to simulate the absent authority that should have, after all, made promotion unnecessary. If all was well, he wouldn't have to act like this. Pound acting like a prick shows that modernist promotional machinery works best if the "thing" is suspiciously lacking. "The abandon, the suggestion of jolly power, and the slight posing of that, are typical of his character," Rupert Brooke writes in his 1909 review of *Personae*.[87] Whether he is posing as Altaforte, Boaz Bobb, or the Hieratic Head, a crucial part of Pound's performance – as Brooke and others recognized – is that it is pose. Pound can adopt unchallenged male authority, even if he is only pretending, precisely because he is only pretending to be an insufferable prick. The scene of literary promotion is keyed directly into his fantasy of producing himself as the phallus for an as-of-yet nonexistent audience, a fantasy which enables him to engage in hyperbolic self-production, producing himself in the work of producing other authors.[88]

As Ronald Bush notes, Pound's postscript to *The Natural Philosophy of Love* echoes two cognate texts written two years earlier, a passage in Canto 29, which also claims that "the / female / Is a chaos / An octopus / a biological process," and introductory letters and doggerel verse sent to Marianne Moore on 16 December 1918 and 1 February 1919.[89] In the Moore letters, the less public context, these ideas resonate in less menacing terms: "The female becomes a chaos, / the male / is a fixed point of stupidity," he writes in the doggerel.[90] The promotional and self-promotional sub-text here is more acute. Pound lays out the terms for their prospective working relationship in his customary epistolary style:

Dear Miss Moore:
The confounded trouble is that I have come to the end of my funds, and cannot pay for any more mss. for *The Little Review*.

   I think the poems too good to print without paying for them: I know you have contributed to *The Egoist* unpaid. And I have myself done a deal of unpaid work: too much of it.

I hope to start a quarterly here before long (part of the funds are in hand); and to be able to pay contributors . . . [and] give them the satisfaction of being in good company. I will either hold over your two poems for the quarterly and try to pay; or print them in *The L.R.* . . . as you choose or permit.

There are one or two details I should like to ask about. (Yeats and Eliot and various other people have had similar queeries leveled at them, and our friendships have weathered the strain, so don't take it ill of me.)[91]

His letter enacts Pound's insufferably fixated persona, blindly charging headlong towards an unknown, undifferentiated editorial response. Pound claims that Moore's verse is too good to print without paying and, in this, likens her to himself: she has done unpaid work; he has done unpaid work. He wants to retain her work to print in a hypothetical magazine that will pay its contributors. He assumes she has approached him to be her editor: "IF I am to be your editor," he writes later, elliptically omitting the subordinate clause, because his entire letter presupposes her subordination to the work of promotion.[92] In rapid succession, he quizzes her about more than a dozen points. Some are editorial minutiae: *Are you satisfied with the cadence and graphical arrangement here? Is this or that word* le mot juste? *Do you want "its self" or "itself" at the end of strophe 12?* Others pose indelicate and invasive queeries (more about this word later), which dismantle the author and reader divide, and recall Eliot's introductory self-fashioning as the preferred reader: *How much* [of your verse is] *deliberate, and therefore to be taken (by me) with studious meticulousness?? How much the fine careless rapture and therefore to be pot-shotted at until it assumes an* [sic] *wholly demonstrable or more obvious rightness????*[93]

The questions Pound puts to Moore are consistent with the "Manichean" (Pound's word here) dualism of his gender theory.[94] For Pound, *fine careless rapture* equates, in general terms, with the Other, the female chaos, the chaotic tissue of the unknown, undifferentiated response and, in specific reference, with the unpaying, unresponsive literary scene in London. *Studious meticulousness*, however, is phallic, self-sameness everywhere it is found. The curious point is that Pound wants Moore to tell him whether her *studious meticulousness* is commensurate with his phallic approach to it. That he does not seem to know in advance suggests that the *wholly demonstrable, obvious rightness* he proposes to help her attain is little more than mutually agreed upon regard for his editorial prowess. By the second letter, the doggerel sent a month and a half later, he seems to have made up his mind: Moore is "a stabilized female," Pound is "a male who has attained . . . chaotic fluidness," and the equilibrium they share may complicate their working relationship, their "mutual usefulness / is open to the gravest suspicions of non-existence."⁹⁵ Establishing a working relationship with Moore is a matter of precedents and testimonials not dialogue or exchange:

[H]ave you a book of verse in print? And, if not, can I get one into print for you? My last and best work *Propertius* has just dodged two publishers, one of whom wants to print half the book, leaving out the best of it . . . [S]till, I have got Joyce, and Lewis, and Eliot and a few other comforting people into print, by page and by volume. At any rate, I will buy a copy of your book IF it is in print, and if not, I want to see a lot of it together. You will never sell more than five hundred copies, as your work demands mental attention. I am inclined to think you would "go" better in bundles about the size of Eliot's *Prufrock and Observations* [*sic*].⁹⁶

The fixation is all-encompassing; the cerebral book, as an unsellable commodity, confirms phallic self-sufficiency, too. It is also a solid object marked by its exteriorized, physical properties wholly removed from another undifferentiated and purportedly feminized domain, namely mass commodity exchange. And, on the strength of anecdotal evidence of his relationships with Eliot, Yeats, Joyce, and Lewis, Pound's promise to Moore of 500 potential readers is finally condensed into the absolute self-sufficiency of a relationship with one editor, Pound himself.

    This substitution returns us to Pound's *queeries*; in effect, Pound must queer modernist women in order to promote them. Not by transforming Moore into *a female female transvestite*, as Gilbert and Gubar would have it, but by phallicizing her, casting her both as the phallic incarnation of impossible male literary authority and its most desired durable goods. The way Pound phallicizes Moore seems to support Koestenbaum's contention that literary collaborations manifest anxiously expressed and concealed homoeroticism.⁹⁷ Yet, unlike Koestenbaum, whose chief interest lies in the psychology of male literary collaboration, I think that the logic of modernist collaboration is determined by the cold promotional economics of fetish objects rather than the hot literary erotics of subjects.⁹⁸ Pound's operative assumption is never that he will work side by side with the authors in question producing authorship by joint signature but rather that these authors occasion him to produce self-sameness, to produce producing authorship without publicizing intersubjective interaction as textual work.⁹⁹ Significantly, the relationship Pound proposes with Moore does not so much implicate the production of Moore's work with metaphors of biological reproduction as much as it implicates the production of Moore as literary autogenesis. Pound's intervention will enable Moore to produce herself as durable goods, self-production without reproduction, through a relationship with Pound that is in itself "open to the gravest suspicions of non-existence."

In modernist studies, the relationship between Pound and Eliot inscribed in *The Waste Land* drafts has come to represent a familiar benchmark for modernist collaborative work, a nurturing intersubjective entanglement through which, in the words of Michael Coyle, Pound was able to "discover the coherence that eluded Eliot."[100] Yet, in certain respects, this is a deceptive standard. Despite the prevailing mythology of literary midwifery, Pound's letters confirm that he objectifies and phallicizes his relationship with Eliot in much the same manner as he did collaboration with Moore. Notably, I am referring to Pound's letter to Eliot of 24 January 1922, which includes another brutally scatological and sexualized doggerel, "Sage Homme." The verses indeed propose Eliot as the mother of *The Waste Land*, invoking the poem's difficult birth, but – to take issue with Koestenbaum – they figure Pound as a surgeon not a midwife.

> These are the Poems of Eliot
> By the Uranian Muse begot;
> A Man their Mother was,
> A Muse their Sire.
>
> How did the printed Infancies result
> From Nuptials thus doubly difficult?
>
> If you must need enquire
> Know diligent reader
> That on each Occasion
> Ezra performed the caesarean Operation.[101]

Koestenbaum's explication argues that the doggerel represents *The Waste Land* as a poem "sired in a scene of intercourse between the two men"; moreover, it implies that "Pound, Eliot's male muse, is the sire of *The Waste Land*."[102] Yet the first section emphasizes *The Waste Land* postpartum, not in conception, how the poem will come to be *printed*, not how it was inspired. Pound indeed queers Eliot ("Complimenti, you bitch," he writes in the prose section of the letter) but for the same reason he queers Moore: to underscore that lack of *studious meticulousness* may yet threaten the manuscript with oblivion. Pound, not Eliot, provides the focal point for both halves of the doggerel, figuring in the first as a rigorous, resourceful promoter of finished goods not as a siring muse inseminating a work-in-progress. By 24 January, the date of the letter, *The Waste Land* editing sessions were complete and the negotiations to place the literary product – which Pound brokered, of course – were already underway.[103]

Without a doubt, as Koestenbaum's explication demonstrates, the second half of the doggerel is heavily coded with homoeroticism, but, as he also acknowledges, it is equally coded ("coated" may be a better word here) in autoeroticism. As in his earlier correspondence with Moore, Pound translates a course of editorial work into an idiom of phallic promotion, an idiom which scrupulously aims to prevent bodies from touching ("Balls and balls and balls again / Can not touch his fellow men"), thus ensuring that the relationship of literary promotion is "open to the gravest suspicions of non-existence." To put it another way, editing (like promotion, more generally) must appear plausibly deniable. Whatever evidence there may be of a relationship must always appear *a posteriori*, post-coitus, postpartum, in posterity. This idiom may indeed be motivated by reflexive anxiety – anxiety about homosexuality, not least – but the anxiety is closely linked to promotional acts. Promotion, it seems, attracts various forms of anxiety, drawing on the insecurities that collaborative production occasions about identity vis-à-vis sex, gender, race, and class difference. All four are plainly manifest in Pound's letters with Moore and Eliot, being particularly pronounced in the abject crisis of purpose he exhibits in the second half of "Sage Homme":

> E.P. hopeless and unhelped
>
> Enthroned in the marmorean skies
> His verse omits realities,
> . . . .
> The glasses turn to chalices
> Is his fumbling analysis
> And holy hosts of hellenists
> Have numbed and honied his cervic cysts,
> His follows Yeats into the mists
> Despite his hebrew eulogists.
>
> Balls and balls and balls again
> Can not touch his fellow men.
> His foaming and abundant cream
> Has coated his world. The coat of a dream;
> Or say that the upjut of his sperm
> Has rendered his senses pachyderm.

This section is pure Poundian mythology – ironically self-deprecating, masturbatory bluster in the style of Boaz Bobb – written, as he puts it in the body of the letter, as Boaz is "wracked by the seven jealousies, and cogitating an excuse for always exuding my deformative secretions in my own stuff, and never getting an outline."[104] His doggerel refers to influence having a dilatory, "de*form*ative" effect on literary production. Early notoriety (i.e., with Hellenistic imagism) has damaged his ability to embody himself in his own solid literary objects, over-association with Yeats consigning him to follow Yeats into an undifferentiated, derivative Celtic twilight.[105] The phallus is swamped; Pound has spewed so much, so indiscriminately, he now appears to be drowning in formlessness.

To understand Pound's resignation from form to formlessness, it is necessary to return more attentively to the ideas about gender that he adapts from Gourmont's *Natural Philosophy of Love*.[106] According to his elaborate and eccentric brand of gender Lamarckism ("Insect, utility; bird, flight; mammal, muscular splendour; man, experiment"), the brain and the "spermatozoid" are composed of common matter, shared evolutionary origins which carry over into phallic forms of cultural labor: "the power of the spermatozoid," he writes, "is precisely the power of exteriorizing a form."[107] True to form, then, this conception of brainwork has two implications, one involving "discharge," the other "retention": most "men apparently stupefying themselves . . . by excess," while "other cases discharging apparently only a surplus at high pressure; the imbecile, or the genius, the 'strong-minded'."[108]

This distinction provides Pound with a basis for both his theory of genius and his theory of promotion. In essence, the two theories are one: the strong-minded have the power to experiment, to exteriorize form, and, above all else, to "fecundate" "a generation of minds," to produce themselves in the production of new authors; the remainder merely spill their spermatozoid.[109] In the spirit of symmetry, claiming to be "neither writing an anti-feminist tract, nor claiming disproportionate privilege for the spermatozoid," he also "ascribe[s] a cognate role for the ovule": "A flood is as bad as a famine; the ovular bath could still account for the refreshment of the female mind . . . [,] where one woman appears to benefit by an alluvial clarifying, ten dozen appear to be swamped."[110] With both the spermatozoid and the ovule brain apparently, uncontrolled excess represents the debasement of originality, the failure of the authorial self as exteriorized form. For Pound, lining up authors under specific "internalized" signs of gender difference is less crucial than establishing which authors, among men and women, conform to his exteriorized – at once phallicized and phallicizing – standard of literary production, a definition which holds retentive, literary originality as an autogenetic mechanism of literary reputation, the author encased in durable literary goods as if in a kind of vulcanized covering.[111]

The upshot of Pound's letter to Eliot is a crisis occasioned by Eliot's exteriorized final product. With Eliot's completed *Waste Land* in sight, the process to place it underway, Pound writes about how *he* has failed to exteriorize *himself* sufficiently. Next to *The Waste Land*, he feels undifferentiated from the undifferentiated literary flood, a condition in which he conflates menstruation and ejaculation. Four years earlier, he tells Moore, "Thank God, I think you can be trusted not to pour out flood (in the manner of dear Amy [Lowell] and poor [Edgar Lee] Masters)."[112] Elsewhere, he associates Lowell's verse with ejaculate, calling her imagist work "Amygism," a term which makes Lowell herself manifest the supposed inadequacies of her free verse and the deformation of the imagist movement in her formlessness. In his 1917 "Retrospect" to the imagist manifesto (printed in *Make it New* as "A Stray Document"), Pound locates the undoing of imagism ("Amygism") in the widespread disregard for his second imagist principle prescribing scarcity of words: the founding imagist

school [was later] "joined" or "followed" [by] numerous people who, whatever their merits, do not show any signs of agreeing with the second specification. Indeed *vers libre* has become as prolix and as verbose as any of the flaccid varieties that preceded it. It has brought faults of its own. The actual language and phrasing is often as bad as that of our elders without even the excuse that the words are shovelled in to fill a metric pattern or to complete the noise of a rhyme-sound.[113]

In 1932, when discussing his relationship with Eliot in retrospect in *The Criterion*, Pound frames the relationship not with the work of *The Waste Land* in 1921, but with their shared departure from Amygism's flaccid deformation in 1917. He chooses a narrative that appears, from his point of view, at once, more phallic and more fluid-retentive. "T. S. Eliot," Pound writes,

displayed great tact, or enjoyed good fortune, in arriving in London at a particular date with a formed style of his own. He also participated in a movement to which no name has ever been given.
   That is to say, at a particular date in a particular room, two authors, neither engaged in picking the other's pockets, decided that the dilution [*sic*] of *vers libre*, Amygism, Lee Masterism, general floppiness had gone too far and that some counter-current must be set going . . . Remedy prescribed "Émaux et Camées" (or the Bay State Hymn Book). Rhyme and regular strophes.
   Results: Poems in Mr. Eliot's *second* volume, not contained in his first ("Prufrock", Egoist, 1917 . . . also "H. S. Mauberley". Divergence later.[114]

The collaborative work with Eliot, which Pound publicly underscores and sanctions in 1932, is their mutual decision in 1917 to appropriate the "chiseled line" of Théophile Gautier's *Émaux et Camées*, a formal commitment to formalism yielding *two* durable literary goods, the quatrains of Eliot's *Ara Vos Prec* and the quatrains of Pound's *Hugh Selwyn Mauberley*.[115] *Pace*

Koestenbaum, this narrative of collaborative work does not concern two authors in intersubjective entanglement nor does it concern the relations of mentor and protégé; rather, it promotes the material self-sufficiency of two fully formed and fully "modernized" objects, in Pound's words, "at a particular date in a particular room." Once again, we're with the Hieratic Heads planted in the muck of an overwhelmingly indifferent, undifferentiated, and feminized literary landscape.

For those who would see Pound and Eliot working shoulder to shoulder, like Wordsworth and Coleridge, jointly modeling their poems on common sources, Pound's comments of 1932 have been a crucial piece of evidence.[116] Yet, the key phrase in Pound's account is probably *divergence later*, for it cues us to the extent that their association involves *a posteriori* promotion of their literary careers. Thirty years later, in his *Paris Review* interview with Donald Hall, Pound represents his relationship with Eliot the same way, stating offhandedly, "Oh, Eliot and I started diverging from the beginning."[117] Eliot also privileges 1917 as the time of closest interaction.[118] No doubt, both Pound and Eliot tirelessly promoted their coupling; for instance, the blurb on the dust-jacket of Pound's *Selected Poems* (1928), Eliot's Faber edition, claims "No two poets have been so closely or so long associated as Mr Ezra Pound and Mr T. S. Eliot." Yet, their coupling also entailed their perpetual uncoupling. Their association became more and more prominent as the two quarreled, first over Pound's 1919 "conversion" to social credit economics, and then over Eliot's 1927 conversion to Anglicanism. Pound's Canto 46 is fairly typical of the sarcastic jibes made at Reverend Eliot's expense in *The Cantos*: "And if you will say that this tale teaches . . . / a lesson, or that the Reverend Eliot / has found a more natural language . . . you who think / you will / get through hell in hurry."[119] Moments where the poets explicitly address one another's work, such as Eliot's prefaces to Pound's *Selected Poems* (1928) and *Literary Essays* (1954), Pound's ripostes to Eliot in *The Cantos*, or the many essays the one devoted to the other, document the dynamic of a relation that was at once increasingly public and increasingly apocryphally mediated.

Insofar as Pound and Eliot have been glorified as the *parents* of an Anglo-American modernist poetics, the principal evidence (until 1971) has been Eliot's *Waste Land* dedication, "For Ezra Pound / il miglior fabbro," and hearsay about Pound's editorial input during the composition of Eliot's *Waste Land*. For example, G. W. Stonier titles his anti-Pound piece in a 1938 issue of *Purpose* "The Mystery of Ezra Pound," the mystery being why the "spluttering typewriter" still commands any literary attention whatever: "The dedication of *The Waste Land*, 'il miglior fabbro,' no doubt

has something to do with it; a tip like that, to the Eliot initiate, was far too
good to miss":

> He has served as Poe to Eliot's Baudelaire: that is the relationship, more awkward
> from the fact that in this case both poets are living. I don't deny Eliot's sincere
> admiration for Pound any more than I would question Baudelaire's admiration
> for Poe; and Pound, like Poe, deserves the credit of an originality great enough to
> feed a better poet. . . . Pound *is* a master – a little master – of his sort. Dismiss his
> drivel, fake learning, fake classicism, fake dialect . . . He is the master of the small
> effect: image and epigram.[120]

In the next issue, Eliot's writes in to disabuse Stonier of his misreading of
the epigraph:

> Mr. Stonier seems to assign to me the chief responsibility of having put over
> Mr. Pound on a snobbish and gullible public. He says, of Pound's expanding
> reputation, "the dedication of *The Waste Land*, 'il miglior fabbro,' no doubt has
> something to do with it; a tip like that, to the Eliot initiate, was far too good to
> miss." Mr. Stonier, apparently, is not an Eliot initiate: or he might have discovered
> that the phrase, not only used by Dante, but as quoted by myself, had a precise
> meaning. I did not mean to imply that Pound was only that: but I wished at that
> moment to honour the technical mastery and critical ability in his own work, which
> had also done so much to turn *The Waste Land* from a jumble of good passages into a
> poem.[121]

As the Pound initiate knows, "il miglior fabbro" also represents a specific
reference in Pound's literary promotional theory, referring to *The Spirit
of Romance*, Pound's first critical volume, that recuperates Arnaut Daniel
using Dante's act of homage, "il miglior fabbro," as a chapter heading.
When Eliot inscribed Pound's copy, "for E.P. / il miglior fabbro / from
T.S.E. / Jan 1923," this was surely the personal resonance. As I discussed
in the previous chapter, Pound's heuristic of reputation, first published in
January 1923 (in the *Criterion* number immediately following the *Waste
Land* number), places Arnaut Daniel above Dante: "The 'predecessors,'
inventors, discoverers of fragments which are later used in masterwork;
Arnaut Daniel and the better Troubadours, the hypothetical ballad writers
who went before Homer, etc.," come first.[122] Eliot's homage gives Pound on
Pound's own terms – *il miglior fabbro*, the better maker, predecessor, forerunner of the forerunner, inventor, discover of fragments, *il miglior fallo* –
terms Pound himself formulated as he edited the better object, that is, *The
Waste Land*. Ironically, reading Eliot on Pound's terms only becomes possible *post facto*, in 1925, when Eliot turns the private inscription into a public
dedication.

Notwithstanding, Pound's editorial *queeries* into Eliot's work were partially hidden, promotional mythoi long before they were obtainable. Dual authorship only becomes fully legible after the fabled Quinn manuscript is rediscovered in 1968 and published by Valerie Eliot in 1971. In his brief preface to the text, the octogenarian Pound aptly describes the significance of the *Waste Land* typescripts and manuscripts as mythological, describing them as "the occultation of 'The Waste Land' manuscript": "'The mystery of the missing manuscript' is now solved," he writes.[123] Tellingly, Pound sticks to the old script; the rediscovery will implicate Eliot studies rather than his own reputation or his relationship with Eliot: "The more we know of Eliot, the better."[124] The preferred story remains 1917 not 1921, for it provides a better parable for Pound's promotion of literary autogenesis by providing specific foils among literary contemporaries.

The prerogative of literary autogenesis draws on a narrative of opposition rather than shared labor: *wholly demonstrable, obvious rightness* cast against *fine, careless rapture*, form against formlessness, male fixity against female oblivion, the phallic author against the great passive vulva of the London literary scene, Pound, Moore, and Eliot against Amygism, Lee Masterism, and diluted floppiness. However vulgarly generalized this dualistic essentialism, its symptoms and remedies are narrowly fixed, retentive, and consciously promotional. Not surprisingly, as the Moore letters show, Pound advances deliberate strategies for countering literary oblivion, which involve consciously differentiating oneself from one's contemporaries, an invasive procedure of self-hardening (or *pot-shotting*) applied to the most minute lexical particles. He urges Moore, to cite a particularly excruciating example, to steer clear of the word "pneumatic" in the poem "Old Tiger," even though it is "*le mot juste*":

Eliot has just preempted it in Grishkin's "pneumatic bliss." . . . [I]n so close a circle (you are in it willy nilly, by the mere fact of writing verse for the members of the reading public capable of understanding). Also T.S.E. has jaguar'd – quite differently, but still . . . we *must* defend the camp against the outer damnations.

T.S.E. first had his housemaids drooping like the boas in my "Millwins," and it was only after inquisition of this sort that he decided, to the improvement of his line, to have them sprout . . .

(. . . I am rejecting imitators of T.S.E. who would be only too ready to rend anyone they might think at their preserve.) In the words of W. L. [Wyndham Lewis] send us one to catch our fleas.[125]

New words must be divvied up among the literary group. As I have argued in chapter two, the modernist distribution of words as scarce commodities is commensurate with the modernist sense of the scarcity of *the reading public capable of understanding*. Pound makes participation in this economy the defining feature of the modernist community and hints that Moore's participation is a forced choice: if Moore chooses to heed the editorial correctives, if she avoids certain lexical property, she becomes part of a camp, which already includes Pound, Eliot, Lewis, Yeats, Joyce, and others. If not, she becomes a parasitical *imitator*, one of Lewis's flea-catchers, part of the undifferentiated morass of *outerdamnations*. Significantly, the case makes no explicit appeal to aesthetic principles, but only to pragmatism and testimonials: meticulously maintained originality – self-hardening – is the surest means to literary posterity, a literary group is defined by each member's phallically exteriorized self-sufficiency – all the better, if the self-sufficiency tacitly presupposes group dynamics and turf boundaries that are quietly negotiated behind the scenes under the cover of plausible deniability.

Without doubt, Pound's theory of promotion creates an uncongenial environment for women modernists. We can gauge some of its effects on Moore. She indeed becomes part of Pound's closed modernist network "willy-nilly," not merely by attending to his questions with changes, which she did, nor by accepting his tutelage, which she did not. Instead, she joins by internalizing his theory ("My contemporaries are welcome to anything they have come to first"), even as she confesses that she has "at times objected to [*his*] promptness with the cudgels."[126] Following Pound's lead, she produces her own reputation by actively encouraging other writers to follow a phallomorphic regime of literary promotion in order to gain access to a closed literary network of the *first-rate*.[127] She writes a letter to Allen Ginsberg in 1952, for instance, which echoes the letter she received from Pound in 1919. There is the fixation on a particular order of technical minutiae ("This is too juicy . . . Adjectives are dangerous"), the ingenuous apology conferring literary solidarity and presuming that Ginsberg can stand the pot-shotting, the warnings that he should avoid other writers' turf (this "is William C. Williams instead of (or as well as) Allen Ginsberg"), and the veiled threats that not listening may endanger chances for literary posterity.[128]

As a performance of self, the buffoonish mimicry and the impossible embodiment of disembodied patriarchal authority are decidedly uncomfortable, not least for a woman writer, whose relationship to phallic, patriarchal power is, needless to say, already more vexed, yet it was not unfeasible . . . and herein lies the detrimentally misogynistic logic of the regime. In Pound, the idiom achieves what might called be its ultimate literary, theoretical, and promotional expression, but, that said, it was more than an esoteric idiolect. There is also something of it in Eliot's position at Faber, the businessman poet-critic, posing himself as an impossible dialectical synthesis between the "tiresome, inferior . . . beings known as Authors" and the literary-historical form of necessity known as the bottom line.[129]

Harold Monro describes the stifling effects of Victorianism for his literary generation using language about brainwork as distinctly phallomorphic as Pound's, if perhaps less deliberately so: "By 1910 the numbing effect of the Victorian period [seemed] finally to have relaxed its pressure on the brain of the rising generation."[130] Further, it was not difficult to read the entire thrust of modernist aesthetic innovation as phallic self-performance, like Ford Madox Ford (then still Hueffer) in 1921:

> The Cubists, Vorticists, Imagistes, Vers Libristes . . . said simply: "All this attempt to hypnotise the Public is mere waste of time. An Artist attracts; gets a Public or royalties from sales because he is a clever fellow. Let him begin by saying: "I am a clever fellow . . ." And let him go on saying: "What a fellow I am!" Conspuez the Subject! A bas all conventions of tale-telling! We, the Vorticists, Cubists, Imagistes, Symbolists, Vers Libristes, Tapagistes are the fine, young Cocks of the Walk! We and we only are the Playboys of the Western World. We and we only shall be heard.[131]

What makes Ford's description revealing is its striking incongruity, the way he connects the *Cock of the Walk* – a figure of authoritarian male individuality, which promotes the exteriorized singular artist – with collective literary factions – promotional constructs based on networks of many artists such as imagism and vorticism. Wyndham Lewis strikes the same note in the "Long Live the Vortex" section of *Blast*, emphasizing that "Blast [i.e., an organ of the literary group] presents an art of Individuals."[132] New types of anthologies, which began to emerge in the years leading up to the First World War, were key instruments in fostering this dynamic, advertising networks of authors – literary brands, so to speak – as suitable staging grounds for advancing the solitary genius. "The object of the *Group*," writes Monro in 1920, "is generally the attainment of wider publicity by a combination of forces . . . The members of English Cliques meet less at supper than in periodicals and anthologies, less in private than in public."[133] The attainment of the kind of literary publicity described by Monro and Ford (and dominated by Pound and Eliot) depends on a notion that literary careerism is a function of textual embodiment.

Monro's sense that the new literary groups meet neither as bodies nor as texts but as bodies-in-texts is an appropriate segue to the next chapter, which moves from the imposing role of imprimaturs between individual modernist contemporaries to its placing among them as they become hypostatic brand names. And "imposing" is the right word in both settings. As the "downstream" work sanctioned by Eliot and Pound illustrates, the help Eliot and Pound provided contemporaries was, at best, a long-term imposition on their careers and, at worst, invasively and punitively phallomorphic, marking them as merely contemporary, derivative, and unrepresentative. Their work, in Eliot's chestnut of damning praise, only renders *a state of mind contemporary with the author*. Above all, these practices serve to maintain the self-same claims of Pound and Eliot to representative distinction, like feedback loops, feeding some of the output reputation back into the input of the system. Lionization – securing elite modernist prestige, a project under scrutiny in chapter four, "Promotional networking" – was another matter. Partly because Eliot and Pound were already lionized by the twenties, partly because of the specific, mutually-conferring dynamics of their lionizations, escaping each other's imprimaturs was never a precondition of their renown over the long literary *durée*. There was neither pressing need for Pound to escape Eliot's introductions nor for Eliot to escape Pound's editing protocols, because, as detailed above, their period of association was over from the beginning.

CHAPTER 4

Promotional networking

Like the previous chapter, this chapter examines a side of the modernists' habitual recourse to collaborative work. Again, the encounter under examination tends to happen "downstream" in modernist apocrypha, sites which are implicitly and explicitly marked by gender. The last chapter focused on how micro-techniques of sustaining modernist reputation operate through protocols about introducing and editing individual contemporaries. In these undervalued literary labors, modernist phallocrats like Eliot and Pound established the stubborn, punitive phallomorphism of the elite literary career. The assistance Pound and Eliot offered other authors often played out as categorical impositions on their careers. Such obligatory reiteration and citation of certain careers on others both defined what it meant to *be a representative* of a "grrrreat litttterary period" – to invoke Pound's memorably sanguine phrase – and substantiated the specific claims of a small selection of authors like Eliot and Pound to *being representative*, simultaneously thinning out the field of competitors.[1]

This chapter follows this line of argument into a frontier designated in the second chapter as modernism's ultimate spatial and ideological construct, its diagrammatically distorted lists of famous names, the closed system of mutually dependent, inter-signified imprimaturs required for circulating emergent imprimaturs as elite currency. In particular, I seek this space on the contents pages of new kinds of poetry anthologies, which began to appear in England shortly after F. T. Marinetti foisted his futurist anthology onto the still nascent public for avant-garde poetry in 1912. Despite the often divergent aesthetic agendas practiced by anthologists like Edward Marsh, Ezra Pound, Amy Lowell, and Edith Sitwell, brands such as the "Georgian" anthologies, the "imagist" anthologies, and the "*Wheels*" anthologies shared a promotional logic that indicates a shared provenance. Promising unheard-of exposure, the inexpensive, polemical anthology of contemporary poetry quickly became one of the preferred vehicles for publicity among modernist poets and their contemporaries. The appeal of the new anthology traded on its role as simulation of literary society; the names on the contents page stood for working relationships in an imagined bohemia. The very formal qualities of these anthologies embedded individual authors in propaganda about new literary brand names, schools, movements, generations, and periods. Hierarchies of literary reputation among contemporaries became material artifacts, and originality and representativeness became a group fetish.

Putting aside the diachronic axis, then, this chapter shifts to a synchronic line of inquiry. Rather than examining how particular modernist idiosyncrasies calcified into dominant protocols of reputation *between* literary figures, I want to investigate how the formal logic of new poetry anthologies helped institute a modernist logic of literary networking by placing the representative (male) modernist (that is, the singular artist, the solitary genius) *among* groups of putative subordinates, literary fellow-travelers, and also-rans. The more general point here is that, although the new anthologies were particularly good at finding some literary figures, they were even better at losing others. If the new anthologies transmit narratives about finding and placing individual literary stars in larger literary constellations, why did they serve certain literary careers so well and misplace others? More to the point, why did so many anthologized women get lost in this mode of presentation that lies at the very core of the lionization narratives of a number of their male counterparts? After all, many of the new anthologies – with the noted exception of Edward Marsh's *Georgian Poetry* (1912) – presented a deliberately more balanced picture when it came to women poets than monumental Victorian predecessors like F. T. Palgrave's *Golden Treasury* (1861). The representation of women writers in the new anthologies points to a more gender-inclusive literary scene, but mere representation did not necessarily translate into access to the elite registers of modernist reputation. One obvious explanation – made plain by the roll call of poet-soldiers in the three analogy franchises – is that the new forms of poetic anthologizing found a resonant, promotional connection with commemorating the male names of the First World War, but this answer alone is inadequate, because the new anthology system was well in place beforehand. Its overriding rhetoric of literary factionalism, its prerogatives of originality and representativeness, and its warrants about the anthologist's authoritative subject position counteracted whatever measure of pluralism the anthology form promised by including more women poets. The gap here, measuring the distance between representation as a pluralistic ideal of reputation and the fictions of representativeness as modernist rules of capricious inclusion and omission, shows, among other things, that, first, the "fix was in," so to speak, from the very beginning against modern women poets and, second, this fix was regulated by a specific mode and means of literary presentation.

In her posthumously published memoirs, *A Poet's Life* (1937), Harriet Monroe makes a connection between her commitment as the editor of *Poetry* to the careers of new poets and the emergence of a new, potentially lucrative, literary system, based on anthologies. I quote at length her unflinchingly materialistic account of *Poetry's* contribution to this new economy:

The two most widely quoted poems we ever printed, Helen Hoyt's "Ellis Park" and Joyce Kilmer's "Trees," appeared on consecutive pages during our first year, when Kilmer wrote, "Six dollars will satisfy me for 'Trees.' For 'Trees,'" which has coined money for . . . everybody but the author, who was killed soon after . . . The head of a motto-card firm told me long after that for years he had paid sixteen hundred dollars or more annually in royalties to its publisher, to be shared with the poet's estate. That is what it means to write two lines which the people take to heart and can never forget.

Helen Hoyt's first published poem has become a prime necessity for all anthologists. So many requests for the use of "Ellis Park" came to *Poetry*, and were referred to her, that she stopped answering them in sheer fatigue, and finally . . . she rose to the point of demanding – and getting – twenty dollars for each consent. Agnes Lee's lovely lyric, "A Statue in a Garden," became another favorite of anthologists; "A Lady" and "A Gift" from Amy Lowell's first long group; . . . Ezra's "Dance Figure" and "The Garden"; and the inimitable "Psychological Hour"; Frances Shaw's "Who Loves the Rain"; Sara Teasdale's "Debt" and "Morning"; T. S. Eliot's "La Figlia che Piange"; . . . and many other poems which, emerging quietly at first, gradually focused the light of fame, and became remembered, the much-quoted, the brightly colored jewels of their generation.

My anthology, *The New Poetry*, led the way . . . [It] was the first of the twentieth century collections which now fill four five-foot shelves of our poetry library.[2]

In 1936, Pound – Monroe's one-time *agent provocateur* and *Poetry's* one-time foreign correspondent, whose epistolary exhortations to Monroe were published in the magazine's very pages – would hardly be pleased with most of the literary company he is made to keep. Nor would he be likely to swallow a lyrical standard that measures success by the acquisitions of greeting-card manufacturers. Monroe's equation of literary fame with anthology popularity (*Poetry's* poets as *the much-quoted, the brightly colored jewels of their generation*) owes something to the Victorian lyrical ideal established by F. T. Palgrave's *Golden Treasury of the Best Songs and Lyrical Poems in the English Language* (1861), the best-selling anthology, published by Macmillan, which went through numerous reprintings, sold hundreds of thousands of copies,

and inspired a host of imitators in the late nineteenth and early twentieth centuries. As Frank Lentricchia and Cary Wolfe have both observed,
Palgrave's recognizable brand name and the market hegemony of its
recipe for nondescript, compact, and seemingly timeless Tennysonian lyrics
("more golden than gold"), which promised mass consumers escapist, "lyrical transcendence," furnished a generation of modernist poets with "considerable antithetical motivation," and apparently provided Pound, on at
least one occasion, with a specific nemesis in literary superstructure.[3]
    Lentricchia calls it "the representative literary anecdote of [Pound's] lit-
erary career": in 1931 in "How to Read," Pound recalls approaching a literary agent in 1916 to propose an anthology "to replace that doddard [*sic*]
Palgrave," something like the National Gallery of London with the history
of poetry exhibited in "a twelve-volume anthology in which each poem
was chosen not merely because it was a nice poem or a poem Aunt Hepsy
liked, but because it contained an invention, a definite contribution to the
art of verbal expression."[4] Unfortunately, the agent unwittingly forwards
Pound's proposal to Palgrave's publisher, "X . . . & Co.," the fortunes of
which are sustained by none other than Palgrave's *Golden Treasury*. The
homily that Pound draws out of this cuts to the quick of his program
for aesthetic *qua* social *qua* monetary reform: "there were thousands of
pounds sterling invested in electro-plate, and the least change in public
taste, let alone swift, catastrophic changes, would depreciate the values of
those electros . . . Against ignorance one might struggle . . . but against a
so vast vested interest the lone odds were too heavy."[5] Not coincidentally,
he uses the story to explain a downturn in his own literary fortunes in
England, suggesting seriocomically that his against-all-odds confrontation
of the un-restructured Victorian anthology industry may have led to his
being black-balled.
    Pound's encounter with this system was significantly more complicitous
than he lets on (and the anthology market was significantly more varied).
In 1912, Sir Arthur Quiller-Couch (1863–1944), alias "Q," then the doyen
of English letters (venerable literary journalist, anthologist, popularizer,
and academic; head of Cambridge English from 1912 until his death),
approached Pound for submissions for *his* replacement to Palgrave, *The
Oxford Book of Victorian Verse*. Pound was sufficiently pleased to pass the
news on to Harriet Monroe as a kind of testimonial: "This is no small
honor – at least I should count it as recognition. Nevertheless he had hit
on two poems which I marked 'to be omitted' from the next edition of
my work . . . If a man writes six good lines he is immortal – isn't that
worth trying for?"[6] Pound's last rhetorical question indicates his complete

comprehension (however cynical) of the cultural logic of anthology-sized verse. Whether or not his words are measured to suit his correspondent's literary proprieties, the sentiment he voices circa 1912 participates in the same Palgravian logic as Monroe's assessment of literary renown circa 1936 – *the much-quoted, the brightly colored jewels of their generation*. Given Pound's comprehension of the logic, it is fair to take the poems that made it into the Quiller-Couch anthology as Pound's equivocal bid for anthology immortality, lyrical transcendence, a hedging of bets in case his belief in the "*modern* stuff" proves wrong from the start.[7] Twenty-four years later, Yeats writes to apologize in the introduction to his edition of *The Oxford Book of Modern Verse* (1936) that Pound is "inadequately represented": he is simply "too expensive even for an anthologist with the ample means the Oxford University Press puts at his disposal."[8] Along with "The River Merchant's Wife," Yeats includes excerpts from "Homage to Sextus Propertius" and Canto 17.[9] However much Pound may have scorned the hegemony of "Aunt Hepsy's" taste in poetry, he clearly saw possibilities both in anthology work as a means of literary promotion and in the anthologist's work as means of configuring literary networks and setting exchange rates.

As Wolfe points out, Aunt Hepsy's role in Pound's Palgrave anecdote is not as a figure "for the denial of manhood so much as the denial of *self* hood": Aunt Hepsy is not a figure of the *ewige Weib* so much as a figure for specific, anthology contingent tastes, namely the tastes of the petty bourgeois woman, "literature as 'embroidery' and 'decoration,' as something that demanded about as much investment of self as the clubby status-mongering of 'ladies' societies,'" something which achieves its most far-reaching expression inside greeting-cards. According to Wolfe, Aunt Hepsy becomes the characteristic surface symptom for Pound of a "feminized culture," "backed by that economic power which patriarchy almost always figures as masculine," the old dotard Palgrave, the X & Co. stockpiles of anthology electroplates.[10] Recalling his appeal to Monroe and his approach to the feminized literary scene in the postscript to *Natural Philosophy of Love*, Pound's work, his point of intervention, so to speak, lies with Aunt Hepsy, inside anthologies, his name interspersed among the kind of Aunt Hepsyian literary company Monroe proposes. Remaking feminized tastes from within *new* anthologies was a crucial means for Pound and other upcoming literary figures to acquire and consolidate phallic literary authority through a privileged relationship to the literary promotional system.

By the mid-thirties, as Harriet Monroe's bookshelves testify, the market dominance of Palgrave's *Golden Treasury* was in ruins. It was challenged by a series of more historically thorough anthologies edited by Q, first appearing in 1900, and then was broken by degree by successive new verse anthologies, appearing at an alarming pace between 1912 and 1940.[11] Q's *Oxford Book of Victorian Verse* already announced its own departure from Palgrave, whose anthology abruptly ends in 1850, by defining the Victorian period as inclusively as possible, and including "any English poet, born in our time, under the great name Victorian," a principle which makes new verse by any poet over the age of eleven fair game.[12] Yet, the modern (if not to say, modernist) anthology offensive began in earnest in England in December 1912 with Edward Marsh's enormously successful anthology *Georgian Poetry*.[13] If the lyrical standard of Marsh's *Georgian Poetry* now seems indistinguishable from Palgrave's *Golden Treasury*, it is largely because the cagey promotional work of rival anthologists obscured its break with Palgravian Victorianism:

This volume is issued in the belief that English poetry is now once again putting on a new strength and beauty . . . This collection, drawn entirely from the publications of the past two years, may if it is fortunate help the lovers of poetry to realize that we are at the beginning of another "Georgian period" which may take rank . . . with the several great poetic ages of the past . . .[14]

Following *Georgian Poetry* into the breach, four more volumes of the *Georgian Poetry* franchise were published (1915–22); numerous "Georgian" spin-offs and imitations; Pound's imagist anthology, *Des Imagistes* (1914); its "successor" volumes edited by Amy Lowell, *Some Imagist Poets* (1915–17); Pound's *Catholic Anthology* (1915); six numbers of Edith Sitwell's *Wheels* (1916–21); scores of war poetry anthologies;[15] two volumes of Alfred Kreymbourg's *Others* (1917, 1919); Monroe's *New Poetry*; Louis Untermeyer's *Modern American Poetry* (1919) and *Modern British Poetry* (1920); J. C. Squire's *Selections from Modern Poets* (1921); Lawrence Binyon's updated *Golden Treasury of Modern Lyrics* (1924); E. V. Lucas' *Joy of Life* (1927); Harold Monro's *Twentieth Century Poetry* (1929); Ford Madox Ford and Glenn Hughes' *Imagist Anthology 1930*; Lascelles Abercrombie's *New English Poems* (1931); Michael Roberts' *New Signatures* (1932) and *New Country* (1933); Pound's *Active Anthology* (1933); Yeats' *Oxford Book of Modern Verse* (1936); Roberts' *Faber Book of Modern Verse* (1936); and *Edith Sitwell's Anthology* (1940). The sheer profusion of anthologies after 1912 suggests the emergence of new combative and exclusionary standards among and between anthologists, even as they were bound by the lyrical strictures of anthology form.

According to Marsh, the first *Georgian Poetry* and its successors – all published by Harold Monro – "went up like a rocket."[16] The first run of 500 copies sold out in one day.[17] By Marsh's estimates, the first two volumes, *Georgian Poetry, 1911–1912* and *Georgian Poetry, 1913–1915*, sold 15,000 and 19,000 copies respectively, suggesting to would-be anthologists like Pound and Sitwell, anthology contributors, and anthology publishers alike that inexpensive, exclusive, strictly contemporary anthologies could both sell and afford to give contributors royalties.[18] After *Georgian Poetry*, an anthology-sized poem – in theory, at least – could return exponential gains, especially the sort of gains to literary reputation which come via an expanded circulation. It was possible, in other words, that Pound's six lines could return Monroe's sixteen hundred dollars as well as *the light of fame*. Upon receiving his payment for "Snapdragon" from the first *Georgian Poetry*, D. H. Lawrence describes the unexpected payout in both financial and promotional terms: "Georgian Poetry book is a veritable Aladdin's lamp. I little thought my Snapdragon would go on blooming and seeding in this prolific fashion. So many thanks for the cheque for four pounds, and long life to G.P."[19]

Sometime in late 1912, between Q's *Oxford Book of Victorian Verse* and Marsh's *Georgian Poetry*, Q's inclusive gesture – the poets of "our time" (Yeats, Pound, Brooke, Monro, Walter de la Mare, John Masefield, et al.) alongside the Victorian notables (Tennyson, Arnold, the Brownings, Longfellow, et al.) – becomes undesirable, if not even unthinkable.[20] By contrast, the anthological standard in 1936 is nothing but exclusive: for Michael Roberts, compiling the "most significant poetry of this age" means only using poems published after 1910, including Gerard Manley Hopkins as well as much of the Faber modernist stable and omitting Helen Hoyt, Joyce Kilmer, and all poets who seem "to have written good poems without having been compelled to make any notable development of poetic technique."[21] Anthologies such as Roberts', despite their promise to bracket the entire modern period, become elite reserves for a generally male register of names.[22] Not surprisingly, given the similarity of this standard not only to general modernist notions of originality but also to Eliot's specific condemnations of *Georgian Poetry* in *The Egoist*, the "Georgians" figure prominently among the conspicuous omissions. By 1949, Geoffrey Grigson writes that he "does not presume" to call his influential *Poetry of the Present* anthology

"a selection of modern verse" as though the elder poets such as T. S. Eliot had now drifted out of modernity. "Modernity" is made up of several generations. When I was sixteen I bought a selection called "An Anthology of Modern Verse"; and then – it was compiled in 1921 – "modern" could still bracket poets back from Masefield and de la Mare [i.e., "Georgians"] to Arthur Symons and Robert Louis Stevenson . . . Since then the generations have slipped by. I aim in this book to include the good poets of what appear to be the last three poetic generations, the last three instalments [*sic*] of modernity – since Eliot. No poet herein was born earlier than 1904.[23]

The book jacket for Grigson's deliberately post-Eliotic anthology calls this approach "a freshening vision." It was *Georgian Poetry* that first created the staging ground for replacing pretensions of comprehensiveness or complete-ness with pretensions of selectivity. According to Marsh's "Prefatory Note" dated October 1912, *Georgian Poetry* has "no pretension to cover the field. Every reader will notice the absence of poets whose work would be a neces-sary ornament of any anthology not limited by a definite aim."[24] Ironically, the *Georgian* anthologies themselves helped create the conditions for the obsolescence of the generation of poets marked with its "ranch-brand" (to borrow Robert Graves' characterization).[25]

   To understand this dialectic, one must look beyond Marsh's fairly mod-erate manifesto in the first *Georgian* anthology (his superficial evocation of "new strength and beauty") and his Palgravian appeal to economical packag-ing (i.e., that "few *readers have the leisure or the zeal to investigate*" new poets) and instead examine the "Georgian" innovation as a literary promotional logic. The difference between the Georgian Poetry brand and, say, the Pre-Raphaelite Brotherhood as a literary-aesthetic is that "GP" is conceived first as a common brand-name with shared characteristics only deduced later, whereas the "PRB" presumes fixed, shared characteristics from the outset. In other words, with the "GP" brand, the entire notion of the group is a retroactive reconstruction. For all subsequent critical discussion about unifying characteristics among the "Georgians," a group which eventually includes forty poets (thirty-eight men; two women, Fredegond Shove and Vita Sackville-West), the ultimate built-in commonality is the recogniz-able brand, the implicit standards that strictly correspond to Marsh's own under-theorized tastes. Q's standards are also under-theorized, but where Marsh is implicit, Q is explicit, calling them the "old rule," "choosing what seems to me the best, and for that sole reason." Marsh, however, stumbles on the idea of disguising the old rule under the auto-authorizing machinery of a brand-name. His "proud ambiguous adjective 'Georgian'" works as a brand-name by justifying itself recursively as a literary generation, a literary movement, a literary periodization, and, most significantly, in contrast to the sprawling 700 pages each of Palgrave and Q, by invoking suggestions of shared influences and collaboration among the anthologized authors.[26] The new economized anthology, in other words, is based on standards of radical, sometimes even haphazard, exclusions.

The success of *Georgian Poetry* and the effects of this success on the anthology market followed from an aggressive, nationwide onslaught of brand propaganda, detailed in Marsh's letters, a campaign which was actively designed to galvanize the entire British literary establishment to the "Georgian" cause.[27] According to Robert H. Ross, Marsh

planned [the advertising campaign] to the last detail: which journals would be asked to publish reviews; which among influential friends would be given pre-publication copies and requested to mention the book publicly, either orally or in writing; and even which tone would be suggested for each review.[28]

Significantly, Ross's analysis is not *a posteriori* reconstruction; the "Georgian" campaign was conceptualized as a promotional construct. Brooke writes in a letter to Marsh in late 1912:

I have a hazy vision of incredible Reklam, secured by your potent wire-pulling & ingenious brain . . . I feel sure you ought to have an immense map of England (vide Tono Bungay) & plan campaigns with its aid. And literary charts, each district mapped out & a fortress secured.[29]

Like the sham tonic of *Tono-Bungay*, H. G. Wells' 1909 novel, Marsh's "Georgianism" emphasized both packaging and quasi-militaristic brand saturation on a nationwide scale (after the unofficial Tono-Bungay motto, perhaps, "the cheapest thing possible in the dearest bottle").[30] Each contributor was called upon to solicit favorable notices from places "where [his] influence was likely to be most effectively felt." Marsh, for example, took care of the *TLS*; John Drinkwater called in favors at the *Birmingham Post*; Wilfred Gibson promoted the anthology on his lecture tour of Scotland; Lascelles Abercrombie reviewed it himself in the *Manchester Guardian*, as did D. H. Lawrence in *Rhythm* and Walter de la Mare in *The Edinburgh Review*; and so on.[31] It seems that "Georgian" contributors were sought largely on the strength of their connections to various literary quarters, which explains the presence of John Masefield, T. Sturge Moore, Robert Ross, and G. K. Chesterton in the first volume and the attempts to secure such diverse figures as Ezra Pound, A. E. Housman, and, in a subsequent volume, Ford Madox Ford. The sequence of dedications in the five volumes, given to eminent authors (Robert Bridges and Thomas Hardy), to eminent literary journalists and critics (Edmund Gosse and Alice Meynell), and "in memoriam" (Rupert Brooke and James Elroy Flecker), also bears witness to the central role of making connections – configuring literary networks within and without – in the anthology's promotional work. The circuit is closed not merely through intertextuality but also through textually exteriorized connections, constructing an economy of publicity through the circulating introductions between critics, editors, anthologists, and publishers, sending names out in order to bring demand for names back to the source, in this case, "Georgian" poets and poetry anthologies available at Harold Monro's Poetry Bookshop. Moreover, the role of *Georgian Poetry* as an advertisement for Monro's Poetry Bookshop cannot be overlooked; the volumes are embossed with "The Poetry Bookshop" in quarter-inch gilt lettering on the cover and a "PB" crest, which appears sometimes on the cover and sometimes on the spine (more about this connection later).

Career secretary to Winston Churchill until 1937, Marsh was, without doubt, a well-connected establishment figure. In a sense, networking was not only a prerogative of ruling-class privilege but also his chief form of professional expertise. The most notorious example of the closing of this circuit may be Churchill's famous obituary for Rupert Brooke, published in *The Times* on 26 April 1915, three days after his death:

During the last few months of his life . . . the poet-soldier told with all the simple force of genius the sorrow of youth about to die . . . He expected to die; he was willing to die for the dear England whose beauty and majesty he knew; and he advanced towards the brink in perfect serenity, with absolute conviction of the rightness of his country's cause . . .

The thoughts to which he gave expression in the very few incomparable war sonnets which he has left behind will be shared by many thousands of young men moving resolutely and blithely forward into this, the hardest, the cruellest, and the least-rewarded of all the wars that men have fought. They are a whole history and revelation of Rupert Brooke himself.[32]

In his death, their deaths.[33] In Churchill's comments, which immediately followed Marsh's own anonymous obituary for Brooke, the gesture of *promoting* poetry consumption is undifferentiated from promoting a specific interpretation of Brooke's death for the nation at war and promoting a specific interpretation of Brooke's war sonnets.

Though never mentioned, Churchill's referent is clearly the fifth, most famous sonnet of Brooke's war sequence, "The Soldier":

> If I should die, think only this of me:
> That there's some corner of a foreign field
> That is for ever England. There shall be
> In that rich earth a richer dust concealed;
> A dust whom England bore, shaped, made aware,
> Gave, once, her flowers to love, her ways to roam,

A body to England's, breathing English air,
Washed by the rivers, blest by suns of home.
And think, this heart, all evil shed away,
A pulse in the eternal mind, no less
Gives somewhere back the thoughts by England given;
Her sights and sounds; dreams happy as her day;
And laughter, learnt of friends; and gentleness,
In hearts at peace, under an English heaven.[34]

A relatively slight poem concerning patriotic indoctrination – the very sentiment excoriated by Wilfred Owen's *the old Lie: Dulce et decorum est / pro patria mori* – becomes something more uncanny as Brooke in death becomes "a whole history and revelation of Rupert Brooke himself" (to crib Churchill's words).[35] Like Poe's M. Valdemar, the question here, which is both unsettled and unsettling, is *how is it that the dead can speak?* How is it that Brooke stages his own death? The photographs of his grave in Skyros in *some corner of a foreign field*. The bodiless memorial at Rugby carved by Eric Gill, engraved with this sonnet as the sole explanation (Brooke's profile in relief matching the photograph in the frontispiece to *1914 and Other Poems*). Who stage-manages this involuted interpretation? Is Churchill supplying the framework for Brooke, or is Brooke supplying the framework for Churchill? Such questions are not meant to be answered; the fortuitous collusion of Edward Marsh's interests in *both* questions, however, is worth noting. As both the secretary to the Lord of the Admiralty and Brooke's literary executor, he provides the hub, as it were, for the promotional network.[36]

In what may be called, somewhat crassly perhaps, one of the most successful product tie-ins in history, Churchill's comments leave *Times* readers with one instrumental question: *where can I get a copy of Brooke?*[37] Those who saved newspaper clippings already had one. Three weeks before Brooke's demise, the dean of St. Paul's recited "The Soldier" on Easter Sunday and, on April 15th, *The Times* put it on the front page.[38] In a sense, the Brooke hagiography began prematurely, that is, even before his demise; as Karen Levenback observes, "the death of Brooke was most timely, his popular deification having begun [beforehand] with a *Times* account of Dean Inge's Easter sermon at St. Paul's, which included lines from one of Brooke's 'War Sonnets.'"[39] The "War Sonnet" sequence was first published in December 1914 in *New Numbers* (the microscopic "Georgian" magazine run by Gibson, devoted to himself, Brooke, Abercrombie, and Drinkwater). This ran out shortly after Inge's sermon, so new readers could not find "The Soldier" there.[40]

They had to wait until June 1915 when Marsh brought out Brooke's *1914 and Other Poems*, which includes an authorizing note from Marsh (signed with the same "E. M." as in the first *Georgian Anthology*), explaining that "the Author had thought of publishing a volume of poems this spring, but he did not prepare the present book for publication." As if not to disappoint demand, Marsh takes the "War Sonnets" out of the chronological sequence of the volume and puts them first. For similar reasons, the second volume of *Georgian Poetry*, appearing in November 1915, incongruously includes "The Soldier" among Brooke's earlier South Seas poems and leaves out the rest of the "War Sonnets." When one considers the general absence of poetic response to the war in the collection, the placement can be explained only as a deliberate appeal to publicity generated by Brooke's death. Brooke's death overseas during wartime was not only supreme publicity for *1914 and Other Poems* (eventually selling hundreds of thousands of copies), the second *Georgian* volume (becoming the best-seller of the series), and *The Collected Poems of Rupert Brooke, with a Memoir by Edward Marsh* (1918) (going through eighteen impressions before 1929) but also, as Marsh's role in all these books suggests, the decisive point in Marsh's own literary self-fashioning, his most conspicuous attempt to define himself through editing, assembling, and networking the work of male literary others. The third edition, *Georgian Poetry: 1916–17*, shifts noticeably in the direction of soldier-poets, including work by Siegfried Sassoon, Robert Graves, Isaac Rosenberg, and Robert Nichols, further postponing the noticeably overdue inclusion of women poets such as Charlotte Mew, Rose Macaulay, and Edith Sitwell despite advocacy by certain *Georgian* contributors. Marsh's approach to the brand was already defined and confirmed in the first two anthologies such that it anticipated the inclusion of war poetry but impeded the inclusion of women.

From the very start *Georgian Poetry* was strategized as an aggressive, quasi-militaristic, all-male advertising campaign. To draw apocrypha from John Drinkwater's account, the "Georgian" strategy, hatched by Marsh, Brooke, Monro, Drinkwater, Gibson, and Arundel del Re in the fall of 1912, was "that England must be bombarded with the claims of new poets."[41] Improbable though it sounds, this strategy of bombardiering – if not the reluctance about blasting the entrenched establishment – came straight from the model of the futurists, whose "battle" for the future of poetry was waged and won, according to Arundel del Re, with "self-advertisement, organisation, persecution . . . the power and vitality of their message" and, perhaps more to the point, anthology sales.[42] There is evidence of direct contact between Marsh and Marinetti. In a letter reprinted in his memoirs,

Marsh writes to Brooke of attending a Marinetti performance in November 1913 in the attic of Monro's Poetry Bookshop.[43] Marinetti, he writes, "is beyond doubt an extraordinary man, full of force and fire, with a surprising gift of turgid lucidity, a full and roaring and foaming flood of indubitable half-truths."[44] In other words, he is the model of the elite purveyor of literary patent medicine. As Marsh's description suggests, Marinetti was doubtless an object of keen interest for both Marsh and Brooke, a prototype cock of the walk for the "Georgians" as well as for Ezra Pound, Wyndham Lewis, and, for that matter, the bulk of the English cultural scene during 1913 and 1914.[45] Although they all rejected specifically futurist poetics (or, in Lewis's case, visual aesthetics) sooner or later for separate reasons, they also all drew on futurism's "extraordinary inventiveness," particularly concerning literary publicity.[46] "He [Marinetti] has a marvellous sensorium, and a marvellous gift for transmitting reports," Marsh tells Brooke, "but what he writes is not literature, only an aide-mémoire for a mimic." His performance was "a very good farmyard-imitation – a supreme music-hall turn" but not likely to dislodge "the position of *Paradise Lost* or the *Grecian Urn*" from the anthologists' canons.[47] This was surely not Marsh's and Brooke's first encounter. As early as spring 1912, for example, before futurism made its big splash in London, Brooke writes back from Berlin as if futurism were already old news, his evidence that Berlin is "*frightfully* out of date" being that the "thrillingly latest sensation" is (what else!) a futurist exhibition: "Signor Marinetti delivered his famous lecture on Monday . . . Fancy being pursued by those old phantoms!"[48]

Harold Monro was the conduit for futurism among the "Georgians" and a major conduit for futurism in England at large. Before returning to England from Europe in 1911, it is likely he procured a copy of Marinetti's anthology of manifestos, extracts, and hostile press-clippings, *Le Futurisme* (1910), and perhaps even read the futurist manifesto when it appeared on the front page of *Figaro* on 20 February 1909. Not only did the Poetry Bookshop host Marinetti during his visit of November 1913, but also, two months earlier, in the editorial to the futurist number of Monro's magazine *Poetry and Drama*, Monro declares himself a futurist.[49] The futurist number includes translations (by Monro and del Re) of Marinetti's recent manifesto and "freely rendered" samples from *I poeti futuristi* (1912), the futurist poetry anthology, replete with revolutionary typography and free and expressive orthography. All the same, Monro's sense of futurism's revolutionary implications – its particular claims for the attention of the British public – came from its sales not its poetics, the 35,000 copies the futurist anthology already sold: "O Parnassus and ye Muses!":

[O]ur present hope [for the future of poetry] lies rather in circulation than innovation. We desire to see a public created that may read verse as it now reads its
newspapers . . . [W]e look for the establishment in the future of a new kind of
Broadside and Chap-book for the circulation of the best poetry, with a clearly
defined scope, and aims that shall be in no danger of overlapping those of the
newspapers and magazines. Such publications require to be accessible, portable,
unconfusing, and, above all, inexpensive. They are meant to be sold anywhere
and everywhere, carried in the pocket, read at any spare moment, left in the train,
committed to memory and passed on. They should be put up for sale in large
quantities; they should reproduce *only* verse of an obviously high standard: when
the public is roused, its spirit of offensive criticism will soon become keen enough
rigorously to oppose all imposture and commercial charlatanism.[50]

Monro is indifferent to the futurist machine cult or its oppositional call for
institutional destruction. He has few problems, for example, with praising
the choice of Robert Bridges as poet laureate in the same futurist issue (he
would have "preferred the abolition of the official laureateship" but "[h]ow
appalling if the choice had fallen on Kipling!").[51] The side of futurism that
holds Monro's attention implicates the mode and means of publication:
linking cheap, mass-produced commodity obsolescence with elite literary
authorship, the very combination that yielded *Georgian Poetry* one year
earlier, the experience he elliptically invokes at the end of the passage cited
above.

About the time of *Georgian Poetry*, November 1912 – two months after the
six men first conspired in Gray's Inn to organize *Georgian Poetry* – Monro
includes a special editorial about the impending opening of the Poetry
Bookshop on 1 January 1913, in the penultimate issue of *Poetry Review*.[52]
Part prospectus, part advertisement, his editorial explains the plans for the
Poetry Bookshop along the very lines he sets out in the futurism number
of *Poetry and Drama*, citing the cracking reception of Italian futurism as
evidence of new literary markets:

Perhaps the public needs startling; yet, if so, let it be by beauty, not mere novelty;
may the surprise excite wonder, not fizzle out in satisfied curiosity.
    We have seen the Italian futurists palming off their tremendous jokes on a
flaccid yet credulous public, wondering to ourselves whether they have the power
of laughter up their sleeves. We have watched Impressionism in poetry dwindling
down into a mere intellectual record of erotic and nervous emotions, or an excitant
for stimulating them; and in the end we see the creed of Art for Art's Sake hollow,
decaying, swamped by the rising tide of Life for Life's Sake . . .[53]

Until the advent of the Poetry Bookshop, it seems, the literature-consuming
public in England has been "unorganized, scattered and strangely

unguided," prey to the pernicious influences of "the Universal Provider in literature" and "the Newsagents." "Specialization is essential."[54] With the advent of the Poetry Bookshop, a nexus of integrated developments in publicity, publishing, and marketing, the public will be organized and revolutionized ("The Poetry Review has leased the whole of an eighteenth century house, where beside the shop, the offices of the Review will be established, lectures will be held, and rooms will be let at a moderate rate to those with sympathies with our aims").[55] Monro's Bookshop is, on paper at least, an integrated, centralized approach to literary production and consumption – the new literary review to be published at the Bookshop will include coupons for readings by authors who are, quite literally, "put up" there. And, despite Monro's attempts to debunk aspects of futurism (both here in 1912 and in November 1913, after Marinetti's visit to the Bookshop disabused Monro of any hopes for an English alliance with the futurists), he is also quite explicit about adapting this strategy from futurist models.[56] The Monro brand of promotional futurism is, at best, a Girondist alternative to Marinetti's Jacobism, reluctantly destructive, maintaining that the "true revolutionary is only a conservative endowed with insight . . . [who] brings his vision to the market-place and urges the people to destroy their city and rebuild it."[57]

One of the projects that falls within the scope of Monro's "futurist" conception of the Poetry Bookshop was publishing, promoting, and selling the *Georgian Anthology*. He stood to take half the proceeds, as mentioned above. Indeed, it is no accident that prominent advertisements for both ventures appear together on the back cover of the November 1912 *Poetry Review*; from Monro's perspective, they were part of an integrated campaign to remake the literary marketplace in time for the Christmas shopping season of 1912. The relevant inquiry addresses were, of course, the same; not only will E. Marsh's *Georgian Poetry* be "Ready 1st December," orders to be taken at "The Poetry Review, 35 Devonshire St, Theobald's Road, W.C.," but also "[f]rom the First of December, 1912, the public is invited to inspect the new premises of The Poetry Review at 35 Devonshire Street, and orders for books or periodicals will be received."[58] In this respect, it is less far-fetched than it may initially sound to call "Georgianism" a species of futurism, at least, of the aspect of futurism which registered with Monro, its integrated onslaught of brand promotion. Contemporary reviews comparing the "Georgians" to the futurists – however preposterously ill-conceived about "Georgian" poetics – are cannily perceptive when it comes to the origins of its promotional logic.[59] Moreover, considering the runaway success of these tactics, it makes sense that Pound turned to Monro and the Poetry Bookshop in

1914 when it came to launching his claims for anthology brand recognition, *Des Imagistes*.[60]

Other commentators have painstakingly detailed both imagism(e)'s debt to Italian futurism and its logic as a promotional brand-name. The key reference point about the latter is the conflict between Ezra Pound and Amy Lowell over her use of the imagist "brand" to plug herself as the "foremost member of the 'imagists' – a group of poets that includes William Butler Yeats, Ezra Pound, Ford Madox Hueffer."[61] The critical prominence of Pound's break with Lowell (and the remaining imagists) over a matter of publicity often serves to shelter Pound from the charge of publicity – as if he were not practicing it wholesale by publicly staging his outrage at Lowell. This emphasis on Pound's rejection of Lowell obscures the extent imagism (well before Lowell "took over") owed its promotional *modus vivendi* to the publicity-centered take on futurism mediated by Marsh, Monro, and the Georgians. It also obscures how *Des Imagistes* and its successor volumes, in turn, served as crucial points of mediation for subsequent derivatives such as Edith Sitwell's *Wheels* (more about which shortly). The physical properties of their two durable goods, *Georgian Poetry: 1911–1912* and *Des Imagistes: An Anthology*, mark the common provenance of the two "movements." Dimensions, paper covers, cheap paper quality, inexpensive price, centered titles, prominent frontal position of the publisher's promotional colophon are all practices which consciously emulate the design of *Le Futurisme* and *I poeti futuristi*. This demonstrates, in short, that the "Georgians" got to futurism first, and, in the case of the anthology market, even mediated the imagistes' approach. Inside *Georgian Poetry*, the layout draws heavily on the model of *I poeti futuristi*. Just as Marinetti's anthology contains thirteen authors, arranged alphabetically, each with his own separate title page; so too, Marsh's anthology contains seventeen authors, arranged alphabetically, each with his own separate title page (like *Le Futurisme*, *I poeti futuristi* also includes supplementary documentation, reviews, bibliographies, etc., a practice copied by subsequent Georgian volumes, *Des Imagistes*, *Wheels*, as well as other new anthologies). Considering these similarities – together with Arundel del Re's admiring comments on "the *Ars Poetica* of futurism, [which] contains the work of some thirteen poets, all reaching a very high standard of achievement, worthy each of attentive study" – it is hard to imagine that Monro and del Re did not design *Georgian Poetry: 1911–1912* with *I poeti futuristi* in hand.[62]

Whereas *I poeti futuristi* contains its thirteen futurists under Marinetti's imprimatur, both *Georgian Poetry* and *Des Imagistes*, in effect, offer literary brands with dual imprimaturs, Marsh's seventeen and Pound's eleven being supplemented, as it were, by the colophon of Monro's Poetry Bookshop.[63] For the futurist avant-garde – and their allegedly unrelated Anglo-American "contemporaries," as F. S. Flint famously described the "non-relationship" between imagism and futurism in *Poetry* – anthologies had a distinct promotional appeal; they created promotional environments for the literary group, which were inescapably contentious: potent mixtures of the anthologist's authorizing imprimatur, recursive networking, and aggressive brand publicity, which encouraged hostile, revisionist sectarianism inside and outside the literary group. The anthologized are always already breaking ranks, coming out on their own, revealing themselves to be literary individuals, self-contained, self-sufficient authors, *disjecta membra* – as Eliot titled a review of Amy Lowell's post-Poundian Amygism.[64]

One crucial departure in both *Georgian Poetry* and *Des Imagistes* is their rejection of futurism's heavy-handed and quasi-bureaucratic organizational schema, which Marinetti printed opposite the cover page in the futurist anthology, the "Direzione del Movimento Futurista," including directorates for "Poesia," "Pittura," "Musica," "Scultura," and, curiously, an "Azione Femminile," a female movement, staffed by one member, "La poetessa, Mme Valentine de Saint-Point." Instead, both Pound and Marsh make concerted efforts to obscure the apparatus of male literary authority. This is a point emphasized by Flint (who, it seems, was following Pound's dictation): imagisme "had not published a manifesto" *per se*; "they were not a revolutionary school."[65] Marsh's imprimatur can only be discerned by his signatory initials on the preface. Pound's imprimatur is even more submerged. One must refer to the auxiliary documentation, an unsigned poem concerning the poetic hardships of E.P., archeological fragments about the pre-history of the "movement," and insider references to comments in the appendix of *Ripostes*, published in October 1912 (that is, the "prefatory note" to *The Complete Poetical Works of T. E. Hulme*, "As for the future, *Les Imagistes*, the descendants of the forgotten school of 1909, have that in their keeping"), which cast imagisme back to apocrypha, meetings with Hulme, F. S. Flint, and others at the Eiffel Tower restaurant, "the cenacle of 1909."[66] (Pound also departs from the alphabetical listing of authors practiced by both Marinetti and Marsh, a practice which Lowell took as a sign of Pound's capricious authority.[67]) The phallus, in the case of "Georgianism" and imagisme as elsewhere, is veiled, the outward signs of authority hidden, tacit, and consequently more mystified and tenacious.

As the "Azione Femminile" directorate suggests, the possibility of women futurists was something of an afterthought, an uneasy anomaly under the futurist superstructure. No women appear in *I poeti futuristi* itself. Pound's descriptions of creative work in the late teens and early twenties detailed in chapter three sound almost bland next to the misogyny and premeditated anti-feminism of the futurist manifesto of 1909: "*We will glorify war* – the world's only hygiene – militarism, patriotism, the destructive gesture of freedom-bringers, beautiful ideas worth dying for, *and scorn for women.*"[68] Although "Georgianism" does not suggest futurism's programmatic hostility towards women, the first three volumes of *Georgian Poetry* were nevertheless almost contemptuously devoid of women. Compared with the exclusively male standards of futurism and "Georgianism," Pound's imagisme was far more gender-inclusive merely by counting two women poets, H. D. and Amy Lowell, among its ranks. Even compared with Q's pre-"Georgian" standards, Pound's paltry two of eleven (18 percent) (rising to 30 percent, if one considers the percentage of poems written by women, the substantial number by H. D.) was an improvement. Although Q includes forty women poets in his anthology, this number represents only about 15 percent of the total.[69] (Under Palgrave, women writers fare even worse.[70]) Symbolically, perhaps Q's forty outweighs Pound's two, but, because of the new anthology's implications about group work, the presence of two women among eleven has more representative value than the presence of forty among 275. The implication that H. D. and Lowell are collaborators and co-conspirators of Pound, Flint, Aldington, Ford, Joyce, and the rest is not available with Q or Palgrave. But does this slight shift matter, given the kind of regime of literary authority that sanctions it?

Edith Sitwell's *Wheels* anthologies, six "cycles" published annually between 1916 and 1921, allow us to examine the new anthology phenomenon as practiced by a woman author and editor (albeit one with somewhat dubious feminist credentials and commitments). Bracketing all other matters, only considering the number of women poets represented in the first "cycle" of 1916, we see a relative increase compared with its predecessors. Of the nine poets in the first "cycle," four are women, Edith Sitwell, Nancy Cunard, Iris Tree, and Helen Rootham, accounting for more than half the poems. At the end of six "cycles," however, after Sitwell has eliminated Cunard and added only a single other woman, this fraction decreases to under a fifth.[71] Still, even accounting for the relatively balanced gender representation of the first "cycle" and the significance of having a woman as anthologist, Sitwell's *Wheels* is inexorably bound by the system of sectarian exclusivity characteristic of the anthologies edited by Marinetti, Marsh, and Pound. As a promotional construct, it registers the developments of its predecessors both through genealogy – *I poeti futuristi*, *Georgian Poetry*,

Des Imagistes – and through individually mediated influences, the promotional implications of Rupert Brooke's demise, to cite a particularly
revealing example, are extended to Wilfred Owen in the third "cycle" of
1919.

Wheels follows the new anthology precedents named above: dimensions, price, inexpensive paper and binding, cover titles, author placement,
strategic dedications, submerged editor (at least in the first two "cycles"),
supplementary documentation, including, like the futurists, hostile press-
cuttings, replete with arch replies from "the Editor of 'Wheels,'" such as
the following: "NOTE. – The Editor of 'Wheels' will shortly answer *all* the
attacks in a pamphlet to be published separately. The attackers are properly
in for it."[72] In one respect, *Wheels* departs significantly from its predecessors:
its integration of visual art, such as the "Wheels" diagrams included on the
cover pages and jarringly avant-garde cover art and endpaper illustrations.
The cover art, in particular, evidences the aggressive, oppositional spirit
of futurism and what is, arguably, its main English analog, vorticism, led
by Pound and Lewis; Sitwell commissioned vorticist work from Laurence
Atkinson and William Roberts with aggressive and militaristic overtones as
well as later work from the founding futurist painter, Gino Severini (though
not work of his futurist period).[73] In his review of the first "cycle," Pound
picks up on Sitwell's strategy, noting the "pleasingly satiric cover, bright yellow, displaying a scraggy nursemaid and a makeshift perambulator . . . The
proper sort of ink-pot to hurl itself in the face of senile pomposity."[74] This
rhetoric is quite similar to Pound's mytho-misogynist description of his
London literary audience; or William Carlos Williams' comments about
the first appearance of the *Others* anthology stateside, "Valueless as the
Others anthology may or may not be, it is at least a fine thrust out into
the dark"; or, for that matter, Marinetti's hurling defiance unto the stars,
"Poetry must be conceived as a violent attack on unknown forces, to reduce
and prostrate them before man."[75] Sitwell cites Pound's comments approvingly in the appendix of the second "cycle." In the third "cycle," with
similar approval, she records a somewhat less congenial response: "The
very cover of the volume is calculated to establish a reign of terror on any
respectable bookshelf. Within, the dazed readers' impression is of a riot
of many-coloured figures, violently gesticulating, with here and there a
tract of impenetrable gloom, pierced by the shrieks of tortured victims."[76]
Covers were clearly selected to elicit this sort of response, provocations,
which, more often than not, come out of new war experiences – William
Roberts' "Gun Drill," with its garish red and black stick-soldier humanoids

and cannon, his red, Tyro-like Cyclops, his angry dart-playing drunks, and Atkinson's "Sky Pilot," a machine-like pile of girders and scaffolds.

The *Wheels* diagrams, figuring the authorized authors into the spokes of a wheel, printed on the title page of each "cycle" save the sixth, provide Sitwell with another promotional mechanism, one which was also eventually connected with the war experience. Like Pound, Sitwell favors a non-alphabetic listing of authors; the diagram seems to make her organizational principles less authoritarian and more "democratic" than Pound's, because it is initially offered as a figure of solidarity within the literary group. In the first diagram, each spoke contains an author's name; the hub contains the date; the rim contains the title and publisher, "Wheels: An Anthology of Verse – Oxford: B. H. Blackwell." Cunard takes up the theme in the prefatory poem of the first "cycle," suitably called "Wheels":

> Now in the scented gardens of the night,
> Where we are scattered like a pack of cards,
> Our words are turned to spokes that thoughts may roll
> And form a jangling chain around the world,
> (Itself a fabulous wheel controlled by Time
> Over the slow incline of the centuries.)[77]

The connection, moreover, was readily available to readers, as the reviewer of *The Southport Guardian* indicates (as recorded in the "Press Notices" of the second "cycle"): "It is not easy to find the axle – '1916' – into which the several spokes of this wheel of verse fit; indeed personal friendship rather than poetic kinship would seem to have been the sole condition for admission."[78] The diagram serves to support fictions of a common working group – whether it be of *personal friendship* or of *poetic kinship*, the suggestion of collaborative contact is made. Yet, over the six "cycles" the diagram and its significance for the *Wheels* group changes. The systematic basis of literary authoritarianism comes to the surface, as if as a kind of increasingly perceptible stain. In the second "cycle" (1917), things are much the same as in the first, but now Cunard has been spun off the wheel, Huxley has been added, and the wheel appears to be turning subtly. In the third "cycle" (1918), the wheel is spinning more rapidly, kicking up leaves and mud; now Edith Sitwell occupies the wheel's hub, replacing the year. *The fabulous wheel controlled by Time* is now controlled by Sitwell, and a second page documents her editorship bibliographically. In the fourth cycle (1919), the one which contains Wilfred Owen's posthumous war poetry, the wheel is now whirling violently, as if on fire, thrashing up earth, with

Figure 5a *Wheels* diagram, 1919.

Sitwell still occupying the hub on the title page, a fixed center to the vortex (see Figure 5a).

In late 1919, Sitwell writes Susan Owen, Wilfred Owen's mother, to "assure" her about the imminent success of her son's posthumous poems: all of "London will be 'on fire' when *Wheels* comes out – at least *all* London that cares about poetry, and a great many people who have never read poetry before."[79] And that her brother, Sacheverell, the budding futurist ("not at all of your son's school, but like the Italian Futurists"), has recognized Owen's genius is especially significant: "it shows that *all* the schools will regard your son as a supreme master. I have never known Sachie so overcome; he can think of nothing else; and he has always been entirely out of sympathy with 'war poems'. He says these are the greatest poems of the kind that he has ever seen, and that their beauty and poignancy are absolutely overwhelming. I agree with him."[80] In the twilight of literary factionalism, all London will be burning! Sitwell's nightmarishly ecstatic predictions are not calibrated by the gravitas of Owen's verse, nor are they carefully measured with postwar anomie; rather they follow from a wholly uncritical pattern of exaggeration commensurate with the marketing blitz of patent medicine in H. G. Wells' novel *Tono-Bungay*. Even in the face of

Owen's war-death, aggression, violence, and war are but rhetorical strate-
gies, tried and tested for provoking widespread interest and consumption.
Sitwell's framing of Owen in the fourth "cycle" is studiously modeled on
Marsh's framing of Rupert Brooke in *Georgian Poetry: 1913–1915*, beginning
with a dedication dutifully noting Owen's military honors: "We Dedicate
This Book / To The Memory / Of / Wilfred Owen, M. C." In case the
relevant point is missed, Sitwell makes it again in the page headings above
Owen's section: "WILFRED OWEN (killed in action)" – as if to emphasize
that the *Wheels* group has a soldier-poet, too, and can finally fill the pages
reserved for him posthumously. Owen's late letters establish a chronology
confirming that his inclusion in *Wheels* anticipates his death: in June 1918,
the Sitwells send "an urgent request" to Owen's barracks in Scarborough to
solicit poems; in July, he is trying to obtain an examination copy of *Wheels*;
in August, he is writing verses expressly for *Wheels*; and, in November, a
week before Armistice, he is killed at the front.[81] In mid-March 1919, four
months later, Sitwell is negotiating with Susan Owen to secure Wilfred's
"very beautiful poems" for the fourth "cycle": "I am particularly anxious
to have the honour of producing some of the war poems," Sitwell writes,
"if you do not mind my saying so, I consider them among the very finest
poems of the war."[82] At the end of July, she writes her again: "I should like
to dedicate this year's *Wheels* to the memory of your son – as a tribute. Will
you . . . send me a photograph of him? I should value it as one of my prized
possessions."[83] By September, she writes that *Wheels* "will awaken all those
who care for poetry to the fact that [Owen] is by far our greatest war poet":

your son's poems appear to me – simply as the greatest poetry of our time. Though
shorter than Dante's *Inferno*, they rank with that poem . . . Each time I write to
you, I write with the kind of reverence and humility with which I should have
written Dante's mother. You have given the world the greatest poet of our time.[84]

In subsequent letters, Sitwell reports to Susan Owen of the strategic com-
mendations of Arnold Bennett, Edmund Gosse, and John Middleton
Murry ("an *exceedingly* powerful man") and her unrelenting tactical exertions for Owen's cause: "I met several critics and publishers' readers at Mr
Edmund Gosse's house . . . and they all rushed up to me, and said 'I hear
there is a wonderful new poet.' I said to them 'He is the one genius the war
has produced.' Soon, all London will be ringing with it."[85]
    The private history of literary propaganda detailed in Sitwell's correspon-
dence suggests the action of Lewis's painting "The Crowd" (1914–15), which
is, ironically, a more expansive rendering of the visual idiom of Roberts'
"Gun Drill," the cover art of the Owen number. In Lewis's painting,

various factions of matchstick humanoids, each led by avant-garde standard-bearers, mount offensives in closed, lattice-like spaces, and the rearguard of the factions become increasingly indistinguishable from the grid on which they mount their offensives. The *Wheels* anthology practices a type of group-promotion that gathers together the avant-garde aggression of futurism, chucking insults into the void, and the rearguard networking of "Georgianism," desperate for the approval of Gosse, Bennett, Murry, and the rest of the literary establishment. Recalling her early comments about Wilfred Owen's appeal to her brother Sacheverell, the futurist manqué, Edith Sitwell's tactical exertions explain literary factionalism, at last, as the annihilation of factionalism, the return of a closed, undifferentiated, authoritarian literary system for throwing out geniuses, not least Sitwell and her brothers. It represents the new anthology pattern *par excellence*, potently mixing an anthologist's authorizing imprimatur, recursive networking, aggressive brand publicity, and a group of anthologized authors (Cunard, Huxley, Lewis, Pound, Graves) breaking ranks publicly and privately. That Edith Sitwell, a woman, presses the imprimatur does nothing to alter, undermine, or open up the male authority of which she makes use. Consequently, *Wheels* demonstrates how the new anthologies persistently sanction forms of male literary authority, drawing on overstated masculinist rhetoric of war, violence, and aggression, whether or not the agent conferring the editorial imprimatur is male.

And, in a sense, all this is to say that F. R. Leavis is right in his memorable dig at Osbert, Sacheverell, and Edith in *New Bearings in English Poetry*, that "the Sitwells belong to the history of publicity rather than poetry."[86] Like Lowell, nothing shields Sitwell from the charge of too much publicity. This was, of course, no secret; one of the press-cuttings Sitwell approvingly includes in the fifth "cycle" makes the same point: "The publication of 'Wheels' is regarded by all right-minded people as more of a society event than a literary one."[87] The obvious satire here is lost on readers like Leavis. When it comes to minority culture, nothing fails like success. Modernist publicity must be good but it can't be too good. In this history of modernist promotion, Sitwell was hardly unique; it was only that it was damningly difficult for her to other her own publicity.

The following brief critical history is, by now, celebrated apocrypha in its own right. In the seventies and eighties, feminist scholars of modernism – in particular, Shari Benstock, Susan Stanford Friedman, Jane Marcus, and Sandra Gilbert and Susan Gubar – began to appraise the work of women modernists, whose literary reputations, if not exactly forgotten, had not until then been so embraced in university English departments as those of male contemporaries like T. S. Eliot, Ezra Pound, and James Joyce. During this period, H. D., Djuna Barnes, Mina Loy, and others – writers who at one time or another in their own lifetimes had appreciable literary renown – became literary celebrities once again, albeit of a different sort. They became subjects of academic knowledge, increasingly appearing as subject matter for articles in the MLA bibliography, required reading on literature course syllabi, literary durable goods available from campus bookstores. The reputations of writers like Virginia Woolf and Gertrude Stein, never in actuality out-of-print, were also resurgent. New editions were published, less familiar works became available.

The arguments for this project drew largely on a narrative of neglect. Bonnie Kime Scott, for example, dedicates *The Gender of Modernism: A Critical Anthology* to "the forgotten and silenced makers of modernism." One scholar summarizes it like this:

[the] androcentric vision of literary modernism distorted a history in which women have in fact been central, as authors, critics, editors, and publishers; they rediscovered the work of long-neglected women writers and asserted that in addition to the established mandarins of masculine modernism – T. S. Eliot, James Joyce, Ezra Pound – women like Djuna Barnes, H. D., and Mina Loy were writers who deserved inclusion in any canon of modernism.[88]

This narrative, in fact, has two components. The first, more conspicuous part derives its notion of literary reputation from a pluralistic ideal of proportional representation, stemming from the same democratizing impulse as Lowell's declaration of imagism's independence from King Ezra. Finally, this standard of fair play amounts to no more than a story of structural replacement, because it does not purpose a critique of the disparity between literary labor and literary reputation. If the literary works of Barnes, H. D., and Loy are on a par with those of Eliot, Joyce, and Pound in terms of both formal experimentation and aesthetic merits, Barnes, H. D., and Loy should be apportioned an equivalent measure of renown. Yet, to the dominant system of literary reputation, these assertions are less shocking than a second part of the project alluded to above: the revaluing of stubbornly devalued literary labors.

Shari Benstock's *Women of the Left Bank* made the second case first and perhaps most forcefully. In the opening pages of her landmark book, she includes a full page listing her main subjects, twenty-two literary figures, all women, from "the artistic community that formed on the Paris Left Bank early in the twentieth century."[89] The names are alphabetized (thus following Lowell's plan for disrupting anthology hierarchy): Margaret Anderson, Djuna Barnes, Natalie Barney, Sylvia Beach, Kay Boyle, Bryher, Colette, Caresse Crosby, Nancy Cunard, H. D., Janet Flanner, jane heap, Maria Jolas, Mina Loy, Adrienne Monnier, Anaïs Nin, Jean Rhys, Solita Solana, Gertrude Stein, Alice B. Toklas, Renée Vivien, and Edith Wharton. Referring to this list, Benstock writes:

> Their literary contributions – which include major works of prose, poetry, drama, critical and journalistic essays, autobiographies, *pensées*, and memoirs – display wide-ranging interests and diverse talents. In addition to their own writing activities, several of these women set up bookshops, publishing houses, little magazines, and artistic salons through which they advertised and marketed the products of literary Paris.[90]

In fact, as I have argued in chapter two, Benstock is invoking two different kinds of literary production, each charged with a different style of literary prestige: upstream work (which includes *major works of prose, poetry, drama*) and downstream work (which includes *critical and journalistic essays, autobiographies,* pensées, *and memoirs* as well as setting up *bookshops, publishing houses, little magazines, and artistic salons*). One of Benstock's chief critical accomplishments is to read these labors side by side, giving the downstream work of advertising and marketing literary goods (by women) its proper due as a necessity of literary production. Roughly speaking, this means reading H. D.'s work of poetry, essays, and magazine editing alongside Bryher's work of memoirs, financing, and magazine editing. As I have argued in chapter three, there is a second key distinction within the field of downstream production between promotional work focused on literary durable goods (literary criticism, introductions, editions, anthologies) and promotional work focused on apocrypha (literary relics, sacred memorabilia, autobiographic accounts of collaborative work). "Reclaiming" literary figures like Margaret Anderson, Sylvia Beach, Bryher, Caresse Crosby, Nancy Cunard, and jane heap is potentially more disruptive than "reclaiming" Djuna Barnes, H. D., and Mina Loy, because it means turning the tables of a literary value system based on subordinating low literary labors of promotion in order to isolate, individualize, and reify the high literary labors of literary durable goods. Yet, despite Benstock's premise, such table-turning has not taken place; the devalued genres, which narrativize modernist collaborative work, have remained devalued partly because undoing this work would mean ignoring the dominant message of these texts, a message which, more often than not, undermines the very instrumental work these narratives describe.

Margaret Anderson, Maria Jolas, jane heap, Natalie Barney, Sylvia Beach, Bryher, Caresse Crosby, Nancy Cunard, Harriet Shaw Weaver, Harriet Monroe – like Robert McAlmon, Eugene Jolas, Henry Crosby, William Bird, Malcom Cowley, Gilbert Seldes, Thayer Scofield, Harry McBride, Harry Crowder, Harold Monro, A. R. Orage, Eddie Marsh – long held as secondary figures continue to appear as secondary figures, because anything else would spell the end of the reign of signed masterpieces, focusing too much attention on literary promotion in its lived, negotiated, and trespassed complexity. These "celebrities" – like Amy Lowell or Edith Sitwell – suffer from an excess of promotion. Their claims for recognition entail subordination vis-à-vis the authors they have known. Caresse Crosby, for example, describes her memoir, *The Passionate Years*, as a mode of entry into public life, a means of documenting being there. In this framework, the memoir occupies imaginative space between two apocryphal worlds, being half-remembered and being well-known. To the first world, a world Crosby seems to associate only with men, she apologizes for her imminent departure: "One or two personalities who are now in public life may feel I have forgotten them – but to tell the world that a man remains magnificent in a woman's memory might complicate his career as much as if she was to say the contrary." About the second, which she also associates with men, she writes: "Each artist, however, is plentifully identified; for I have observed that no matter how good or how bad an artist may be, he believes that his every expression, public or private, is history."[91] Crosby's memory, which she calls "the woman's memory," exists precariously between these two, neither of which purports to need her remembering. Serving notice that the stories circulating in public life do injustice to personal memory, she nevertheless refuses to tell the stories that seemingly need most remembering. She is certain that the artists with lasting implications remember themselves. Apparently, they do not need her help. The overwrought insistence on the self-sufficiency of her subjects comes close to an admission that sabotages her particular claims to be heard as a recorder of anecdotes about other people.

This sentiment about "being there" also marks Margaret Anderson's memoir of the *Little Review, My Thirty Years' War*. "I won't be cornered and I won't stay suppressed," she writes.[92] The specific valence of this assertion, no doubt, is the *Little Review*'s defiance of the censors, suppressed multiple times for publishing James Joyce and Wyndham Lewis. Yet, the struggle at the fore of Anderson's text is the struggle to be known, documenting the "there-ness" of Margaret Anderson and jane heap alongside the literary celebrities whom they helped to make known. The structure of *My Thirty*

Years' War sets the tone for the genre. First, it describes the calling, an untraditional upbringing, early contacts with bohemia, sources for the desire to assist the artist; second, the business, picaresque adventures of setting up the journal (i.e., press, bookstore, coterie), financial, legal, and other headaches, various analgesics applied, contacts with idiosyncratic artists, and projects devised for boosting their reputations and, by implication, the business; third, the business in decline, gradually becoming eclipsed by literary celebrity itself. As Anderson moves eastward from Chicago to New York to Paris, the memoir is increasingly devoted to her encounters with the stable of *Little Review* contributors as literary bodies and the famous literary acquaintances they enable. The work of publishing literary worthies whom she has never seen (a point noted repeatedly) is gradually replaced by making visual contact and seeing where the work was done. By the time Anderson arrives in the Left Bank, proximity to celebrity bodies eclipses literary texts in her narrative. Anderson and heap do not so much make the rounds in Parisian space as they trace the closed circuit of (mostly male) artist celebrities: first Ezra Pound, then James and Nora Joyce, then Gertrude Stein, Constantin Brancusi, Francis Picabia, Ernest Hemingway, Jean Cocteau, and André Gide. With each encounter, Anderson notes the subject's relation to the *Little Review* and carefully describes his or her physical appearance, habits, and habitat, producing passages which come over like equal parts bibliography, celebrity ethnography, and *Klatsch*:

> [heap] and I went . . . to see our foreign editor Ezra Pound . . . He was dressed in the large velvet beret and flowing tie of the Latin Quarter artist of the 1830's. He was totally unlike any picture I had formed of him. Photographs had given no idea of his height, his robustness, his red blondness – could have given no indication of his high Rooseveltian voice, his nervousness, his self-consciousness.[93]

> In 1922 the *Little Review* had published a Brancusi number . . . Constantin Brancusi lives in a stone studio . . . His hair and beard are white, his long working-man's blouse is white, his stone benches and large round table are white, the sculptor's dust that covers everything . . .[94]

Not only were figures like Anderson, heap, and Crosby "there" – among the "makers of modernism" – but they were also instrumental in making the "makers of modernism," that is to say, making these very narratives, i.e., Pound in his over-large tie, Brancusi covered in dust, Stein and her Picassos. If nothing else, this kind of apocrypha supplies documentary evidence, and, as I mentioned in the introduction, for this reason, these labors were not secret nor were they, strictly speaking, ever lost. Their role has always been

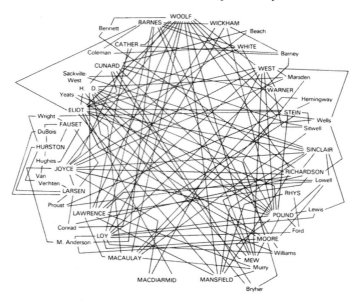

Figure 5b "A Tangled Mesh of Modernists."

instrumental to the reputations of high literary labors. Similarly, the high literary labors of women modernists like H. D., Barnes, and Loy were never, strictly speaking, suppressed; H. D., Barnes, and Loy had substantial access to the modes and means of literary production – upstream and downstream – used to effect by Pound, Eliot, and Joyce. Indeed, at various points, all six – H. D., Barnes, Loy, Pound, Eliot, and Joyce – were fellow-travelers and experimenters in a common literary environment; knowing, assisting, publicizing one another; sharing acquaintances, comparable notoriety, space in memoirs; publishing in the same journals; being reviewed by the same reviewers – a point well-illustrated by Scott's "Tangled Mesh of Modernists," her diagram in *The Gender of Modernism*, the essential collection of primary documents and essays on this topic (see Figure 5b).[95] How and when did H. D., Barnes, and Loy get derailed, then? Sometime between the late 1920s and the early 1960s is the usual answer; sometime between *Nightwood* and *The Antiphon*, which is to say, approximately the time of Hugh Kenner's *Poetry of Ezra Pound* (1951). "Modernism as we were taught it at mid-century," Scott writes, "was perhaps halfway to truth. It was unconsciously gendered masculine."[96]

One problem with this explanation lies in the deliberate vagueness of its mechanism of reputation. The failure of Barnes, H. D., Loy, and other seemingly viable literary figures to maintain their reputations by mid-century (while Eliot, Pound, Joyce, and others not only maintained modernist celebrity status but also appreciably legitimated and institutionalized it) helps explain the workings of celebrity as a promotional system. It suggests that their literary celebrity depended less on actual high literary efforts than on facility with promotional apparatus, its institutional agendas, and accompanying discourses. Status was derived not from the quality of their high literary labors *per se* but from their capacity to *stay news*, to keep their imprimaturs extant, to keep enough of their durable literary goods in print, and, above all, to make the transition to academic institutionalization after the Second World War. Unlike Eliot, Pound, and Joyce, Barnes, H. D., and Loy were not able to promote imprimaturs that would have enabled works like *The Antiphon*, *Trilogy*, and *The Lost Lunar Baedeker* to flourish in that other masculinist literary regime of scarcity, implicit subordination, invasive and deniable collaborative relationships, and radical exclusivity and elitism: the postwar Anglo-American university. Unlike Eliot, they lacked a fixed position of enunciation, backed by a publishing house, from which literary reputation could be promoted as a permanent monument, repeatedly superimposed on a cross-section of a literary generation. They refused to follow Pound in his inflated phallomorphic pose of hyperbolic self-promotion in editorial work and submit to the program of meticulously maintained originality that it entailed. They lacked Joyce's hierarchical network of male acolytes and female benefactors, willing to carry the promotional work of the literary brand downstream – posthumously, if necessary. Unlike Sitwell, whose literary reputation was embarrassingly intact at mid-century, they had no occasion to recycle old work and pitch new anthologies in less productive years after the Second World War. These were the requisite promotional techniques. The literary reputations of women modernists were poorly served by the restrictive promotional system of introducing, editing, and anthologizing, for which men like Eliot, Pound, Marsh, et al. served as gatekeepers. When the rare woman modernist like Sitwell muscled in, her placement became marked and undeniable; there could be no *divergence later* from promotional work.

For these reasons, the epigraph to *The Gender of Modernism* – "to the forgotten and silenced makers of modernism" – is a somewhat mystified and mystifying formula, obscuring several key questions. Are *being forgotten* and *being silenced* two operations or just one? If a single operation, should it not read "silenced" first and then "forgotten"? If a dual operation, how are the two related? The two verbs seems to suggest a fall from reputation, pointing backwards to a utopian condition of once being well-remembered and often-heard, placed romantically, albeit impossibly, at the moment of creative inspiration. By what means did the well-remembered and often-heard become unremembered and unspoken? And, perhaps most crucially: how can we account for the utopian state before the fall? In effect, the formula "forgotten and silenced makers of modernism" returns us to McAlmon's excised sentence, which began chapter three: "Somewhere, silently and without fuss or desire for réclame there is quite apt to be a man or a woman who will turn out the masterpiece that puts to shame all the intriguers or politicians." As McAlmon's sentiment suggests, modernism re-organizes the romantic cult of the solitary literary genius by linking it with the imperative to suppress its own conditions of production, specifically, the collaborative work of making and promoting modernists. Making modernism – that is, making the single modernist artist – is a promotional project that relies on others being occluded yet requires them to be never entirely blotted out. The narrative of neglect, like McAlmon's sentiment, upholds this promotional dynamic at the same time as it complains of it, presenting the work of putting aside old literary goods, as if it were an enviable result of individual creative acts rather than a great deal of fussing and réclame.

Scott's "Tangled Mesh" is, then, a profoundly ambiguous representation of working connections between male and female "modernists." Like Anderson's account of her trip to Paris, which follows a celebrity circuit envisioned in the pages of *The Little Review*, the diagram offers a distorted cartography of modernist collaboration. It circumscribes a closed, inter-related circuit akin to Harry Beck's 1933 diagrammatic map of the London Underground, the design of which distorts the "true scale" of geographic London as if through "a convex lens or mirror, so as to present the central area on a larger scale [giving] needed clarity to interchange information" (see Figures 6a–b).[97] Like Beck's map, the "Tangled Mesh" is a network determined by oversimplified distortions instrumental to "information needs," for it is determined by the literary figures the anthologist–editors elect to bring up most often in their articles: "Each time an important connection was made in an introduction in a primary work in the anthology, a line was drawn between the writers."[98] The web, redrawn as a network diagram, approximates not the auratic organicism of "creative stimulation," mutual interest and influence among authors, editors, and publishers, but the claims that the reputations of a central line of anthologized "modernists" continue to register as inter-associated objects among a survey of literary scholars. The most "connected" – Ezra Pound, T. S. Eliot, Virginia

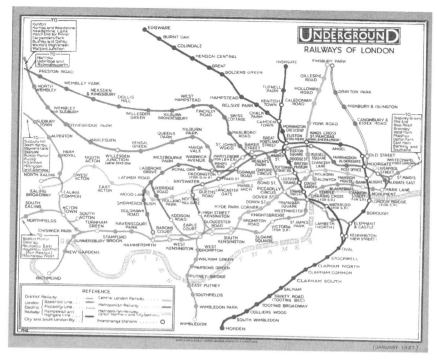

Figure 6a F. H. Stingemore's Pocket Underground Map, 1927.

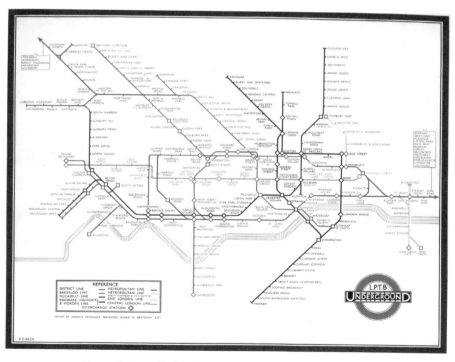

Figure 6b Harry Beck's diagrammatic Underground Map, 1933.

Woolf, James Joyce, Marianne Moore, H. D., D. H. Lawrence, Mina Loy, Dorothy Richardson, Rebecca West – provide the network interchanges, through which the reputations of less "connected" writers are made to circulate. Thus redrawn, it is a perfect emblem for a text like *The Gender of Modernism* that is, above all, aimed at reapportioning renown. In her introduction, Scott instantly puts to rest any doubts about introducing, editing, and anthologizing not being institutional vehicles of reputation, describing the nineteen introducers, editors, and anthologists of the book as "archival explorers of the late twentieth century," their mission to "relocate lost and neglected textual treasures and draw connections between them," and then to advance them for "academic recirculation."[99] If nothing else – and, make no mistake, the anthology has much to offer readers – this mission demonstrates the durability of the modernist brand. Despite its shortcomings, it seems that the brand remains a viable promotional construct: "in relation to gender modernism has a great deal of unassessed vitality and content, with its own intricate and varied theory."[100] Compared with the early anthologies, which hinged on recursive points of departure and revaluations, little has changed. The brand is still literary patent medicine that promises to be four things at once – a fiction of shared work, a generation, a period, and a movement – but that, in fact, works as a controlling mechanism for ordering literary networks vis-à-vis implicit literary hierarchies of work.

CHAPTER 5

Institutions, outrages, and postcards

In 1938, after the Royal Academy refused his portrait of T. S. Eliot, Wyndham Lewis appeared in the pages of *Time*. As a result, in the words of *Time*, the "black-hatted" and "black-witted" Lewis "suddenly became celebrated." There is a note of almost Lewis-like *Schadenfreude* to it: *Guffaw! Look at the so-called "Enemy" now! Undone for dabbling in portraiture, that most institutionally sycophantic of genres!* Hadn't he blasted Lionel Cust, the one-time director of the National Portrait Gallery, and the rest of the museum establishment in *Blast* in 1914? Wasn't his bilious aesthetic *modus operandi*, rooted in the heady days of the English avant-garde, manufactured to shock this very sort of cultural constellation out of existence? In the accompanying photograph, the self-described "Enemy" looks docile, a bit too respectable, the over-eager portraitist for a poet *Time* calls "the most gift-stricken . . . of his time."[1]

Again, we see celebrity as authorial self-fashioning *in extremis*. The point when *self*-fashioning becomes impossible is where Lewis is inscribed in the banalities of mass magazine celebration. Avant-garde scandal sheds its shock value and instead becomes readily consumable. This chapter investigates the complicity of modernist reputation in the arts and culture superstructure emerging in interwar England. More specifically, it examines the productive tension between Lewis's avant-gardist disdain for existing cultural institutions, on the one hand, and his bid to remake the London museum establishment as a *de facto* modernist portrait gallery, on the other. My discussion centers on his theory and practice of portraiture, re-reading his famous repudiation of abstraction less as a retreat from modernist aesthetics than as a modernist effort to distort the prevailing portraiture ideal and retool its institutional logic to accommodate the promotional logic of the imprimaturs forged in the anti-institutional promotional and political culture of interwar Britain. It focuses on the artist–author's professed point of occupational departure, *Blast* (1914) – the manifesto-like organ of the "English Vortex," promised in messianic–revolutionary boldface as the END OF THE CHRISTIAN ERA – examining the promotional ideology of Lewis's signature publication-event in relation to, first, the arguably more explosive prewar blasts issuing from suffragette agitation for political representation; and, second, his programmatic theory and practice of (self-)portraiture as it develops before and after the war.

The modern past's heroic geniuses are fast becoming the postmodern present's celebrities. Point of information: the latest best-selling postcard in the British National Portrait Gallery (hereafter NPG) gift-shop is none other than Virginia Woolf.[2] So much for modernism's legendary iconophobia and institutional antagonism. "Virginia Woolf" is outdistancing all other postcard-rack worthies, from the famous portraits of Shakespeare and Elizabeth to the latest head-shots of British sports heroes and pop stars. In *Virginia Woolf Icon*, this development helps Brenda Silver argue for the ascendancy of a postmodern Woolf. Where Daniel Boorstin reads the transformation from heroic genius to mass celebrity as hollowing hero-worship, Silver sees promising new forms of liberational identification: "undecidability," an "undoing of borders and categories," an "emphasis on the circulation of meanings." Among its beneficial consequences, the loss of fixed content, the "star *as* hero in a productive sense: a site of identification and/or rejection, interpellation and resistance."[3] In fact, Silver does not reject the calculus of hero-worship at all. Instead, she envisions a taxonomy that substitutes the non-coercive, consumer-friendly, ready-to-wear notion of the "icon" for the one-size-fits-all coercions of the "hero-genius." Even as she discards hero-worship's elitist and masculinist connotations, she preserves much of its compensatory narrative about emulating the good and the great. Great signs replace great men, but the encounter remains intact. Old-style hero-worship was also predicated on perceived "identification and/or rejection, interpellation and resistance." Both kinds of "consumers" become "producers," but only insofar as they are fixated by their spectacles, which serve as so many screens for worshipers to misrecognize their productive labors without noticing the institutional frameworks and ideological agendas served.

Perhaps the characteristic site for seemingly non-coercive appropriation of elite cultural commodities is the museum gift-shop. At the NPG, for instance, visitors can purchase an assortment of Virginia Woolf paraphernalia: from postcards and refrigerator magnets to novels and literary critiques.[4] Here, the low-end Woolf trades on an image of a high-end Woolf retrenching cultural capital in ever more accessible,

extra-curricular forms. The marketing wisdom of the refrigerator magnet
is that it confers the ubiquity of collective enthusiasm on Woolf by encouraging the reproduction of the institutional logic of NPG in unconsecrated,
domestic space: every visitor can have his or her own NPG on his or her
refrigerator door.

Using NPG postcard sales as a yardstick of popular esteem for literary
worthies is hardly new. Such popularizing and personalizing rhetoric has
long been a distinctive element of the NPG's mission and marketing strategy
since its inception in the mid-nineteenth century. The latest Woolf blitz
is only the most recent marketing incarnation to capitalize on the NPG's
"annual list of people's favourite pin-ups from the past" – as one of their
campaigns was described. In 1932, the highlights of the collection were
offered *en masse*, a set of 400 postcards, couched in the same message of
institutionalized populism:

With a little shuffling and by taking the appropriate cards out of the "miscellaneous"
containers, the happy possessor can reconstruct a fascinating gallery; indeed by
permutations . . . he can rig up a perpetual variety of exhibitions in miniature . . .
now [by] date, now profession, now sex, [etc.]. The cards are much more obedient
to their owner's whim than the pictures on the wall can be to the visitor, and
they invite more human treatment . . . They can be turned into a delightful game
for evenings at home into which any amount of tragedy and comedy, humour
and pathos, fact and fancy can be worked, making as profitable an English night's
entertainment as anything handed down about the brave days of old.[5]

"None can despair of his or her country," as the copy puts it, if its gallery
of eminent faces is so intimately tangible.

A good part of this thinking about images of dead literary worthies
is residual, stretching back at least to Thomas Carlyle and Parliament's
founding of the NPG in 1856. The sway of the ideas expressed in *On
Heroes, Hero-Worship, and the Heroic in History* (1841) and *Past and Present*
(1843) on the founders of the museum is well known (so well known that
the connection scarcely needs substantial repetition here).[6] Recall Carlyle's
crowning example of hagiolatry, the "culminating moment" in the life of
Abbot Samson of Bury St. Edmunds in *Past and Present*: the happy possessor
exhibiting his apotheosis, taking the corpse of St. Edmund out of the
miscellaneous containers, cradling his head, stroking his fingers, counting
his toes.[7] Admittedly, the act of unpacking plays out more austerely in
Carlyle's account than it does in the advertisement for the NPG postcard set.
Still, both ally the analgesic effects of hero-worship with human treatment,
hands-on experience, and personal contact. The idea is that a strong dose

of intimate contact with prelapsarian heroes mitigates against the spiritual crisis of the modern age and re-consecrates the quotidian.

In an early proposal for a "home of all the National divinities," Carlyle describes the importance of portraiture as follows:

> one of the most primary wants [in writing history is] to procure a bodily likeness of the personage inquired after; a good *Portrait* if such exists; failing that, even an indifferent if sincere one. In short, *any* representation, made by a faithful human creature, of that Face and Figure, which *he* saw with his eyes, and which I can never see with mine, is now valuable to me.[8]

Portraits are valued not as aesthetic objects *per se* but for the sincerity of their implied connection to the sitter, their capacity to represent lived identity as once experienced first-hand. Such transference from spectator to portraitist to sitter is inescapably retroactive. The best portraits are the ones that best frame their subjects as objects of worship, and thus viewing portraits – that is, seeing eminent physiognomy in them – serves as its own reward. As Paul Barlow writes, this portraiture ideal promises the spectator a chance "to look the past in the eyes" by drawing on a myth of unmediated contact between sitter and portraitist: the experience of being in the presence of the portrait represents "a sacramental act, [which reiterates] a mysterious and complex transaction between artist and sitter [that] is neither stable nor easily readable."[9] The experience of enchantment presupposes that "celebrity" be taken with absolute sincerity, that prominence and eminence are, in the final analysis, presumed one and the same.

In fact, the NPG existed virtually first, making itself available in intimate, handheld proportions well before the campaign led by Carlyle and others conferred it with official legitimacy. Heads of "illustrious and eminent personages" called "National Portrait Galleries" were sold in book form as early as 1830. By the early 1840s, with the emergence of illustrated newspapers, the virtual portrait gallery became a popular staple of even broader dissemination.[10] It is in these contexts, in particular – more than Carlyle's lectures, perhaps – where notions of eminence as elite embodied value and prominence as public exposure become cemented (and, I would also argue, later become unhinged). Carlyle helped make precise the terms of the connection and impress their legitimacy upon the ruling classes. In 1856, a motion was tabled in the House of Lords for "forming a Gallery of the Portraits of the most eminent Persons in British History." Earl Stanhope stated that "[t]here ought not to be in this collection a single portrait as to which a man of good education passing round and seeing the name in the catalogue, would be under the necessity of asking 'Who is He?' Such a question ought to be decisive against the admission of the portrait. The success of the whole scheme depended on confining the gallery to men of real distinction, real fame."[11] Here, the test of "real fame" is no less than virtual exposure – the proposition that the eminent have been always already rendered prominent. The core of the NPG project entails exposing the minds of the remainder ("all classes, descending even to the lowest") to the salutary effects of intimate contact with greatness ("encouragement should be given . . . on that rugged path that [leads] to fame").[12] Yet, the scheme cannot manage to conceal its most pressing and anxious ideological contradiction: namely, that making certain personages illustrious and eminent now depends on making them more ordinary, exposing the illustrious and eminent downward through the class structure. This kind of contact becomes possible only when it becomes necessary (and vice-versa).

These circumstances shaped the NPG's so-called "authenticity rule":

The rule which the Trustees desire to lay down to themselves, in either making purchases or receiving presents, is to look to the celebrity of the person rather than to the merits of the artist . . . Nor will they consider great faults and errors, even though admitted on all sides, as any sufficient ground for excluding any portrait which may be valuable, as illustrating the civil, ecclesiastical, or literary history of the country.[13]

This stipulation effectively bars two matters from active deliberation: first, the portraitist's ability and, second, perhaps less obviously, the legitimacy of the sitter's celebrity. Authentic celebrity must go without saying. As the stipulation suggests, it must go without substantive, potentially partisan discussion about the merits of celebrity. Instead, the committee's work involves establishing the provenance of the virtual *experience* of celebrity, the "authenticity" of the spectator's experience of the portrait indexing, as it were, the portraitist's experience of the sitter.

NPG ideology carries with it a ready-made institutional logic, one which realizes public confidence in national institutions by presupposing it. It is, in effect, what Terry Eagleton terms "pseudo-propositional discourse."[14] This "pseudo-proposition" of public confidence comes across in both Carlyle and NPG governance, as shown in the following distillation by Lord Palmerston, for example:

There could be no greater incentive to mental exertion, to noble actions, to good conduct on the part of the living than for them to see before them the features of those who have done things worthy of our admiration, and whose example we are more induced to imitate when they are brought before us in the visible and tangible shape of portraits.[15]

Of course, this means more than indiscriminate techniques for collective national edification; the mediations between individual human beings and the power-structure manifest themselves as personalized, analogical connections with the dead worthies, the NPG, and the nation. Barlow explains this ideology as a bid "to consolidate [the] unstable realm of public discourse, [by] defining the new gallery as a site of officially sanctioned celebrity and significance."[16] It institutionalizes Carlylean hero-worship, realizing his idea of "*Hero*archy," in particular, as an official institution of the state.[17] If the NPG helps the modern state consecrate its political institutions, the analogy also works the other way, securing a rhetoric of popular representation and legitimacy for the NPG. The "pseudo-proposed" pantheon of national heroes becomes pseudo-democratized, the "test of time" serving as a metaphor for the consent of those "governed" by heroes. So long as eminence and prominence remain interchangeable, this constellation of legitimizing analogies – the gallery as a representative institution, the government as a representative institution – retains its credibility and symbolic magic.

In or about December 1910, it no longer quite does (to reintroduce Virginia Woolf's date stamp of modernist aesthetic rupture, more about which below). About this time, the hortatory messages about portraiture and hero-worship come unstuck in time. This is not to say the ideal becomes utterly alien, for much of it survives today however residually. Take the following blurb from one of the NPG's recent coffee-table books, printed under Humphrey Ocean's portrait of Philip Larkin:

The artist . . . found Larkin "not the misanthrope of public note," reporting that at their first meeting "halfway through lunch, he produced the postcard . . . of my [Paul] McCartney picture . . . took my sleeve like a fifteen year old girl and whispered: 'Tell me ALL about him' . . . from then on nothing was too much trouble."[18]

True to Carlyle, today's NPG functionaries select an experience of transformative frisson between sitter and artist, mediated by the artist's eyes. The reader is invited to imitate Ocean's experience of Larkin's experience of (Ocean's experience of) McCartney by flipping the pages back to Ocean's McCartney portrait. The account reiterates the old rule of authenticity, suggesting the requisite detail of the authentic celebrity (the universal Larkin is anything but "the misanthrope of public note"), but, tellingly, this humanizing gesture (he is "like a fifteen year old girl") refigures the experience of sitting for an NPG portrait as a trip to the postcard rack in the NPG gift-shop, a browse through the subtleties of the commodity fetish. This

is the experience we are being induced to imitate. The parting of eminence and prominence, in other words, is affected not when Larkin joins
McCartney in the virtual pop hero-archy of Thatcherite Britain but when
Larkin himself engages half-ironically in the hagiolatry of a pop star ("Tell
me ALL about him"). The celebrity must now experience celebrity himself
to authenticate his own authenticity. And it is the guilty pleasure of it all
that announces the twilight of idols, the knowing wink that prominence is
no longer self-evidently paired with eminence because the combination is
unseemly for the democracy of tastes.

If Virginia Woolf has amounted to little more than "one of 1990's more
unusual calendar girls" (for "the man who has outgrown Pirelli," as *The
Daily Telegraph* odiously puts it) – whither Wyndham Lewis, modernism's
self-styled anti-hero?[19] The Enemy's postcard, one suspects, has not yet
encroached on the sales leaders of the NPG's pin-up list. Lewis is available
in the NPG gift-shop, a postcard reproduction of his 1932 ink and wash
self-portrait created for *Thirty Personalities and a Self-Portrait* (see Figure 7).
The Wyndham Lewis barometer has been rising: witness an important new
biography (Paul O'Keeffe's *Some Sort of Genius: A Life of Wyndham Lewis*)
and a significant monograph on Lewis's literary and artistic work (Paul
Edwards's *Wyndham Lewis: Painter and Writer*), the continued appearance of new editions of his works, and a spate of academic publishing,
including a special number of *Modernism/Modernity*. Still, of the "Men
of 1914" – James Joyce, T. S. Eliot, Ezra Pound, and Wyndham Lewis –
Lewis, the phrase's originator, remains the least self-evident. Of the four,
he was most willing to make his promotional work conspicuous, never
more prominently than in his two late autobiographical ventures, *Blasting and Bombardiering* (1937) and *Rude Assignment* (1950). Both take pains
to unhinge familiar conventions of autobiography, eschewing biographical
self-fashioning and bibliographical text-fashioning. Instead, Lewis frames
the two as autobiographies of a career, an appealing term of description for
Lewis because it hybridizes and objectifies author and work. He calls *Rude
Assignment* "an account of my career as writer and artist" undertaken not
"to speak of my work" but to speak "about *the nature of this type of work*, and
about the paradoxical position of the workman – not myself alone – engaged
in *it*."[20] This rhetoric enables a degree of self-irony. He likens *Blasting and
Bombardiering* to a history of a career in literary gossip.[21] "I am out to pop-
ularise Pound, to jack up Joyce's stocks, and make my own alarming name a
little less horrific," states Lewis in a draft of the preface.[22] In this suggestive
document – another sidelined story of modernist promotion – Lewis does

Figure 7 Lewis postcard image: Wyndham Lewis by Wyndham Lewis, ink and wash, 1932.

more than lament the undoing of a career in modernist "gossip"; he lays claim to these narratives, actively employing them to restructure his imprimatur vis-à-vis his more successful familiars, Joyce, Eliot, and Pound. Lewis's often fractured career as writer and artist, though never as abject as McAlmon's nor as wrecked as Loy's, necessitated a more visible stake in his own promotional labors than those of his "Men of 1914" cohorts.

   This chapter contends that modernist imprimaturs depended on the emergence of a particular stance to dominant cultural institutions, a stance of ironic accommodation far more complicit in these institutions than the often supposed posture of avant-garde antagonism. The last chapters described the use-value and exchange-value of modernist imprimaturs, signatures of hierarchical authority which effectively serve as functional substitutions for celebrity images. The first chapter argued that imprimaturs – even now – tend to regulate scenes of reading of modernist "masterpieces." The subsequent chapters explained how imprimaturs draw on a two-tier system of literary labor. To fix "masterpieces" in new economies of cultural prestige, modernists called upon a matrix of secondary bibliographic work paired with a generative distinction between legitimate literary work, based on exclusionary standards of literary reputation and originality, and illegitimate literary work, based on the punitively collaborative work of promotion. The most "successful" modernists did not so much repudiate so-called "hack work" as they selectively distanced their imprimaturs from it, by adopting the stance of plausible deniability. Obviously, this posture drew on familiar anxieties about culture and class. Lewis provides a modernist case in point. His career is based on the fixed proposition that a substantial portion of his writings and art ("accessible" autobiographical writings and NPG-friendly portraiture, in particular) don't really count.

According to Thomas R. Smith, Lewis framed his aborted preface to *Blasting and Bombardiering* as gossip as a sop to middlebrow readers, "to accommodate himself to middle-class readers who buy books at railway-station bookstalls":

This was a challenge for an artist whose career, since the days of *Blast*, had moved forward while he ignored, dismissed, analyzed, and flouted just such tastes. In the rejected preface, we see Lewis struggling to come to grips with the new opportunities and dangers of finding common ground with readers to whom he felt he had very little real interest to offer, except gossip.[23]

Smith reduces the impetus for memoir writing to "hack work." It represents no more than financial necessity, the same necessity which leads the modernist artist to portraiture:

In August of that year [1936] Lewis was in serious financial trouble; he owed money to his doctor for one of several operations to correct complications from gonorrhea. By 16 October, his lack of money had grown urgent. Lewis told Oliver Brown, the dealer for his paintings, to arrange for a sitter: "One relatively well-paid portrait – or two ill-paid ones – would . . . settle all my illness debts." Lewis was eager to compromise his artistic principles for ready cash. He wrote Brown, "To hell with these experimental 'difficult' contraptions, [. . .] which are hard to sell – I will do no more [. . .] until I am solvent. I will really do dreams of beauty, which will sell themselves, as I am bringing them down to the Gallery."[24]

On one side of the divide is self-fashioning aligned with ready cash, popular taste, gonorrhea, gossip about literary personalities, and the portrait gallery; on the other side, self-effacement with the unsaleable commodity, abstraction, difficulty, blasting, and bombardiering. It is worth noticing that Lewis's career repeatedly shuttles across this divide. Indeed, Lewis's simultaneous turn to portraiture and gossip came not in the late thirties in the twilight of modernist invention but much earlier in Lewis's career, well before his supposed "underground" period of the early twenties after *Kermesse, Blast, Tarr,* and the war paintings. Before the war, Lewis already began to articulate his particular approach to portraiture, hatching what eventually amounted to a promotional strategy for remaking the London museum establishment as a *de facto* modernist portrait gallery in the twenties and thirties.

Much of the legitimate "Wyndham Lewis" originated in the apocryphal tissue of portraiture and gossip laid down during this campaign. Take, for example, the received idea that Lewis got lost in the center of the modernist vortex, the idea that the few people who read or viewed Lewis (Pound, Eliot, Henry Moore, Herbert Read, John Rothenstein, Hugh Kenner, and so on) played a crucial role in modernism's development, a proposition which remains almost perfunctory in Lewis studies. It is already present in Hugh Kenner's *Wyndham Lewis* (1954), his path-breaking study written for the New Directions series appropriately titled "The Makers of Modern Literature," in which Kenner dutifully makes the point that "[n]o historian's model of the age of Joyce, Eliot, and Pound is intelligible without Lewis in it." After explaining Lewis's tendency to be boycotted, Kenner's narrative places him in the high waters of modernist innovation:

He is one of the great painters of the twentieth century – in the perhaps unguarded judgment of Walter Sickert "the greatest portraitist who ever lived." He has written *The Revenge for Love,* a twentieth-century classic; *Tarr,* "the first book of an epoch," a novel of sporadic power; and *Time and Western Man,* one of the key books for the student of modern thought.[25]

Lewis himself, of course, originates the idea of his central role in modernist innovation with his promotional phrase "the Men of 1914" – the phrase which Kenner alludes to but does not mention – fudging the dates and extent of the Joyce–Eliot–Pound–Lewis acquaintance and productivity in order to associate them more closely with the Great War. In a sense, this received wisdom, Lewis gossip *par excellence,* originates in *Blasting and*

Bombardiering, the late masterstroke of modernist occupational portraiture. The painted portraits began earlier as part of an ironic theory of portraiture ironically conscious of the erosion of institutional values.

1910 AND/OR 1914

The last scandal of Lewis's career is so appropriately acrimonious, it is almost uncanny. In 1956, the Tate held the first major retrospective of his artwork, "Wyndham Lewis and Vorticism" ("Have had a big Retrospective Show Picture Exhibition at the Tate, with your portrait prominent, and greatly admired," he wrote Pound).[26] Vorticism being his most enduring artistic association in the mid-fifties, the exhibition did much to exploit its double billing – "Wyndham Lewis *and* Vorticism" – but it also did little to justify it. It ranged across his entire oeuvre, well beyond 1914 and the advertised framework, and included a perfunctory selection of "other vorticists," admitting co-signers of the vorticist manifesto like William Roberts, Henri Gaudier-Brzeska, and Edward Wadsworth as well as sundry members of the English avant-garde like David Bomberg, Frank Dobson, and E. McKnight Kauffer. The exhibition catalogue, which Lewis authored, belittled vorticism as such by explaining it in strictly personalized terms: "Vorticism, in fact, was what I, personally, did, and said, at a certain period."[27] As Richard Cork observes, Lewis's assessment is fundamentally duplicitous; it simultaneously marks vorticism as "a cooked-up art-political conspiracy, which does not deserve to be described as a movement at all" and takes all the credit for it.[28] In a single sentence, Lewis claims sole authorship of the vorticist movement and the interpretive privilege to disclaim its status as movement, at once owning and disowning it as a superseded tactical maneuver along the career of the single artist.[29]

William Roberts took particular exception to the version of English avant-garde fostered by Lewis and the Tate. To rebut their revisionism, he almost immediately published an indignant pamphlet called "The Resurrection of Vorticism and the Apotheosis of Wyndham Lewis" and eventually produced an even more definitive reproof in the form of a large group portrait, *The Vorticists at the Restaurant de la Tour Eiffel: Spring 1915* (see Figure 8).[30] The visual deployment of the modernist memoir, the portrait seeks to document Roberts' presence in the center of the London Vortex in the heady days of *Blast*. In the scene, the "other vorticists" – Pound, Wadsworth, Cuthbert Hamilton, Frederick Etchells, Jessica Dismorr, and Helen Saunders – join Lewis at the vorticist "cenacle" at the Restaurant de la Tour Eiffel to examine newly published copies of *Blast*.[31]

Figure 8 The vorticist cenacle: *The Vorticists at the Restaurant de la Tour Eiffel: Spring, 1915,*
by William Roberts, oil on canvas, 1961–2.

Lewis sits in the center of things, but it is the puce monster that organizes
both the gathering and the composition: its cover, the screeching pink of
the first number launched in summer 1914 (not the muted tan of the second
number issued the following year), is the first clue that Roberts is misdat-
ing his memories.[32] There are three copies of *Blast* in the painting – none,
strictly speaking, in the possession of Lewis. Etchells displays one to the
restaurant owner. Saunders comes through the door holding another under
her arm. Roberts himself, seated between Pound and Lewis, folds his hands
assuredly on a third, his belly pressed against the very cenacle itself. This is
my copy, he seems to be saying. I signed the manifesto, too. I was there for
the cooked-up art-political conspiracy and all the promotional networking.
And, to prove it, he cooks up an image of the cenacle in his post-vorticist
Légeresque figure style, commemorating (that is, affectionately mis-
remembering) himself among the familiar, apocryphal signs: the Restaurant

de la Tour Eiffel with its vorticist decorations, the goateed Pound with ziggurat haircut and walking-stick, the black-hatted and black-coated Lewis, and the bright puce monster emblazoned with its revolutionary typography.

This is surely the image fit for institutionalization and collective edification; not surprisingly, the portrait went almost directly from Roberts' easel into the Tate in 1962.[33] In fact, it does little to set the vorticist record straight; instead of challenging Lewis's promotional framework, it merely confirms the hypostasis of that framework by asserting Roberts' own role as an original consumer of vorticist publicity and propaganda circa 1914 rather than as a producer of vorticist aesthetic objects *per se*. In other words, he only confirms his role as a (re)producer of aesthetic publicity and propaganda. And *Blast* itself helped to generate this framework. Appearances of collective reaction aside (activities for which Lewis acts only as an editor), it is not accidental that *Blast* itself, in addition to the traditional publisher's colophon, is stamped with a discrete place of creative origin: "Copies may also be obtained from – MR. WYNDHAM LEWIS, Rebel Art Centre, 38, Great Ormond Street, Queen's Square, W. C. (Hours, 11. a.m. to 1 p.m.)."[34] At the center of the "Great London Vortex" is the Rebel Art Centre and at the center of the Centre is Wyndham Lewis. The *Blast* copies represented in Roberts' portrait already circulate in the economy of dissemination, because they have already left 38 Great Ormond Street. By commemorating a scene of dissemination rather than a scene of authorship, conceptualization, or production, Roberts elects to circumscribe himself within this circuit. The rebuttal to Lewis's sentence ("[v]orticism, in fact, was what I, personally, did, and said, at a certain period") amounts to little more than a recapitulation of the art-political conspiracy of *Blast* (cooked-up by Lewis in 1914). Notice the regulative nature of the *Blast* framework; it even organizes Roberts' resistance to Lewis hype. At this point, "vorticism" no longer prescribes permanent institutional violence, revealing instead its colors as a conditional ironic stance to existing modes of cultural presentation, a stance which has been institutionally integrated by the sixties. In effect, the institutions have learned to accommodate the modernist author function and the regulative protocols of modernist authorship.

Like Roberts, first- and second-order descriptions of modernism are habitually prepossessed – indeed structured – by conjecture about the *annus mirabilis* and the *anno mundi*. Which year witnessed the creation (the pinnacle? the undoing?) of the modernist world? Where to locate the split in time? 1909? 1910? 1914? 1922? 1928? Each designates a specific program of promotional augury and eschatology, a set of actors, episodes, portentous key texts, resonant world-historical turning points, and self-interested annalists. The whereabouts of modernist actors during these revolutionary scenes must be ascertained. The revolutionary calendars in turn inscribe themselves in scenes of modernist reading and not-reading. The practice not only requires strategic generalities, omissions, and wishful thinking; it also proceeds from a number of informal fallacies. Hasty Generalization: the revolutionary symptoms are too narrowly circumscribed, too much explanatory weight rests on a singular, temporal cause, and often too much cultural transformation is presupposed. The precision of the date identified belies the indefiniteness of the asserted changes. *Post hoc, ergo propter hoc*, the fallacy of mere temporal succession: the defining events in question come before other modernist events "therefore" they cause them. Complex Question: the question "When did the modernist revolution take place?" effectively resembles "When did you murder the defendant?"; the dubious character of the temporal break in itself goes without saying. And, in the same vein, False Dichotomy, perhaps the most typical case: the modernist temporal break either takes place in 1910 or it takes place in 1914, as if these two alternatives were jointly exhaustive.

As should be clear by now, 1914 signifies Wyndham Lewis's contribution to this brand of conjecture. Lewis's *Blast* was conceptualized as a revolutionary event, a violent calendric disruption to serve as a fixed framework for orienting subsequent cultural work. This is established even before its publication in July of 1914; advance advertisements that April foretold the "END OF THE CHRISTIAN ERA."[35] Following Lewis, 1914 indexes Pound, Eliot, and Joyce – that is, the major authorial axis of this book – and a host of promotional associations, which I will explain at length momentarily. By contrast, 1910 indexes Bloomsbury, but, like Lewis's "Men of 1914" comment, Virginia Woolf's "in or about December, 1910" organizes a whole way of seeing modernism. The phrase comes from "Mr. Bennett and Mrs. Brown" (1924). In this landmark essay, Woolf makes her famous "assertion" with notorious pseudo-precision:

in or about December, 1910, human character changed . . . All human relations have shifted – those between masters and servants, husbands and wives, parents and children. And when human relations change there is at the same time a change in religion, conduct, politics, and literature. Let us agree to place one of these changes about the year 1910.[36]

These sentences come early in the essay. Woolf keys the temporal break to certain changes in human relations, which entail changes in class, gender, and generational roles. These changes, in turn, inform more categorical change, namely to religion, conduct, politics, and literature, in other words, wholesale institutional change. Woolf puts human change ahead of institutional change, yet, throughout the essay, she gives the expression of human change a decidedly institutional character, associating it with disillusionment, impertinence, and outrage, that is, the very modes of expression that tend to disrupt preexisting institutions of religion, conduct, politics, and literature. The structure of feeling recalls Pound's observation in *Mauberley* that "[t]he age demanded an image / Of its accelerated grimace."[37]

It is significant that Woolf, writing from the perspective of 1924, places this temporal break four years before the Great War, the association crucial to the Lewis framework. Lewis underscores the link somewhat heavy-handedly in *Blasting and Bombardiering*, which opens with him being grilled about the subtleties of avant-garde praxis by a camp adjutant: "Are you serious when you call your picture *Break of Day – Marengo*? Or are you pulling the Public's leg?"[38] The implication here is that Lewis has disenchanted himself well in advance of his military betters. *Blast* anticipates trench cynicism: "the months immediately preceding the declaration of war were full of sound and fury, and . . . all the artists and men of letters had gone into action before the bank-clerks were clapped into khaki and dispatched to the land of Flanders Poppies to do their bit. Life was one big bloodless brawl, prior to the Great Bloodletting."[39] Inevitably – with the requisite quantum of indefinite precision – the link also bears on the narrative of Lewis's own lionization:

At some time during the six months that preceded the declaration of war, very suddenly, from a position of relative obscurity, I became extremely well-known. Roughly this coincided with the publication of *Blast*. I can remember no specific morning upon which I woke and found that this happened. But by August 1914 no newspaper was complete without news about "vorticism" and its arch-exponent Mr. Lewis.[40]

Taking cues from this very promotional work, some have lumped the violent rhetoric of Lewis's manifesto with the masculinist butchery acted out on Flanders' fields. The connection between "the vorticist reveling in violence in publications like *Blast*" and "the horror of the Great War" is thus read as a damning elective affinity.[41] One need not strain too hard to find evidence of blistering nationalism, misogyny, and homophobia in *Blast*. Still, even counting expressive connections between symbolic violence and physical carnage – acknowledging the materiality of symbolic violence, on the one hand, and the symbolic consequences of violence to bodies, on the other – it is worth discriminating between two functionally different uses of the rhetoric of violence. One proposes to destroy human relations in the name of national institutional integrity; the other proposes institutional violence to reintegrate human relations. *Blast*'s message, the second message, is far too critical of existing national institutions to be readily equated with facile patriotism and patriotic gore.

It is less that *Blast* anticipates the unprecedented violence to bodies on the battlefields than that it anticipates the unprecedented symbolic violence to British national institutions in the war's aftermath, the ritual murders of postwar disillusionment. Otherwise stated, Lewis's 1914 is "all of one piece" with the prewar patterns of oppositional culture that Miriam Hansen – drawing on George Dangerfield's *Strange Death of Liberal England* (1935) – identifies with the "large-scale dissatisfaction with liberal democracy," including suffragette militancy, the Orangemen agitation, and the strike movement: "What made Suffragettes, Orangemen and the labor movement . . . comparable . . . was their tendency to shift political action from the chambers of Parliament to streets, factories, courtrooms and secret meeting places."[42] As Hansen notes, these three coordinates share little ground politically, save one crucial commonality: their individual stances vis-à-vis national institutions presuppose "open display[s] of violence" and "unabashed calls to direct action."[43] The suffragette movement, in particular, employed a mode of symbolic violence that has obvious affinities with avant-gardist technique: the practice of impertinence calculated to offend. The signatures of militant suffragette protest – smashing windows, burning letter-boxes, slashing paintings in public museum space, and blasting assorted national assets and treasures like kiosks in Regent's Park and the pavilion at Kew Gardens – were designed to solicit attention and elicit "outrage." And "outrage" was the characteristic word equally applied to both suffragette and avant-garde activities by the suitably outraged mainstream national press. These family resemblances were no secret. So, it is no great revelation when Lewis writing in 1937 describes himself as a "literary militant" circa 1914; the connection was semi-conscious to begin with.

Before elaborating these connections further, let us establish that Woolf's 1910 does not represent a counter-narrative to Lewis's 1914. Woolf's vision is just as destructive as Lewis's. Moreover, it partly draws on the same source – the link between suffragette violence in the streets and avant-gardist aesthetic experimentation in galleries and books. Woolf describes the high points of the modern ("Georgian" as opposed to "Edwardian," to use her partitioning vocabulary) scene using language more or less directly borrowed from newspaper coverage of suffragette "outrages": "And so the smashing and the crashing began. Thus it is that we hear all round us, in poems and novels and biographies, even in newspaper articles and essays, the sound of breaking and falling, crashing and destruction."[44] Why not in newspaper articles first? Or else, the streets and other public spaces? Surely, the sounds of smashing and crashing, in late 1910 at least, were coming from these sites first, as the women's movement intensified into a campaign of destruction following the Black Friday riots in November.

Jane Goldman draws attention to the proximity of Woolf's temporal break and the massive police brutality and arrests in front of Westminster, noting that Woolf herself joined in a rally immediately prior to Black Friday at the Albert Hall.[45] Certainly, that Woolf's exegetic figure for transformed human relations is a middle-class (even "middlebrow") woman, one Mrs. Brown, a figure who comes to represent an entire class of revolutionary male modernists in Woolf's essay, lends some credence to Goldman's observation. Again, the connection with suffragette militancy presents itself in the manner by which modern artistic activity elicits "outrage," as demonstrated, for instance, in the following passage, quoted at length:

At whatever cost of life, limb, and damage to valuable property Mrs. Brown must be rescued, expressed, and set in her high relations to the world . . . And so the smashing and the crashing began. Thus it is that we hear all round us, in poems and novels and biographies, even in newspaper articles and essays, the sound of breaking and falling, crashing and destruction . . .

But, instead of being gloomy, I am sanguine. For this state of things is, I think, inevitable whenever from hoar old age or callow youth the convention ceases to be a means of communication between writer and reader, and becomes instead an obstacle and an impediment . . . The literary convention of the time is so artificial . . . that, naturally, the feeble are tempted to outrage, and the strong are led to destroy the very foundations and rules of literary society. Signs of this are everywhere apparent. Grammar is violated; syntax disintegrated; as a boy staying with an aunt for the weekend rolls in the geranium bed out of sheer desperation as the solemnities of the sabbath wear on. The more adult writers do not, of course, indulge in such wanton exhibitions of spleen. Their sincerity is desperate, and their courage tremendous; it is only that they do not know which to use, a fork or their fingers. Thus, if you read Mr. Joyce and Mr. Eliot you will be struck by the indecency of the one, and the obscurity of the other. Mr. Joyce's indecency in *Ulysses* seems to me the conscious and calculated indecency of a desperate man who feels that in order to breathe he must break the windows. At moments, when the window is broken, he is magnificent. But what a waste of energy! And, after all, how dull indecency is, when it is not the overflowing of a superabundant energy or savagery, but the determined and public-spirited act of a man who needs fresh air! Again, with the obscurity of Mr. Eliot. I think that Mr. Eliot has written some of the loveliest single lines in modern poetry. But how intolerant he is of the old usages and politenesses of society – respect for the weak, consideration for the dull! . . . For these reasons, then, we must reconcile ourselves to a season of failures and fragments. We must reflect that where so much strength is spent on finding a way of telling the truth, the truth itself is bound to reach us in rather an exhausted and chaotic condition. Ulysses, Queen Victoria, Mr. Prufrock – to give Mrs. Brown some of the names she has made famous lately – is a little pale and dishevelled by the time her rescuers reach her. And it is the sound of their axes that we hear – a vigorous and stimulating sound in my ears.[46]

The kind of insolence Woolf describes resembles the charge of cultural patricide that Arthur Waugh (a bona fide "Edwardian" himself) inveighs against "Mr. Prufrock" and Pound's *Catholic Anthology* in 1916 (discussed in chapter two). One detects a degree of Woolf's own class anxiety in her defense of literary innovation, especially when she discusses Joyce, but, on the whole, her "outrage" is rhetorical, following a rhetorical strategy of establishing common ground with her audience. Outrage is to be presumed, a presumption which gains extra significance in the context of smashing windows and the sound of axes. In effect, this passage displaces the militant suffragettes with the "Georgian" attack, transposing the outrages of the streets into book-covers.

The most familiar gloss of Woolf's "in or about December, 1910" reference is that it alludes to the outrages of gallery space, specifically Roger Fry's exhibition, "Manet and the Post-Impressionists," which opened in the Grafton galleries in November of that year. Although it included a smattering of Picassos and Matisses, the backbone of the collection consisted of Gauguins, Cézannes, and Van Goghs, paintings which, by continental standards, were twenty-five years past avant-garde credentials. Still, the exhibition sufficiently outraged British critics and the British public to justify its association with avant-gardism, the outrages in the streets, and Woolf's cut in time. As Goldman argues, "1910 is a critical moment in the interpenetration of these spheres [the suffragette-political and the modernist-aesthetic] when the art on the gallery walls was brought into dialogue with the political events on the streets outside."[47] The dialogue, however, is not fueled by an intrinsic affinity between the aesthetic program of the exhibition's curators and militant feminist tactics for political emancipation; rather, as Woolf all but points out herself, it is mediated by a shared pattern of response.

Those who come to jeer, in fact, make the implicit commonalities between the contents of the street, the gallery, and the book-covers discussable, as, for example, in the following reviewer's response:

[In a typical painting by Gauguin] hideous brown women, with purple hair and vitriolic faces, squat in the midst of a nightmare landscape . . . A revolution to be successful must presumably revolve; but, undeniably clever as they often are, the catherine-wheel antics of the Post-Impressionists are not likely to wake many responsive chords in British breasts.[48]

Ironically, this response suggests that the "post-impressionist" paintings do exactly that: they wake responsive chords. "Responsive" serves the reviewer as a marked term, meaning a sympathetic response; like suffragette violence, however, the rhetorical structure of the avant-garde exhibition signals that the "response" best serves as an unmarked term, meaning that either response – sympathy or outrage – signals the desired reaction. Fry apparently hung the paintings to become progressively more abstract so that, Laurence Binyon noted, "the shock of the revelation is only administered by degrees": "In the first room you scarcely needed to be uneasy; Manet reigns here, and Manet is already a classic; in the second room the temperature is more exciting, you are in the face of Gauguin and Van Gogh; and only when sufficiently acclimatized need you venture yet further into the wild realms of Matisse and his peers."[49] Consciously or unconsciously, the exhibition was engineered for the throngs of snorting visitors ("outraged philistines" was Fry's prevenient phrase), with whom it became permanently associated.

ELONGATED NOSES

Lewis did not participate in the first post-impressionist exhibition, but, like his contemporaries, he exhibited in its aftermath and thus registered its influences in promotional terms. According to one biographer, Lewis – from after the first Camden Town Group exhibition in June 1911 – collected vituperative notices as so many marks of distinction, anti-laurels earned, above all, for his commitment to figural distortion ("visitors may be shocked at the elongated noses in the squarely drawn heads by Mr. Wyndham Lewis," wrote *The Sunday Times*, for example).[50] Working in and around cubist idiom and futurist technological animus, he perfected an increasingly abstracted, bracingly anti-humanist visual idiolect, which, according to Tom Normand, "marked a clear separation between Lewis and even the most radical of his English contemporaries."[51] Jeffrey Meyers comments that this will to "total abstraction" alone signals Lewis's break with darlings of Bloomsbury like Duncan Grant who retained the "absolute bourgeois" backsliding of representational impressionism.[52] All the while, Lewis provocatively held *pro forma* to his commitment to portraiture. In an April 1914 interview with *The Daily News and Leader*, for example, he insists on the ultimate verisimilitude of *Laughing Woman*: "Although the forms of the figure and head perhaps look rather unlikely to you, they are more or less accurate, as representation. It was done from life."[53] If approaching abstraction, the aggressively grinning figure nevertheless defiantly demands to be recognized as a mask-like "jagged likeness" of Kate Lechmere (a chief "investor" in Lewis's prewar ventures, among other things).[54] This instance itself presents the hapless reviewer ready to praise or bury modern work on strictly formal grounds (early Lewis notices are overlaid with facile evaluations of colors, shapes, compositions, frames, canvas sizes) with yet another cause for outrage.[55] Even *Portrait of an Englishwoman* – the jagged composition of plinths and pillars reproduced in *Blast*, which comes, by critical consensus, at the height of his prewar abstractions – carries a title that suggests a stubbornly representational logic. As Normand argues, despite the stridency of the painting's abstraction, its couching as portraiture challenges received vocabularies of art criticism: "The 'portrait' was no longer to be concerned with the identity, psychology and personality of the individual sitter – instead the 'portrait' was an abstract statement concerning the abstraction 'humankind,' and its manifest destiny."[56] The specific reference of mock portraits of mocking women – particularly his *Portrait of an Englishwoman* presented as it was in the very center of *Blast* – returns us to the prewar public space, where the "manifest destiny" of British "womankind" was waking its responsive chords.

Like Woolf's manifesto-like assertions of 1924, *Blast*'s ties to suffragette militancy are well pronounced.[57] There is, for example, the "blessing" of two of the most prolifically destructive suffragettes, Lillian Lenton ("Lillie Lenton"), arrested for burning down the Kew Pavilion in February 1913, and Freda Graham ("Frieder Graham"), responsible for slashing five paintings in the National Gallery in May 1914.[58] An even more conspicuous reference comes toward the end of the issue, a broadside declaring vorticist sympathy for the suffragette cause:

TO SUFFRAGETTES.
A WORD OF ADVICE.
IN DESTRUCTION AS IN OTHER THINGS,
stick to what you understand.
WE MAKE YOU A PRESENT OF OUR VOTES.
ONLY LEAVE THE WORKS OF ART ALONE.
YOU MIGHT SOME DAY DESTROY A
GOOD PICTURE BY ACCIDENT.

THEN! –
MAIS SOYEZ BONNES FILLES!
NOUS VOUS AIMONS!
WE ADMIRE YOUR ENERGY. YOU AND ARTISTS
ARE THE ONLY THINGS (YOU DON'T MIND
BEING CALLED THINGS?) LEFT IN ENGLAND
WITH A LITTLE LIFE IN THEM.
IF YOU DESTROY A GREAT WORK OF ART you
are destroying a greater soul than if you
annihilated a whole district of London.
LEAVE ART ALONE, BRAVE COMRADES.[59]

As Janet Lyon observes, it is likely that this curious statement of an "anti-bourgeois alliance" was written during the climax of the suffragette gallery raids in May and June of 1914, raids conducted in protest against the inhumane treatment of suffragette prisoners in Holloway Gaol.[60] During the two months, twelve paintings were attacked – including three in the Royal Academy, five in the National Gallery, one in the National Portrait Gallery, and two in the Doré Galleries (the site of a number of significant avant-garde events, including the follow-up post-impressionist and futurist exhibition).[61] Nearly all the targets were figurative paintings. Lyon argues that the oddly combined admonition and endorsement of the vorticists effectively disenfranchise the suffragettes as political agitators, stripping them of the appellation of artists:

[I]n belittling and dismissing the (bourgeois) political aims of the Suffragettes, Lewis's avant-garde manifesto simultaneously enhances his own group's artistic claims to anti-bourgeois autonomy. Indeed, the manifesto embraces only the *formal* properties of the Suffragettes as they discursively reconstrued and compartmentalized in a carefully controlled militant alliance.[62]

Loosely translated: if you can't beat their tactics, steal their tactics, and then patronize their politics. In a similar vein, Paige Reynolds argues that the vorticists floated their offer of conditional solidarity in order to conceal their debts to their promotional militancy. They try to outflank the suffragettes by asserting the primacy of their claim to aesthetic originality.

These interpretations make sense, insofar as *Blast* co-opts much of its promotional strategy from militant suffragism, but only to a point; they do not account for the specific purchase of the vorticist co-optation. In other words: what draws Lewis to suffragette militancy? After all, despite Lyon's claims, the vorticists appear not to warrant suffragette activity as form but to endorse it as content. That is, they claim to support, however condescendingly, the political aims of women's suffrage and to disapprove, at least conditionally, of the formal means by which suffragettes design to achieve it. It is important to note, moreover, that this disapproval does not hinge on the destruction of art *per se*: Graham is blessed not blasted for terrorizing the National Gallery. Instead, the disapproval concerns the absolute sincerity that the painting-slashers bring to their targets. The specificity of this address becomes clear in light of the well-publicized explanations given by the perpetrators of the attacks. "Every night pictures by the greatest artist of all are being defaced in our streets," explained Graham at her arraignment.[63] These words echo Mary Richardson's even more widely disseminated statement made after she slashed the "Rokeby" Venus the previous March: "I have tried to destroy the picture of the most beautiful woman in mythological history as a protest against the government for destroying Mrs. Pankhurst, who is the most beautiful character in modern history."[64]

Richardson justifies her actions by equating the image she has destroyed with Emmeline Pankhurst, the imprisoned leader of the movement. This is her implied argument: no "beautiful women" should be exhibited in the nation's galleries when beautiful souls like Pankhurst are subjected to such destructive conditions. Graham raises the stakes of this metaphor, likening the insides of the nation's museums to the extremity of women outside in the nation's public spaces. For Graham, Richardson, and many of their apologists, the outrages in galleries, thus, become commensurable with the outrages in the streets.

The symbolism of the acts of protest relies on an absolute belief in the legitimate authority of galleries as national institutions. To destroy art represents a kind of nationally mediated self-abnegation. Lewis takes issue with precisely such justifications, when he frames the objection in the suffragette's vocabulary: "IF YOU DESTROY A GREAT WORK OF ART," he warns, "you are destroying a greater soul than if you annihilated a whole district of London." The suffragettes' error, from his point of view, is not the choice to destroy paintings *per se* but the choice not to choose which paintings deserve destruction. Blast "Thomas Carlyle" – slashed in the National Portrait Gallery in July – but, perhaps, bless "Henry James" – slashed in the Royal Academy in May. Blast "Rokeby." Bless "Portrait of an Englishwoman." A campaign of seemingly indiscriminate art destruction, in other words, begins, ends, and ultimately reinforces the very kind of perfunctory institutional authority that Lewis and company seek to undermine. Consequently, the relevant binarism – *pace* Lyon – is not between form and content but between deeds and words. Lewis, in effect, objects to the suffragettes' words, their self-justifications. Unlike

Blast, which poses objective targets for rhetorically heterodox violence, they propose orthodox rhetorical aspirations for precisely targeted objects. Almost without fail, these explanations depend on an always already sacralized notion of symbolic value, value guaranteed, as it were, by a framework of national institutions in which it is embedded. In their own words, at least, suffragettes seek little more than to substitute one sacred object for another (substituting Pankhurst as Venus for the "Rokeby" Venus). At last, Lewis opposes suffragette attacks against art for the same reason he blasts so much of the London museum establishment: its representational logic is obediently institutional. In effect, Lewis argues that there is no representational critique without institutional critique.

Rowena Fowler proposes that suffragettes attacked certain works of art because of "a proto-feminist awareness of the sexual politics of art and connoisseurship which we are only now able to recognize and to articulate."[65] The crucial qualification to this claim is that in 1914 this awareness is still politically unconscious. Even though paintings of female nudes and male celebrities are "obvious target[s] for a feminist attack," there are no words to articulate these attacks as feminist representational critique circa 1914. "Henry James" is not attacked because he represents an "overbearing image of male authority"; the perpetrator, Mary Wood, has no idea who James is (the irony of which the writer of "John Delavoy" no doubt appreciated).[66] Nevertheless, the rhetorical position is not without a subtle awareness of institutional power, for it aims to shift the struggle from the non-legitimized, public space outside in the streets to the hyper-legitimized, public space inside the gallery: "I have tried to destroy a valuable picture," Wood announces, "because I wish to show the public that they have no security for their property nor their art treasures until women are given political freedom."[67]

It is not surprising, then, that the perpetrators of these "outrages" make their political aims comparable – indeed, commensurable – with the objects they destroy. The newspapers stressed the monetary costs as property damage; suffragettes often responded in kind, arguing that the damage, in fact, would eventually serve to supplement the paintings' financial value by adding the symbolic patina of association with their cause.[68] Margaret Gibbs, for example, who attacked Millais' unfinished portrait of Carlyle in the National Portrait Gallery with a "butcher's cleaver," testified that now it "will have an added value and be of great historical interest because it has been honoured with the attentions of a militant."[69] Of the cases Fowler cites, none explicitly verbalizes either the subjects of the paintings or the paintings themselves as *deserving* of execration.

BLASTING AND BLESSING

The last among the gallery raids, the attack on Millais' unfinished portrait of Carlyle in the NPG, has a different resonance than the others. Even though Gibbs' *post facto* justification resembles the others, the deed is different in kind. Millais' unfinished portrait of Carlyle is not just another portrait. Given the instrumental role of Carlyle in the founding ideology of the NPG, his portrait's "victimization" in the NPG at the hands of suffragette violence demands special consideration. The portrait is – as Paul Barlow observes – "directly influenced by Carlyle's theory of authenticity."[70] Only the cragged features of his face are complete. His crisply realized, almost crumbling physiognomy hovers over the unfinished remainder – "twisted, agitated" hands, a suggestion of a walking stick, and a murky background.[71] For Barlow, the immediacy of this contrast typifies the Carlylean portraiture ideal:

> The paint itself acts out the unresolved meeting of the body of pigment with the body of the subject, itself a sign of the engagement of one personality with another. [. . .] The signs of common humanity, age, care, the body, are the very means by which the artist signals the encounter with the sitter. The viewer is encouraged to identify with mortality and physicality. The reality of bodily decay merges with the transcendent triumph of complex identity. This is the nearest portraiture can approach to Abbot Samson's devotion to both the mortal remains of St Edmund and to his undying spiritual presence.[72]

On these terms alone, Gibbs' destructive act defies the apparent lack of discrimination that occasioned Lewis's earlier disapproval. Add to this significance its placement inside the nationally sanctioned space for repositing a nationally sanctioning ideology of portraiture – ideology that the portrait itself exemplifies and that the portrait's sitter originated – the overdeterminacy is striking. Axing *this* portrait, one imagines, was no accident.

Goldman connects this particular "outrage" to Woolf's "in or about December, 1910" comments. In "Mr. Bennett and Mrs. Brown," immediately after introducing the idea of a shift in human relations, Woolf invokes the domestic misery of the "married life of the Carlyles": "bewail the waste, the futility for him and for her, of the horrible domestic tradition which made it seemly for a woman of genius to spend her time chasing beetles, scouring saucepans, instead of writing books."[73] Goldman speculates that Woolf's memories of temporal rupture in 1910 may have also registered the "suffragette scorn for Thomas Carlyle," which "result[ed] in" the outrages to Millais' unfinished portrait in 1914.[74] Causality, as we have seen, is even more shadowy than even this tentative speculation admits. Still, a more definitive point of reference establishes a precedent for suffragette interest in Carlyle's NPG portrait along the lines Goldman proposes: the "Famous Women" Pageant of the Women's Coronation Procession in June 1911. Dressed as famous women from history – among whom, "Mrs. Carlyle" – the suffragettes first marched and then held a rally in the Royal Albert Hall.[75] "The Historical Pageant of women," explained *Votes for Women*, "will not only be a wonderful sight from an artistic point of view, it will also be instructive: it will seize the imagination and suggest many trains of thought."[76] Like Woolf's reference to Jane Carlyle, recovering "the woman of genius" buried under a lifetime of futile domestic labors, the "Famous Women" Pageant works to recover a lost procession of female worthies. The rhetoric is of one piece with the NPG; it is self-evident that the calls for political emancipation and political representation entail analogous changes in the "Government of Heroes." The ideology of the NPG remains intact.

Goldman, like Fowler, reads suffragette violence as representational critique, which means, in the case of the Carlyle portrait, reading its destruction via an implicit substitution: the slashed canvas of the portrait signifies that this is where *a woman of genius should be.* For Goldman, this substitution connects Woolf with the suffragette militancy in the gallery circa 1914. Even if this interpretation is not borne out in the justifications of the suffragettes *per se*, there remains, nevertheless, as Fowler observes, an unarticulated undercurrent of representational critique to the attacks. This interpretation has a far more literal basis. Above all, it lies with the physical agency of the deeds in themselves: the penchant for axing "exposed flesh," "decapitating heads," and gouging out eyes. Here – in the anatomy of the attack, as it were – property damage against costly masterpieces becomes ritual murder of unclothed goddesses and eminent worthies. The *Times* coverage of the Carlyle attack registers this undercurrent when it describes the portrait's "mutilation": "One cut extends from just below the right eye to below the beard, another begins just above the head and passes through the left eye, while the third is on the extreme left of the forehead."[77] In the same sensationalistic vein: "The blows were delivered with lightning-like rapidity," writes *The Morning Chronicle*, "and before she could be restrained [she] made three large cuts on the face and head of the portrait."[78] The sub-text is entirely consonant with the institutional logic of portraiture, which derives, not without some irony, from Carlyle himself, but it deliberately turns this logic against itself. The specific murder of "Carlyle" *qua* the authentic encounter with the man of genius does violence to the very institution itself. Mutilating Carlyle seemingly represents a *coup d'état* in the National Portrait Gallery.

Lewis's reaction to the "blasting" of Carlyle's portrait is even more dimly lit than Woolf's presumed response. Unlike the "outrages" of May and June, the mutilation of "Carlyle" came in late July, after *Blast* went to press.[79] His positions vis-à-vis the NPG itself and Carlylean notions of portraiture were certainly antagonistic. As far as the former is concerned, he blasts Lionel Cust, its former director, along with the rest of the museum establishment in the opening pages of *Blast*. For the latter, I have already endeavored to demonstrate Lewis's particular take on the Carlylean portrait ideal, his will to transform, desacralize, and, "dehumanize" the encounter between viewers, artists, and sitters. We can only surmise whether the last outrage of the suffragettes met with his approval, but how could Lewis not approve of its possibilities as an institutional critique of portraiture?

PORTRAITURE REFIGURED

Critics have been at a loss to explain Lewis's turn from abstraction to celebrity portraiture after he was demobilized. It has been variously explained, usually in biographical, even humanistic terms: a personal crisis of abstraction occasioned by the devastation of the Great War, or his unfortunate necessity to do jobbing commissions at the expense of pure experimentation, or an obsequious need for sanction in the emerging, postwar arts and culture superstructure. Anyone who has read Lewis's late promotional memoirs – *Blasting and Bombardiering* and *Rude Assignment* – will not be surprised to learn that Lewis himself both originates and summarily dismisses all three explanations. In his first exhibition catalogue after the war, he explains that the turn from "vexing diagrams" to "eyes and noses" is not merely a sop to a public craving recognizable figure styles. It is rather a rejection of the formalist cant of Fry and Bell that the movement from verisimilitude to "fundamentals of design or colour" represents a process of aesthetic self-purification.[80] Instead, Lewis proposes a rubric of modern art that holds the continuum of his efforts – prewar and postwar, abstract and representational, naturalistic and nonobjective, visual and literary: the modern artist himself signifies the ultimate aesthetic horizon. Lewis's ideal public looks upon solid bits of eyes and noses not to reassemble them as physiognomy. Rather, it looks at eyes and noses in their dissemblance, and here finds the Artist. All figurative painting then – not merely portraiture strictly defined – amounts to a kind of self-portraiture. The process so crucial to the Carlylean experience of the NPG – the transference from viewer to artist to sitter – is effectively short-circuited. Leading up to the war, this idiosyncratic take on portraiture is a consistent part of Lewis's aesthetic output, even at the height of his attempts at abstraction; after the war, it becomes its very cornerstone.

In the twenties and thirties, Lewis produces portraits – images of his benefactors, modernist contemporaries, and the "Men of 1914," especially – at a surprising clip.[81] In the early twenties, as Pound, Eliot, and Joyce produced their most renowned literary works, Lewis produced the drawings of Pound, Eliot, and Joyce that have achieved near "permanent association" (to recall Eliot's phrase of chapter three) with the "Men of 1914" – now endlessly reproduced on postcards and interleaved in modernism's bibliographic record. The circulation of Lewis's modernist portraits – and the NPG portraiture ideology they entailed – served a generation of modernist critics with its promotional marching orders. Hugh Kenner, for example, comments that the pose of Pound reclining in Lewis's 1939 portrait is "utterly characteristic" (see Figure 9).[82] His description of the portrait is absolute Carlyle – inserting Lewis and Pound into the framework of Abbot Samson and St. Edmund:

Ezra Pound is at ease; he seems asleep . . . There is no trace of a mask; the head is solid, understood in three dimensions and stated without simplification. The iconography is casual and exact: a folded newspaper on the table beside the poet who had grown so concerned with newspaper events; three objets d'art – unused ash-trays – one crystalline, one with a dragon emblem, implying glazes and translucencies of vision and language, polarized toward the Orient; in the background, Odysseus' vast sea, but a painted sea; not only painted but represented as being a painting, since the nailheads that hold the canvas to its stretcher run metrically down its left side. And amid artifacts – nothing but an art-world is visible – the man before us dreams, drawn into what he once called "the obscure reveries of the inward gaze," the posture relaxed, the face at ease but intent. There are many ways for a face to be at ease, and this face's way is neither congealed nor vapid. The massive body runs diagonally across the canvas (imagine Dante being painted so!)[. . .] The pose, as it happens, is utterly characteristic; a casual camera in Rapallo reproduced it twenty-five years later. The mounting hair, the majestic forehead, the nose, restate one another's contours; the beard is not a disguise but the face's final cachet of authority, trimmed and asserted on the nearly vertical plane of the lower face.[83]

Kenner's reading not only praises Lewis's ability to capture the essence of Pound's mortal remains, but it also attempts to relive it. Kenner sees (or wills himself to see) the physiognomy of the "authentic" Pound through the artist's eyes (and then imitates the ecstatic experience on his own, via a snap-shot during Kenner's audience with the great man in Rapallo).

Figure 9   Ezra Pound by Wyndham Lewis, oil on canvas, 1939.

Stunningly like un-restructured Carlylean hero-worship, Kenner's narrative
may not be exactly what Lewis had in mind when he set out to combat the
institutional mechanisms of portraiture in or about 1914, but it is entirely of
one piece with Lewis's promotional push after 1914 to remake the London
museum establishment as a *de facto* modernist portrait gallery.

Yet, this eager embrace of Carlylean portraiture ideology should not be
seen as modernist backsliding, because the encounter with Pound is uncan-
nily dehumanized: a survey of ashtrays, mounting hair, and the authentic
massively recumbent pose. These are, in short, the fragments of Lewis's
eyes and noses rather than the unifying connections of Carlyle's toes.
The authenticating factor is the piecemeal detritus of Pound's pre-formed
celebrity; Kenner goes to meet Pound himself in Rapallo and is pleased to
find all the requisite promotional iconography confirmed. Celebrity is no
longer taken with absolute sincerity, the transcendental signifier of an undy-
ing national-spiritual presence; rather, it becomes yet another hypostatic
and reified signature of prominent personality, a literary-artistic semaphore
for both Lewis and Kenner to jack up and popularize. Kenner is a singularly
more acceptable curator of famous portraits than Lionel Cust, and perhaps

this was at least partly the aim: to install an arts and culture establishment more attentive to and compatible with modern work . . . and modernist imprimaturs. Finally, it is Kenner's promotional self-awareness that signals his continuum with Lewis. Each viewer becomes his own portraitist, creating his own transformative frisson as so many trips to the postcard racks.

In *Thirty Personalities and a Self-Portrait*, a folio of lithographs published in 1932, Lewis constructs his own virtual NPG of "miscellaneous heads": among others Anthony Asquith, Stella Benson, Meyrick Booth, G. K. Chesterton, Noël Coward, Augustus John, James Joyce, David Low, Rebecca West, and, above all, with suitable billing, Lewis himself. "There is no selective design," he writes,

> except that every unit of this big bag of thirty is in some way remarkable, I think, and worthy of a place in the home of even the most particular head-hunter . . . The militant feminist Stella Benson alphabetically embraces our only great anti-feminist, Dr. Meyrick Booth. I have not planned these paradoxes; it is just as it happened.[84]

Having long abandoned the leveling destructions and sanctifications of *Blast*, he puts militant feminists and anti-feminists side-by-side. Both share in the seemingly content-free distinction of being "in some way remarkable," aridly echoing the NPG's original mandate, after the possibility of denoting eminence is long foreclosed. The main difference, perhaps, between Lewis's "big bag of thirty" and the NPG's collection of 400 postcards published the same year is Lewis's audacious claim that his exemplars represent "units," making the promotional intentions plain: thirty "units" and one Artist.

When Lewis tries his own hand at the set-pieces of Carlylean portrait interpretation in the preface, it takes on the cast of parody, communicating strictly with degraded celebrity semaphores: "the lionesque splendours of the august countenance of Augustus John"; "the hollow hatchet of the face of Mr. Joyce"; "the mongoloid woodenness of the excellent mime and wit, Noel Coward"; and so on. "I move with a familiarity natural to me amongst eyeless and hairless abstractions," he writes, "but I am also interested in human beings." Lewis's late portraits are, in his own words, "likenesses of people [for whom] elementary structure must be infinitely supplemented by the details of features and the planes proper to the particular head – marking it off from all other heads."[85] For Lewis, in other words, these units are strictly speaking no more and no less than so many incrementally differentiated commodities at different stages of wear – and, in this regard, he understands their promotional work at least as well as the marketing director of the NPG today – even if the work is put to different ends. Lewis's interventions in the struggles over instrumental celebrity do not prevent scenes like his own embarrassment as institutional sycophant in the pages of *Time* but they do help explain celebrity culture's continued discomfort with modernists – Virginia Woolf included.[86] Among other things, the big bag of thirty heads is an obvious play on numismatics, coin collecting: the modernist's big bag of worn coins. At the beginning of this book, I proposed something akin to this as a way to refigure the cunning of modernism's existing claims on the flows of cultural value and reputation. The happy possessor organizes reputations . . . now by size, now by date, now by gender, now by profession, now by politics, now by nationality, and now, last, the defining work, by their commemorative withdrawal from mass circulation.[87]

Epilogue

In his later years, on the wall in his private study beside framed portraits of Paul Valéry, W. B. Yeats, and J. W. Goethe, T. S. Eliot kept a framed head-shot of Groucho Marx.[1] The idea of "Groucho" interspersed among the literary giants over Eliot's work-desk provides a negative of the image with which this book began – the photograph of Marilyn Monroe reading James Joyce. This time, high trades on low: "Groucho" is the literary-biographical factoid that confirms "the Possum" as an object ordinary enough for popular tastes. Granted the selection of the "literary Marx brother" for the function of covert prestige is debatable. The sign of "Groucho" is "high" enough by mid-century to sanction it for elite con-sumption, but isn't that after all the point? The esoteric poet of record reveals himself to be a discriminating connoisseur of mass entertainments. In other situations and quarters of elite culture, the paradigmatic enthusi-asms will be detective fiction, certain genres of popular jazz, comic strips, and other *guilty pleasures* and elite *causes célèbres*. The very idea of a "private" Eliotic hall of fame – an actual collection of portraits hung in his study – returns us to the "Hall of Fame" spreads printed in British *Vogue* in the mid-twenties in which portraits and cameos of the likes of Eliot, Stein, Picasso, Einstein, and Freud were interspersed with heads of Charlie Chaplin, Noël Coward, and Grock.[2] When the Groucho–Eliot factoid appears on the *New York Times* obituary page, the frisson is reversed. Eliot is transferred onto the menus of popular consumption: "He also kept a signed photograph of Groucho Marx, cigar protuberant, in his study at home."[3] We only know about the "Groucho" portrait because of its status as a well-heeled anecdote of modernist promotion (as opposed to, say, the mass publicity dimensions of the Joycean imprimatur used by Monroe, *Esquire*, and company). Its existence as such is supported by the layers of apocryphal tissue seen before – anecdotes, letters, memoirs, obituaries – promotional genres of a sort which alone should signal that there is nothing private about the placement of "Groucho" in the Possum's inner sanctum. By mid-century, the Hall of Fame shakes hands with the Galaxy of Stars.

The pair, it turns out, shared a keen regard for one another's reputations, exchanging letters and celebrity photos in the early sixties, right before Eliot's death. As a correspondent, Eliot ends up lending intellectual prestige to Groucho's collected letters; as a photo, Groucho ends up lending covert prestige to Eliot's apocryphal mantelpiece. At first blush, however, their relationship was hampered by awkwardness about modes of address. What should the lowbrow television and former movie star – known by his humorous stage name – call the highbrow Nobel laureate and modernist apotheosis of two initials – and vice-versa? In *The Dialectic of Enlightenment*, Adorno and Horkheimer write that the flux of high and low that comes with late modernity resolves into a confusion of addresses between the public and the aesthetic: "Formerly, like Kant and Hume, [artists] signed their letters 'Your most humble and obedient servant,' and undermined the foundations of throne and altar. Today they address heads of government by their first names, yet in every activity they are subject to their illiterate masters."[4] Early in their correspondence, perhaps as a matter of form, Eliot and Groucho gingerly address each other with full names: Groucho calls Eliot "T. S. Eliot," and Eliot calls Groucho "Groucho Marx." In 1963, however, Groucho suddenly lapses, addressing Eliot as "Mr. Eliot," and Eliot writes back to say that he finds this development unacceptable:

> It seems more of an impertinence to address Groucho Marx as "Dear Mr. Marx" than it would be to address any other celebrity by his first name. It is out of respect, my dear Groucho, that I address you as I do. I should only be too happy to have a letter from Groucho Marx beginning "Dear T. S. E."[5]

Eliot's excuse for calling Groucho "Groucho" is worth pausing over, for it comes from a desire not to reduce formality but to maintain it.

Eliot's comments indicate that he knows well that respecting "Groucho" does not mean respecting conventions of social propriety ordinarily construed; it means, instead, upholding his currency. That Eliot wanted Groucho to call him "T. S. E." indicates not so much that Eliot wished close acquaintances to call him "T. S. E." – though this may have been true – but that he envisioned the marker "T. S. E." circulating with "Groucho" in one economy. By the 1960s, we find the modernist and the popular partaking in a continuous logic. In a sense, the ease of cross-over between Groucho's star image and T. S. E.'s textual imprimatur in the mid-sixties is the problem that inspired this book. Some fifty years earlier, exchange rates between the cultural economies of the popular and the elite were less self-evident. In fact, the very possibility of doing elite cultural work was in a bad way – at least, this is what still incipient modernists liked to tell themselves. In London in 1915, when the young Eliot asked Pound to write that testimonial to his father about his prospective career choice, there was no sense that deliberately "unpopular writing" could provide any compensable work whatever. Modernists found a loophole. Against the prevailing view that literary life was no occupation, modernists made ostensibly unpopular writing both materially possible and culturally defining by exploiting a form of value speculating in imprimaturs. This surplus of elite cultural authority is, in fact, dependent on a legion of generative promotional and otherwise literary labors that are, to quote Barthes, "apparently most unlike literature," but only apparently.[6]

In "The Task of the Translator," Benjamin likens the source text to a fragment of a broken vessel. To envision a complete work, he suggests, try to imagine all the fragments, of which the source text is but one, glued back together: all actual, possible, and potential versions "restored" into "a greater language," a hypothetical, impossible mode of signification.[7] In this vein, it may be possible, as I have endeavored in this book, to conceptualize the modernist text in a radically more just framework, modernist work – masterworks, commentaries, interpretations, layers of promotional tissue, worn coins of authorship – refigured as the impossibly cosmopolitan object from which the fragmentary modernist masterpiece before you – on your desk, on your bookshelf, in your head – has been splintered.

I continue to have impossible cosmopolitan visions, a transcendental Left Bank in my suburbia. In a Barnes and Noble café in a nondescript strip-mall, I sit drinking Starbucks coffee and find myself admonished once again by two of the visionary figures of this book, T. S. Eliot and James Joyce. The pair of modernists watch me from a mural of thirty literary worthies pried from their works and the particulars of context, history, and geography and inserted in a pseudo-Parisian sidewalk tableau, another incarnation of the literary Hall of Fame, diagrammatically distorting authorship and literary work. I have seen the mural before; a version of it rings every Barnes and Noble café I've been to.[8] A wine-drinking Joyce is sitting *al fresco* with an anonymous woman. Could it be Nora, I wonder? He is being nudged by the elbow of Nabokov, cleaning his glasses at another table. Orwell looks on. Elsewhere in this long visionary cenacle, Eliot cracks a book. No cheese board on offer, apparently. Is he reviewing submissions for Faber? He sits with Faulkner and Steinbeck. Is he reading aloud to these improbable luncheon companions?

Modernists are well represented; at least a third of the total by my count. Still, Pound and Lewis, the other Men of 1914, do not make the cut.

Perhaps they are remanded somewhere in Washington, D.C., or Toronto. A hunch tells me their executors were not approached. Were Pound and Lewis ignored for their politics? obscurity? obscure politics? As might be expected, the modernist others of this book are also missing: Edith Sitwell, Djuna Barnes, Mina Loy, Marianne Moore, Sylvia Beach are all absent, but then so are Samuel Beckett, Gertrude Stein, Wallace Stevens, Joseph Conrad, Ford Madox Ford, E. M. Forster, H. D., William Carlos Williams, Jean Toomer, e. e. cummings, Nathaniel West, Aldous Huxley, Rebecca West, and Hart Crane. Henry James is there. Yeats and Auden are obvious choices for inclusion, but they are missing, too. Did their executors withhold permission? Who else might refuse royalties from the book and coffee trade? Virginia Woolf *is* present; her visionary presence could not be denied, it seems, even if her face is partially occluded by ductwork. And, where, for that matter, is D. H. Lawrence? I've seen him in other versions of this mural, including the one on offer that decorates a coffee mug (see Figure 10).

If visionary figures admonish us, are they admonishing us to buy their books? Are the sales of *Moby Dick* the better for Melville's presence in the mural? What about the sales of Tagore? Are the figures admonishing us to buy each other's books? Read more Zora Neale Hurston, says Isaac Bashevis Singer. Read more Anthony Trollope, says Ernest Hemingway. Call up old Thomas Hardy and ask him what he thinks of J. D. Salinger. In *Aspects of the Novel* (1927), Forster asks us

to visualize the English novelists . . . as seated together in a room, a circular room, a sort of British Museum reading-room – all writing their novels simultaneously. They do not, as they sit there, think "I live under Queen Victoria, I under Anne, I carry on the tradition of Trollope, I am reacting against Aldous Huxley." The fact that their pens are in their hands is far more vivid to them. They are half mesmerized, their sorrows and joys are pouring out through ink, they are approximated by the act of creation, and when Professor Oliver Elton says, as he does, "after 1847 the novel of passion was never to be the same again," none of them understand what he means. That is to be our vision of them – an imperfect vision, but it is suited to our powers, it will preserve us from a serious danger, the danger of pseudo-scholarship.[9]

What do books want? he asks. Forster's answer: they want us to dwell with their half-mesmerized authors. They want us to "look over their shoulders" as the books are being written.[10] His pseudo-scholar – like the "savage tribes" who eat books, he says – does not know that a book wants to be read in this way ("he is moving round books instead of through them, he either has not read them or cannot read them properly"): "The reader must sit down alone and struggle with the writer, and this the pseudo-scholar

Figure 10 Barnes and Noble mural mug.

will not do. He would rather relate a book to the history of its time, to events in the life of its author, to the events it describes, above all to some tendency."[11]

Indeed, it may be exactly the opposite of what Forster says; by all odds, books today may *not* want to be read, hence the feelings of "struggle" with the "geniuses" who make them.[12] In Thomas M. Disch's story, "The Man Who Read a Book," the only readers left are subsidized by a special government agency: "no one *wants* to read books [but] it's a job, isn't it?"[13] Hence: the desperate, messianic hopes that followed talk show host Oprah Winfrey's decision in 2002 to fold her monthly book club.[14] Reporting the news with its usual homey sapience, *Time* pompously and not entirely facetiously rates Oprah's Book Club as the third most significant development in the history of writing, to follow only the printing press and the invention of writing itself: "In a nation where reading serious fiction is always in danger of becoming a specialized pursuit, something like playing the dulcimer . . . [with] 26 million U.S. viewers a week [Oprah has] made reading nearly as popular as professional wrestling."[15] Fittingly, Winfrey cites reasons of literary scarcity for her departure: "It has become harder and harder to find books on a monthly basis that I feel absolutely compelled to share." As I have endeavored to show in this book, utopian and dystopian fantasies of the single literary artifact as a sublime object of monumental inapproachability depend on the strategic effacement of a whole host of other texts, secondary reading operations, and scenes of reading. Forster's *idée fixe*, "all the novelists writing their novels at once," frees us from the so-called "accidents" of relevant context: "They come from different ages and ranks, they have different temperaments and aims, but they all hold pens in their hands, and are in the process of creation."[16] Without history, geography, class, and culture – and, above all, without promotion – reputation appears once again as a spectral form, a form which only appears as a state of inexorable erosion.

There are two prevailing selection principles at work in the mural of visionary authors. First, there is second-order fame – i.e., celebrity, knownness, being famous for being famous. Twain wears his white suit; Eliot, his four-piece one; Joyce, hat and high prescription glasses; Wilde, velvet suit and floppy tie. Second, there are the gestures of representation, that the literary hero-archy must at all costs appear inclusive, even if, in truth, there are a majority of male geniuses, a quorum of modernists, a preponderance of Anglophones, and only one face from outside the Euro-American world. The gesture certainly does not extend to middlebrow and lowbrow authors (save Chandler, long rated a highbrow enthusiasm). There are no representative romance novelists, military historians, or authors of coffee-table books. Yet, judging from their prominence on display tables, I doubt the oversight is much dampening sales. Thus, the message of this collection of visionary figures may be even more banal than my previous queries have implied. On some level, the visionary figures support the most worn of all worn coins, the exhortation to read, a message for which the actual work of the thirty figures on the mural is all but incidental. Read! Read something, read anything, but do please read! If the occasional customer picks up a copy of *To the Lighthouse* great, but then it doesn't really matter, for the exhortation, after all, really amounts to an exhortation to buy, buy, buy. Like the NPG gift-shop, the low trades on the high. As the rearguard mousemats and refrigerator magnets come up behind the avant-garde novels and critiques, so too, the stern glances of George Eliot and Langston Hughes may help move ceramic mugs, calendars, and lifestyle magazines. The imprimaturs of the visionary figures – Oprah included – grease the wheels of a giant accountancy, where, paradoxically – as *Time* tells us – "profits are narrow" despite a surfeit of "hungry mouths to feed."[17]

Notes

INTRODUCTION

1 Walter Benjamin, "Einbahnstraße," in Tillman Rexroth, ed., *Kleine Prosa Baudelaire-Übertragungen, Gesammelte Schriften* 4.1 (Frankfurt: Suhrkamp, 1991), 107.

2 Eve Arnold, *Marilyn Monroe: An Appreciation* (New York: Knopf, 1987), 42. On the photograph's significance for Joyce studies, see Richard Brown, "Marilyn Monroe Reading *Ulysses*: Goddess or Post-Cultural Cyborg," in R. B. Kershner, ed., *Joyce and Popular Culture* (Gainesville: University Press of Florida, 1996), 170–9.

3 For a related point, see Franco Moretti, "The Slaughterhouse of Literature," *MLQ* 61.1 (March 2000), 207–27.

4 Roger Kimball, "Barometer Falling," *First Things* 92 (April 1999), 56.

5 *Ibid.*, 53.

6 *Ibid.*, 56.

7 *Ibid.*

8 Lawrence Rainey, *Institutions of Modernism: Literary Elites and Public Culture* (London: Yale University Press, 1998), 6.

9 Kimball, "Barometer," 52.

10 Rainey, *Institutions*, 4.

11 Roger Kimball, "A Craving for Reality: T. S. Eliot Today," *The New Criterion* 18.2 (October 1999) <http://www.newcriterion.com/archive/18/ct99/eliot.htm>.

12 T. S. Eliot, *The Letters of T. S. Eliot*, Eliot, Valerie, ed. (London: Faber and Faber, 1988), 103.

13 *Ibid.*, 99.

14 Raymond Williams, "Culture Is Ordinary," in Robin Gable, ed., *Resources of Hope: Culture, Democracy, Socialism* (London: Verso, 1989), 4. On the respective case for and against a modernist Williams, see Tony Pinkney, "Raymond Williams and the 'Two Faces of Modernism,'" in Terry Eagleton, ed., *Raymond Williams: Critical Perspectives* (Boston: Northeastern University Press, 1989), 12–33, and John Higgins, *Raymond Williams: Literature, Marxism and Cultural Materialism* (London: Routledge, 1999). For my purposes, the early formula *culture is ordinary* places Williams squarely in a framework of "existing" modernism, namely revaluation, the task of trying to make "arts and learning"

possible in an increasingly instrumentalized modern world. The difference here
between Williams and Leavis – the difference that makes all the difference, I
suppose – is Williams' insistence that the production of culture in the second
sense not be merely a minority concern.

15 Cf. Barbara Herrnstein Smith, *Contingencies of Value: Alternative Perspectives
for Critical Theory* (Cambridge: Harvard University Press, 1988), 17–29. Smith
argues that – excepting Leavis – evaluation as a formal enterprise is banished
from the kingdom of academic English by mid-century. This makes sense but
should not obscure the point – a point that Smith herself makes elsewhere –
that implicit evaluative practices are legion both outside and inside academia.
It may be more accurate to say that evaluation becomes regulative rather than
constitutive – at least, until feminist critics begin a conscious process of second-
wave revaluation in the 1970s.

16 Eliot, *Letters*, 103.

17 Quoted in Kimball, "Craving."

18 For the bearings of the "bibliographic code" on some of these issues, see George
Bornstein, *Material Modernism: The Politics of the Page* (Cambridge: Cambridge
University Press, 2001).

19 This critical turn owes much to Pierre Bourdieu, *Distinction* (Cambridge:
Harvard University Press, 1984) and *The Field of Cultural Production* (New
York: Columbia University Press, 1993). Useful local examples include Rainey's
work; Jennifer Wickes's *Advertising Fictions* (New York: Columbia University
Press, 1988); Mark Morrison's *Public Face of Modernism* (Madison: Univer-
sity of Wisconsin Press, 2000); the essays collected in Patrick Brantlinger and
James Naremore's *Modernism and Mass Culture* (Bloomington: Indiana University Press, 1991), in Kevin Dettmar and Stephen Watt's *Marketing Modernisms* (Ann Arbor: University of Michigan Press, 1996), and in Jani Scandura
and Michael Thurston's *Modernism, Inc.* (New York: New York University
Press, 2001); as well as such essential single artist/author studies as Michael
FitzGerald's *Making Modernism: Picasso and the Creation of the Market for Twentieth Century Art* (Berkeley: University of California Press, 1996), John Rod-
den's *The Politics of Literary Reputation: The Making and Claiming of St. George
Orwell* (Oxford: Oxford University Press, 1990), Lawrence Schwartz's *Creating
Faulkner's Reputation: The Politics of Modern Literary Criticism* (Knoxville: University of Tennessee Press, 1988), and Pierre Bourdieu's work on Heidegger in
The Political Ontology of Martin Heidegger (Stanford: Stanford University Press,
1991) and on Flaubert in *The Rules of Art* (Stanford: Stanford University Press,
1996).

20 Along with Bourdieu, *The Rules of Art*, see Brian Cosgrove, "Flaubert, Schlegel,
Nietzsche: Joyce and Some European Precursors," *Miscelánea* 20 (1999),
193–207. Cosgrove also connects this archly modernist image to Lukács's idea
of the "'self-surmounting' of subjectivity," "that irony is not only a revelation
of the problematic disjunction between subjective aspiration and recalcitrant
fact, but is equally, in the form of willed authorial detachment, the counter-
strategy initiated by the novelist against the perceived problem of 'immanent

meaninglessness'" (194). For many of the modernist value effects I discuss, Bourdieu establishes Flaubert's Paris as a decisive antecedent; the same for Baudelaire's Paris in Walter Benjamin, *The Arcades Project*, trans. Howard Eiland and Kevin McLaughlin (Cambridge: Harvard University Press, 1999), 228–387. Whether such correspondences come from genealogy (shadows of Flaubert and Baudelaire into Anglo-American modernism) or homology (the uneven development of a cultural system first manifest in Paris) is beyond my purview here.

21 Ezra Pound, "On Criticism in General," *The Criterion* 1.2 (January 1923), 147–8.

22 Robert McAlmon, *Being Geniuses Together: An Autobiography* (London: Secker and Warburg, 1938), 5.

23 Jean-Joseph Goux, *Symbolic Economies after Marx and Freud* (Ithaca: Cornell University Press, 1990), 10.

24 For this sort of axiological pragmatism, see Smith, *Contingencies*.

25 Friedrich Nietzsche, "On Truth and Falsity in their Extramoral Sense," in Reinhold Grimm and Caroline Molina y Vedia, eds., *Philosophical Writings* (New York: Continuum, 1995), 92.

26 On the exceptions, particularly Georges Bataille, see Arkady Plotnitsky, *Reconfigurations* (Gainesville: University Press of Florida, 1993), 3–61.

27 See Leo Braudy, *The Frenzy of Renown* (Oxford: Oxford University Press, 1986), 103–6: "When the leader wanted to change his public imagery, he changed his coinage. Coins helped to legitimize power both by asserting the financial solidity of those who issued them and by furnishing a set of recognizable symbols of their authority" (103). Whereas Braudy's is the classic study of fame – the magisterial thematic history from antiquity to the present, the definitive treatment of celebrity – a cultural studies analysis of Hollywood's celestial mechanics is Richard Dyer's *Stars* (London: British Film Institute, 1979).

28 See Thomas Crow, *Modern Art in Common Culture* (New Haven: Yale University Press, 1996). Particularly relevant is his sense that "modernist negation – which is modernist in its most powerful moments – proceeds from a productive confusion within the normal hierarchy of cultural prestige" (33).

29 Peter Osborne, *Philosophy in Cultural Theory* (New York: Routledge, 2000), 18–19.

30 John Harwood, *Eliot to Derrida: The Poverty of Interpretation* (Basingstoke: Macmillan, 1995), 13.

31 Jennifer Birkett and Stan Smith, "Introduction: Modernism's Comings and Goings," *Miscelánea* 20 (1999), 20; and Stan Smith, "Lineages of 'Modernism,' or: How They Brought the Good News from Nashville to Oxford," *Miscelánea* 20 (1999), 35.

32 My contention, then, is that, in certain terms, the idea of "historical modernism" amounts to a failure to think historically.

33 John Frow, *Cultural Studies and Cultural Value* (Oxford: Oxford University Press, 1995), 1.

34 Harold Perkin, *The Rise of Professional Society: England since 1880* (New York: Routledge, 1989). For Perkin, professionals are less class actors than special agents embodying the regulative principle of career hierarchy – "the right to a flow of income," "acknowledged and legitimated claim(s) to other people's labor" – throughout the social system (7).

35 Frow, *Cultural Studies*, 128. See also Perkin, *Rise of Professional Society*, 2–16. For the relationship between the "canon debates" and these issues, see especially John Guillory, *Cultural Capital: The Problem of Literary Canon Formation* (Chicago: University of Chicago Press, 1993). I am less interested here in the status of cultural capital as class vesting instrument and its connection to the problem of "canon" (well covered by Bourdieu, Guillory, Smith, and others) than in the concept's more explicit bearings in terms of cultural labor, surplus value, and the social infiltration of hierarchy and scarcity.

36 See Frow, on this and other inconsistencies in Bourdieu's economics. Also see John Guillory, "Bourdieu's Refusal" and Jon Beasley-Murray, "Value and Capital in Bourdieu and Marx," in Nicholas Brown and Imre Szeman, eds., *Pierre Bourdieu: Fieldwork in Culture* (New York: Rowman and Littlefield, 2000).

37 Frow, *Cultural Studies*, 127.

38 On "the anomalous status of high culture," see Frow, *Cultural Studies*, 14.

39 See Frow, *Cultural Studies*, 95–6. Here, I am also thinking of Benjamin, *Arcades*, 460: "Historical 'understanding' is to be grasped, in principle, as an afterlife of that which is understood; and what has been recognized in the analysis of the 'after-life of works,' in the analysis of 'fame,' is therefore to be considered the foundation of history in general."

40 I. A. Richards, "On T. S. E.," *Sewanee Review* 74.1 (January–March 1966), 21–2.

41 Stephen Spender, "Remembering Eliot," *Sewanee Review* 74.1 (January–March 1966), 77. For more about Forster's stakes as a visionary other, see my epilogue, pp. 202–3.

42 Adam Parkes, "'How Visionary Figures Admonish Us': Virginia Woolf and Roger Fry" (paper presented at the MSA 3: Conference of the Modernist Studies Association, Rice University, Houston, Tex., 13 October 2001), 2.

43 7 August 1939; Virginia Woolf, *The Diary of Virginia Woolf*, vol. V, Anne Olivier Bell, ed. (New York: Harcourt, Brace, Jovanovich, 1984), 229.

44 For the expressive precedent in Baudelaire, see the tissue of citations traced in Benjamin, *Arcades*, 228ff.

45 On Mansfield's role as a visionary other for Woolf, see especially Andrew Bennett, "Hating Katherine Mansfield," *Angelaki* 7.3 (December 2002), 3–16.

46 Parkes, "Visionary Figures," 6.

47 Ford Madox Ford, "On Impressionism," in Jane Goldman, et al., eds., *Modernism: An Anthology of Sources and Documents* (Chicago: University of Chicago Press, 1998), 326.

48 T. S. Eliot, "Yeats," *Selected Prose of T. S. Eliot*, Frank Kermode, ed. (New York: Harcourt, Brace, Jovanovich, 1975), 257, 248. The classic exposition of this point is Richard Ellmann, *Eminent Domain: Yeats among Wilde, Joyce, Pound, Eliot, and Auden* (New York: Oxford University Press, 1967).

49 Brendan Behan, *The James Joyce Society Presents Brendan Behan on Joyce at the Gotham Book Mart, N. Y. C.* [LP] (Folkways: 1962). Thanks to Steven Guthrie for directing my attention to the existence of this recording.

1 IMPRIMATURS

1 T. S. Eliot, *The Letters of T. S. Eliot*, ed. Valerie Eliot (London: Faber and Faber, 1988), 99.

2 Thomas Strychacz, *Modernism, Mass Culture, and Professionalism* (New York: Cambridge University Press, 1993), 25–6.

3 For a definitive elaboration of this historical model, see Harold Perkin, *The Rise of Professional Society: England since 1880* (New York: Routledge, 1989), especially 359–404.

4 Strychacz, *Modernism*, 25.

5 *Ibid.*, 24–7.

6 Andreas Huyssen, *After the Great Divide: Modernism, Mass Culture and Post-Modernism* (Bloomington: Indiana University Press, 1986).

7 Fredric Jameson, "Postmodernism and Consumer Society," in Hal Foster, ed., *The Anti-Aesthetic: Essays on Postmodern Culture* (Port Townsend: Bay, 1983), 114.

8 Compare the reference to Baudelaire's *poncif* ("cliché") in Walter Benjamin, *The Arcades Project*, trans. Howard Eiland and Kevin McLaughlin (Cambridge: Harvard University Press, 1999), 371–2.

9 James Joyce, *Letters of James Joyce*, vol. III, ed. Richard Ellmann (New York: Viking, 1966), 312.

10 Douglas Lane Patey, *The Life of Evelyn Waugh: A Critical Biography* (Oxford: Blackwell, 1998), 3.

11 Joyce Piell Wexler, *Who Paid for Modernism? Art, Money, and the Fiction of Conrad, Joyce, and Lawrence* (Fayetteville: University of Arkansas Press, 1997), xi.

12 David McWhirter, ed., *Henry James's New York Edition: The Construction of Authorship* (Stanford: Stanford University Press, 1995), 1. See also John H. Pearson, *The Prefaces of Henry James: Framing the Modern Reader* (University Park: Penn. State University Press, 1997).

13 Henry James, *The Art of the Novel: Critical Prefaces*, ed. R. P. Blackmur (New York: Scribner's, 1962), 119.

14 *Ibid.*, 221.

15 Henry James, *The Figure in the Carpet and Other Stories*, ed. Frank Kermode (New York: Penguin Books, 1986), 37–8. This edition brings together James's stories on this subject; see Kermode's introduction for the basics on its critical, historical moment.

16 James, *Figure*, 41.

17 James, *Art of the Novel*, 220–1.

18 *Ibid.*, 119.

19 James, *Figure*, 38–41.

20 *Ibid.*, 38.
21 *Ibid.*, 39.
22 Henry James, *The Notebooks of Henry James*, F. O. Matthiessen and Kenneth B. Murdock, eds. (New York: Oxford University Press, 1947), 147–8.
23 Compare Pierre Bourdieu, *The Rules of Art* (Stanford: Stanford University Press, 1996), 29–73.
24 James, *Figure*, 302.
25 *Ibid.*, 307.
26 *Ibid.*
27 *Ibid.*, 309.
28 *Ibid.*, 308–9.
29 *Ibid.*, 349.
30 *Ibid.*, 352.
31 *Ibid.*, 352–3.
32 Henry James, *The Art of Fiction* (New York: Oxford University Press), 11.
33 James, *Notebooks*, 149.
34 *Ibid.*, 220–1.
35 Wolfgang Iser, *The Implied Reader* (Baltimore: Johns Hopkins University Press, 1974), 103.
36 James, *Figure*, 365–6.
37 *Ibid.*, 367.
38 James, *Notebooks*, 245–6.
39 James, *Figure*, 405.
40 *Ibid.*, 414.
41 *Ibid.*, 408.
42 *Ibid.*, 428.
43 *Ibid.*, 408.
44 *Ibid.*, 408, 412.
45 *Ibid.*, 428.
46 Compare Marguerite Harkness, *A Portrait of the Artist as a Young Man: Voices in the Text* (Boston: Twayne Publishing, 1990). It also bears on the broader interpretive nexus filed under the name Flaubert in Bourdieu, *Rules*, 112ff.
47 James Joyce, *A Portrait of the Artist as a Young Man* (New York: Penguin, 1976), 253.
48 Ezra Pound, *Pound/Joyce: The Letters of Ezra Pound to James Joyce with Pound's Essays on Joyce*, Forrest Read, ed. (New York: New Directions, 1967), 44–5.
49 Robert Scholes, "Stephen Dedalus, Poet or Esthete?," *PMLA* 79 (September 1964), 484.
50 Harry Levin, *James Joyce: A Critical Introduction* (Norfolk: New Directions, 1941) and Hugh Kenner, *Dublin's Joyce* (London: Chatto and Windus, 1955). For a good overview of this debate and a compendium of relevant materials, see Chester Anderson, ed., *A Portrait of the Artist as a Young Man: Text, Criticism, and Notes* (New York: Viking, 1968).
51 Levin, *Joyce*, 45.
52 Kenner, *Dublin's Joyce*, 120.

53 *Ibid.*, 112.
54 Wayne Booth, *The Rhetoric of Fiction* (Chicago: University of Chicago Press, 1961), 335.
55 See Booth, *Rhetoric*, 333; and John Kelleher, "The Perceptions of James Joyce," *Atlantic Monthly* (March 1958), 84.
56 Joyce, *Portrait*, 215.
57 Kenner, *Dublin's Joyce*, 198.
58 Joyce, *Portrait*, 253.
59 *Ibid.*, 180.
60 *Ibid.*, 209.
61 *Ibid.*, 247.
62 *Ibid.*, 203.
63 *Ibid.*, 63.
64 *Ibid.*, 189.
65 *Ibid.*, 176.
66 *Ibid.*, 207.
67 Edward Upward, *Journey to the Border* (London: Enitharmon, 1994), 34–5.
68 Upward, *Journey*, 59–60.
69 Joyce, *Portrait*, 253.
70 Perry Anderson, "Modernity and Revolution," in Cary Nelson and Lawrence Grossberg, eds., *Marxism and the Interpretation of Culture* (Urbana: University of Illinois Press, 1988), 325.
71 Christopher Isherwood, *Prater Violet* (New York: Farrar, Straus and Giroux, 1987), 42–3.
72 *Ibid.*, 41.
73 *Ibid.*, 34.
74 *Ibid.*, 49–50.
75 The artist's participation requires identification with the script of heterosexual romance, an identification which is rendered problematic at various points in the narrative, especially Christopher's sexual encounter with J. at the novel's end – "After J., there would be K. and L. and M., right down the alphabet . . ." (*Ibid.*, 125).
76 *Ibid.*, 50.
77 *Ibid.*, 51.
78 *Ibid.*, 96.
79 *Ibid.*, 128.
80 *Ibid.*, 127.
81 *Ibid.*
82 Christopher Isherwood, *Lions and Shadows: An Education in the Twenties* (London: Hogarth, 1938), 7.
83 Maurice Beebe, *Ivory Towers and Sacred Founts: The Artist as Hero in Fiction from Goethe to Joyce* (New York: New York University Press, 1964), 4–5.
84 On Waugh's early commitments to modernist literary experimentation, see Martin Stannard, *Evelyn Waugh, The Early Years, 1903–1939* (New York: Norton, 1986), 79–82, 207–12, 222–5.

85 Stannard, *Evelyn Waugh*, 161.
86 *Ibid.*
87 Evelyn Waugh, *Vile Bodies* (Boston: Little, Brown, 1930), ix–x.
88 Quoted in Stannard, *Evelyn Waugh*, 206.
89 *Ibid.*, 196.
90 *Ibid.*, 204.
91 See Stannard, *Evelyn Waugh*, 134–91. Which is not to say, of course, to borrow the usual turn of phrase of the disavowal, that Fenwick-Symes *is* Waugh.
92 Waugh, *Vile*, 314; Stannard, *Evelyn Waugh*, 205.
93 Waugh, *Vile*, 170–1.
94 *Ibid.*, 84.
95 Christopher Isherwood, *Exhumations: Stories, Articles, Verses* (London: Methuen, 1966), 55.
96 His gender, however, is not masked.
97 See Colin MacCabe, "The Revenge of the Author," in David Simpson, ed., *Subject to History: Ideology, Class, Gender* (Ithaca: Cornell University Press, 1991), 34–7. Like MacCabe, I acknowledge the poststructuralist reading lesson "on the sociality of writing and the transindividuality of its codes" but still see a pressing need to account for the lingering prerogatives of authorship historically (34).
98 Michel Foucault, "Le philosophe masqué," *Le Monde* (6–7 April 1980), 1, 17.
99 Michel Foucault, "What Is an Author?" in *The Foucault Reader*, Paul Rabinow, ed. (New York: Pantheon, 1984), 109–10.
100 *Ibid.*, 107.
101 *Ibid.*, 118.
102 Michel Foucault, "The Masked Philosopher," in Alan Sheridan, ed. and trans., *Politics, Philosophy, Culture* (New York: Routledge, 1990), 323.
103 Eliot, "Tradition and the Individual Talent," in *Selected Prose of T. S. Eliot*, Frank Kermode, ed. (New York: Harcourt, Brace, Jovanovich, 1975), 40–1.
104 *Ibid.*, 42–3.
105 *Ibid.*, 40.
106 *Ibid.*, 39.
107 *Ibid.*, 38–9.
108 Herbert Read, *The Politics of the Unpolitical* (London: Routledge, 1943), 160.
109 Wyndham Lewis, *The Revenge for Love* (London: Secker and Warburg, 1982), 312.
110 Foucault, "Masked," 120.
111 Foucault, "What Is an Author?," 120.

2 ADJECTIVES

1 Ernest Hemingway, *A Moveable Feast* (New York: Scribner's, 1964), 134.
2 Ezra Pound, *The Spirit of Romance* (London: J. M. Dent, 1910), 208.
3 From Canto XLV: Ezra Pound, *The Cantos of Ezra Pound* (New York: New Directions, 1989), 229.

4 Pound, *Spirit*, 105.

5 Ezra Pound, *ABC of Reading* (New York: New Directions, 1987), 22–3.

6 Ezra Pound, *The Guide to Kulchur* (New York: New Directions, 1970).

7 Robert Nichols. "Poetry and Mr. Pound," in *Ezra Pound: The Critical Heritage* (London: Routledge and Kegan Paul, 1972), 165–7.

8 J. A. Simpson and E. S. C. Weiner, eds., *The Oxford English Dictionary*, 2nd edn., vol. VII (Oxford: Clarendon Press, 1989), 134.

9 *Ibid.*, vol. XV, 571.

10 *Ibid.*, vol. XII, 248.

11 John Mortimer, "William Shakeshafte, International Man of Mystery," *The Observer Review* (14 November 1999), 13.

12 There are, of course, conspicuous omissions, authorial adjectives the editors of the *OED* neglected to notice.

13 T. S. Eliot, *After Strange Gods: A Primer of Modern Heresy* (London: Faber and Faber, 1934), 23.

14 C. K. Ogden, "James Joyce's Anna Livia Plurabelle," *transition* 18 (March 1932), 259.

15 For some family resemblances between BASIC and recent ideas about World Englishes, see David Simpson, "Prospects for Global English: Back to BASIC?," *Yale Journal of Criticism* 11.1 (Spring 1998), 301–7.

16 C. K. Ogden, *Basic English: A General Introduction with Rules and Grammar* (London: Kegan Paul, Trench, Trubner, 1936), 7–8.

17 Ogden, *Basic English*, 7–8.

18 See Bernard Crick, notes to *Nineteen Eighty-Four* by George Orwell (Oxford: Clarendon, 1984), 430.

19 George Orwell, *Nineteen Eighty-Four* (Oxford: Clarendon, 1984), 201.

20 John Paul Russo, *I. A. Richards: His Life and Work* (London: Routledge, 1989), 397.

21 Russo, *I. A. Richards*, 401–3; Crick, *Nineteen Eighty-Four*, 430.

22 Ezra Pound, "Debabelization and Ogden," *The New English Weekly* (28 February 1935), 411.

23 Ezra Pound, "How to Read," *Literary Essays of Ezra Pound* (New York: New Directions, 1968), 23.

24 There is reason to believe that Pound did not think Joyce – at least "Work in Progress" Joyce – survived translation into Basic. See Pound's letter to Ogden on 28 January 1935 in which he scolds Ogden for sending him Basic samples, "a mass of light licherachoor" including "Anna havva banYana," rather than hardcore Basic theory: Ezra Pound, *The Letters of Ezra Pound, 1907–1941*, ed. D. D. Paige (New York: Harcourt, Brace, 1950), 265.

25 Pound, *ABC*, 13.

26 For example, see Hugh Kenner, *The Poetry of Ezra Pound* (Lincoln, Nebr.: University of Nebraska Press, 1985), 11.

27 Pound, "A Few Don'ts," *Literary Essays*, 4–5.

28 *Ibid.*

29 *Ibid.*

30 Balachandra Rajan, "T. S. Eliot," in *The Johns Hopkins Guide to Literary Theory and Criticism*, Michael Groden and Martin Kreiswirth, eds. (Baltimore: Johns Hopkins University Press, 1994), 222.

31 Pound, "A Few Don'ts," *Literary Essays*, 12.

32 Pound, "On Criticism," 143.

33 Pound, *Spirit*, 8.

34 Pound, "On Criticism," 147–8.

35 Pound, *ABC*, 39–40.

36 Pound, "On Criticism," 148.

37 Pound, "How to Read," 23.

38 *Ibid.*

39 See Pound's "Prefatory Note" to *The Complete Poetical Works of T. E. Hulme*, both appended to the end of *Ripostes* (1912), in *Collected Shorter Poems*, 2nd edn. (London: Faber and Faber, 1968), 268.

40 Pound, *ABC*, 9, 84. By 1934, the categories were (1) "inventors," (2) "masters," (3) "diluters," (4) "good writers without salient qualities," (5) "writers of belle-lettres," and (6) "starters of crazes" (39–40).

41 T. S. Eliot, *The Sacred Wood: Essays on Poetry and Criticism* (London: Methuen, 1960), 104.

42 Pound, *ABC*, 45.

43 T. S. Eliot, "Tradition and the Individual Talent," *Selected Prose of T. S. Eliot*, ed. Frank Kermode (New York: Harcourt, Brace, Jovanovich, 1975), 49.

44 *Ibid.*, 50.

45 F. R. Leavis, *How to Teach Reading: A Primer for Ezra Pound* (Cambridge: Minority, 1932), 1.

46 Leavis, *How to Teach Reading*, 2–3.

47 Eliot, "Tradition," 49.

48 Kenner, *Poetry*, 28–9.

49 *The Oxford Magazine* (24 January 1929), 318–19.

50 Leonard Woolf, *Letters of Leonard Woolf*, ed. Frederic Spotts (New York: Harcourt, Brace, Jovanovich, 1989), 230–1.

51 Lawrence Rainey, *Institutions of Modernism: Literary Elites and Public Culture* (London: Yale University Press, 1998), 106.

52 *The Dial* 73.4 (October 1922), xxviii.

53 On the prohibitively high price of the first edition of *Ulysses*, see Rainey, *Institutions*, 42–76.

54 Ian MacKillop, *F. R. Leavis: A Life in Criticism* (London: Penguin, 1997), 89. For an account of this interesting episode in the suppression of criticism see 88–91.

55 Michael Arlen, *The Green Hat* (London: Collins, 1924), 22.

56 *Ibid.*, 24.

57 Rainey, *Institutions*, 101.

58 *Ibid.*, 100–2.

59 "Comment," *The Dial* 73.6 (December 1922), 685–6.

60 Harold Acton, *Memoirs of an Aesthete* (London: Methuen, 1948), 99. On the influence of Acton's circle at Oxford see Martin Stannard, *Evelyn Waugh, The*

Early Years, 1903–1939 (New York: Norton, 1986), 67–96. Also see Waugh's "Isis Idol" piece on Acton in *The Isis* (20 February 1924), 7.

61 Acton, *Memoirs*, 147.

62 Anonymous [B. N.], "The Sad Story of the Young Man from M-rt-n," *The Isis* (30 April 1919), 6.

63 According to John Betjeman, in 1925, Acton was the "chief Oxford Aesthete." *My Oxford*, ed. Ann Thwaite (London: Robson, 1986), 65.

64 Arthur Waugh, "The New Poetry" (1916) in *T. S. Eliot: The Critical Heritage*, vol. I, Michael Grant, ed. (London: Routledge and Kegan Paul, 1982), 68. Arthur Waugh was the father of Evelyn and Alec, both Oxonians. Evelyn was one of Acton's chief co-conspirators. Theirs was a family business, for Arthur Waugh was himself a prominent man of letters. These "co-incidences" not only place cubism and Eliot in the same timeframe; they also place them in the same circles, that is, the homes of Oxford-bound youth.

65 Waugh, "The New Poetry," 69.

66 *Ibid.*

67 *Ibid.*

68 *Ibid.*

69 Ezra Pound, "Drunken Helots and Mr. Eliot" (1917), in *T. S. Eliot: The Critical Heritage*, 70.

70 Pound, "Drunken Helots," 71.

71 "Poetical Bread: A Note and Recipe," *The Oxford Broom* 2 (April 1923), 2–3.

72 On the rivalry and differences between *Venture* and *Experiment*, see Thomas M. Sawyer, "Experiment," in *British Literary Magazines: The Modern Age, 1914–1984*, vol. IV, Alvin Sullivan, ed. (New York: Greenwood, 1986), 177–9.

73 Muriel Bradbrook, in *My Cambridge*, ed. Ronald Hayman (London: Robson Books, 1977), 42.

74 *Ibid.*

75 Among Bradbrook's subsequent work on Eliot, her British Council pamphlet, for the "Writers and Their Work" series, is particularly interesting for re-cathecting Mr. Heliot's "juvenile naughtiness." See especially her *T. S. Eliot* (London: Longmans, Green, 1950), 11, 17.

76 Christopher Isherwood, *Lions and Shadows: An Education in the Twenties* (London: Hogarth, 1938), 121–2.

77 See Malcolm Cowley, *Exile's Return: A Literary Odyssey of the 1920's* (London: Bodley Head, 1961), 21–2.

78 See James Tetreault, "Parallel Lines: C. S. Lewis and T. S. Eliot," *Renascence* 38.4 (1986), 258.

79 F. R. Leavis, "Approaches to T. S. Eliot," *The Common Pursuit* (London: Chatto and Windus, 1952), 279.

80 Bradbrook, *My Cambridge*, 42.

81 See Muriel Bradbrook, "I. A. Richards at Cambridge," in Reuben Brower, et al., eds., *I. A. Richards: Essays in His Honor* (New York: Oxford University Press, 1973), 61–72.

82 I. A. Richards, *Practical Criticism: A Study of Literary Judgment* (London: Kegan Paul, Trench, Trubner, 1929), 367.

83 MacKillop, *F. R. Leavis*, 102; F. L. Lucas, "Review," in *T. S. Eliot: The Critical Heritage*, 198–9.
84 Lucas, "Review," 199.
85 MacKillop, *F. R. Leavis*, 102.
86 Lucas, "Review," 199.
87 I. A. Richards, "Mr. Eliot's Poems," in *T. S. Eliot: The Critical Heritage*, 235.
88 MacKillop, *F. R. Leavis*, 103.
89 F. R. Leavis, "T. S. Eliot – A Reply to the Condescending," *Cambridge Review* 50 (8 February 1929), 254.
90 *Ibid.*
91 *Ibid.*
92 For Leavis on Sitwellism, see, among other places, *New Bearings in English Poetry: A Study of the Contemporary Situation* (London: Penguin, 1982), 58, and *For Continuity* (Cambridge, UK: Minority, 1933), 16.
93 Leavis, *New Bearings*, 60.
94 *Ibid.*, 156.
95 Richards, *Practical Criticism*, 3.
96 *Ibid.*, 4–5. M. C. Bradbrook, William Empson, Christopher Isherwood, Edward Upward, T. H. White, Joan Bennett, John Blackie, Francis Partridge, and L. C. Knights were all students of Richards. See MacKillop, *F. R. Leavis*, 75, and Russo, *I. A. Richards*, 708–9, 750.
97 Richards, *Practical Criticism*, 6.
98 *Ibid.*, v.
99 *Ibid.*, viii.
100 It is hardly surprising that a method which subsequently became part of standard English examination practice at Cambridge and beyond was *first* envisioned as a test of reading proficiency, "a good examination for English students to print five extracts of poetry and prose, with no clues as to the author or date, and containing one really *worthless* piece – and ask for comment and opinion." See Russo, *I. A. Richards*, 294.
101 Richards, *Practical Criticism*, 26.
102 *Ibid.*, 257.
103 *Ibid.*, 238.
104 *Ibid.*, 12.
105 Russo, *I. A. Richards*, 299; Richards, *Practical Criticism*, 89.
106 Richards, *Practical Criticism*, 113.
107 *Ibid.*, 115–16.
108 *Ibid.*, 79.
109 MacKillop, *F. R. Leavis*, 74–8.
110 *Ibid.*, 76.
111 Harwood, *Eliot to Derrida*, 13.
112 Peter Nichols, *Modernisms: A Literary Guide* (Berkeley: University of California Press, 1995).
113 The use that consumer culture found in modernist innovation – as in the field of advertising, for example – involves, perhaps, a different set of questions.

114 Michael Kammen, *The Lively Arts: Gilbert Seldes and the Transformation of Culture Criticism in the United States* (Oxford: Oxford University Press, 1996), 356–7.
115 Quoted in Kammen, *The Lively Arts*, 357.
116 Compare Rainey, *Institutions*, 72–6.
117 David Farmer, *Ezra Pound: An Exhibition, held in Humanities Research Center, University of Texas, March 1967* (Austin: University of Texas Press, 1967), 27.
118 Farmer, *Ezra Pound*, 35. Many, including Humphrey Carpenter and Peter Ackroyd, have noted the iconic character of Pound's very signature, seeing even here traces of Gaudier-Brzeska's Pound logotype. Peter Ackroyd, *Ezra Pound* (London: Thames and Hudson, 1980), 40.

3 COLLABORATIVE WORK

1 Robert McAlmon, *Being Geniuses Together: An Autobiography* (London: Secker and Warburg, 1938), 5.
2 Malcolm Cowley, "Those Paris Years," *The New York Times* (9 June 1968), sec. 7, 35.
3 Kay Boyle and Robert McAlmon, *Being Geniuses Together: 1920–1930* (London: Hogarth, 1968, 1984), iii.
4 For a more affirmative reading, see Christine H. Hait, "Life-Giving: Kay Boyle's Innovations in Autobiography in *Being Geniuses Together*," in *Critical Essays on Kay Boyle*, Marilyn Elkins, ed. (New York: G. K. Hall, 1997), 299–311.
5 Sylvia Beach, *Shakespeare and Company: The Story of an American Bookshop in Paris* (New York: Harcourt, Brace and Company, 1956), 60.
6 Lawrence Rainey, *Institutions of Modernism: Literary Elites and Public Culture* (London: Yale University Press, 1998), 4–5.
7 *Ibid.*, 169. Rainey's *locus classicus*, among the many forms of small-scale publishing he examines, is "the limited edition" (see 42–74, 99–103, and 153–4). Considered as a social and discursive space rather than a limited edition *per se*, it functions as an anomalous social niche in which modernists can thrive. "The limited edition," he writes, "established a kind of special productive space insulated from the harsh exigencies of the larger marketplace" (100–1).
8 From Ford's *Thus to Revisit* (1921) to Mary de Rachewiltz's *Discretions* (1971), the sub-genre's catalog is vast.
9 McAlmon, *Being Geniuses Together*, 90.
10 *Ibid.*, 91.
11 *Ibid.*
12 Caresse Crosby, *The Passionate Years* (London: Alvin Redman, 1953, 1955), 191.
13 *Ibid.*, 196.
14 *Ibid.*, 197.
15 Richard Ellmann, *James Joyce* (Oxford: Oxford University Press, 1982), 514–15, 615. Ellmann picks up both anecdotes and significantly seems to find McAlmon's anecdote more threatening than Caresse Crosby's. Only McAlmon merits "a small place . . . in the authorship [of *Ulysses*]," a development

sufficiently disconcerting for Ellmann to include a footnote which reports that Hans Walter Gabler "assures [him] that [McAlmon's] changes were negligible" (514).

16 Douglas Mao, *Solid Objects, Modernism and the Test of Production* (Princeton, N.J.: Princeton University Press, 1998), 11. Burstein perceptively notes that, while endeavoring to get at "the things described in texts, Mao misses out on the life of things that inhabit space": Jessica Burstein, "Solid Criticism," *Modernism/Modernity* 71 (January 2000), 145. Mao gives short shrift to the very materiality of text ("those inky words on white leaves"), modernism's textual hardware itself, and the critical import of the modernist book as a solid object and as a "validation of production" (11). Is there a better thing with which to experience the combination of the "urgent validation of production" and the *fantasy* of an "object world beyond the manipulation of consciousness" than modernism's celebrated textual objects/literary products?

17 Mao, *Solid Objects*, 11.

18 This impossible, modernist object has three faces. First, the book-in-print as a non-obsolescent commodity. During the Cornel West–Lawrence Summers flap at Harvard, for example, this from President Summers: "It would be much better if two more books that stood the long test of time were written over the next decade at Harvard than if we created two new centers on issues of the day" (quoted in Robert Wilson and Scott Smallwood, "Battle of Wills at Harvard," *The Chronicle of Higher Education* (18 January 2002, 8). Second, the sublime, all-consuming work, obviating exchange value. The object of desire for the reader who dreams of a library of just one book, "that ideal Joycean reader who devotes an entire life to the perusal of a single text" (Colin MacCabe, "The Revenge of the Author," in David Simpson, ed., *Subject to History: Ideology, Class, Gender* (Ithaca: Cornell University Press, 1991), 37). Third, the difficult book as unsellable object, impossible to produce, market, and consume. "He who offers for sale something unique that no-one wants to buy, represents, even against his will, freedom from exchange," as noted Theodor Adorno, in *Minima Moralia* (London: Verso, 1997), 68.

19 Roger Conover, "Introduction," in *The Lost Lunar Baedeker*, by Mina Loy (New York: Farrar, Straus, Giroux, 1996), 169.

20 *Ibid.*, xii.

21 *Ibid.*, xix, 172ff.

22 *Ibid.*, xix.

23 *Ibid.*, xviii.

24 *Ibid.*, xiii.

25 Clare Hanson, "Katherine Mansfield," in *The Gender of Modernism: A Critical Anthology*, Bonnie Kime Scott, ed. (Bloomington: Indiana University Press, 1990), 299.

26 T. S. Eliot, *The Letters of T. S. Eliot*, Valerie Eliot, ed. (London: Faber and Faber: 1985), 391.

27 *Ibid.*, 392.

28 "Comment," *The Dial* 73 (December 1922), 685. This is one of the chief criteria for the Dial Prize. In a letter thanking John Quinn for subsidizing the Dial

Prize, Eliot writes magnanimously that Pound "deserves the recognition more than I do, certainly 'for his services to Letters' and I feel that I ought to have been made to wait until after he had received this public testimony" (571–2). Maxwell Bodenheim (1893–1954) appears in Pound's *Catholic Anthology*, represented only "under the signature 'M.B.,' as it was decided that his full name might be objectionable at a time when England was at war with Germany": Pound, *Letters*, 55. In a letter to Harriet Monroe (2 October 1922), Pound brings Bodenheim up in the same promotional context as Eliot, writing that "Bodenheim shows promise" but "is young enough to wait" (64).

29 See Eliot's letter to Pound, 3 July 1920, in which he first claims sympathy for Bodenheim, then writes: "I can't see any means by which Bodenheim might be made self-supporting here; can you?" (388–9).

30 For *The Cantos* parody, see Joyce's letter of 13 June 1925 (*Letters*, vol. I, 227–9; *Selected Letters*, 307), and for *The Waste Land* parody, see his letter of 15 August 1925 (*Letters*, vol. I, 230–1; reprinted in Ellmann, *James Joyce*, 572).

31 Edith Sitwell, *Selected Letters of Edith Sitwell*, ed. Richard Greene (London: Virago, 1997), 58.

32 Edwin Muir, *Selected Letters of Edwin Muir*, ed. P. H. Butter (London: Hogarth, 1974), 175–6.

33 *Ibid.*, 181.

34 Letter of 11 June 1917: Pound, *Pound/the Little Review: The Letters of Ezra Pound to Margaret Anderson*, Melvin J. Friedman, et al., eds. (London: Faber and Faber: 1988), 65–6.

35 T. S. Eliot, "Introduction" to *Selected Poems* by Ezra Pound, ed. T. S. Eliot (London: Faber and Faber, 1959), 19.

36 *Ibid.*, 21. On the fractious history of these late Pound–Eliot encounters, see Michael Coyle, *Ezra Pound, Popular Genres, and the Discourse of Culture* (University Park: Pennsylvania State University Press, 1995).

37 T. S. Eliot, "Preface" to *Transit of Venus* by Harry Crosby (Paris: Black Sun Press, 1931), iv.

38 Peter Ackroyd, *T. S. Eliot* (London: Sphere Books, 1985), 20. According to Read, Eliot expressed some embarrassment about the poem: Herbert Read, "T.S.E. – a Memoir," *Sewanee Review* 74.1 (January–March 1966), 51.

39 T. S. Eliot, "Introduction" to *Savonarola: A Dramatic Poem* by Charlotte Eliot (London: R. Cobden-Sanderson, 1926), x.

40 *Ibid.*, viii.

41 *Ibid.*, vii.

42 *Ibid.*, ix–x.

43 Eliot, "Tradition," 38.

44 Eliot, "Introduction" to *Selected Poems*, 21.

45 Eliot, "Tradition," 38.

46 T. S. Eliot, *Notes towards the Definition of Culture* (London: Faber and Faber, 1948), 133.

47 T. S. Eliot, "Introduction" to *Nightwood* by Djuna Barnes (New York: Farrar, Straus and Cudahy, 1962), 228.

48 *Ibid.*

49 *Ibid.*
50 See Cheryl J. Plumb, "Introduction" to *Nightwood: The Original Version and Related Drafts* by Djuna Barnes, ed. Plumb (Normal, Ill.: Dalkey Archive, 1995), vii–xxvi. Compare Plumb, who makes a persuasive case for Coleman as Barnes' chief editorial mover, with Field, whose Barnes biography casts Eliot in the central role. Barnes, for one, appears to have preferred and even promoted the fiction of the Eliotic imprimatur and, according to Field, was taken aback by Coleman's all too apparent wish for more credit: Andrew Field, *Djuna: The Life and Times of Djuna Barnes* (New York: Putnam, 1983), 219. That Barnes dedicated her final work *Creatures in an Alphabet* (1982) to Coleman says much about Barnes' debt to her (Plumb, "Introduction," xxv). That Barnes submitted *Antiphon* (1958) to the following equivocating blurb by Eliot explains more about the "authorized" relationship with Eliot: "It might be said of Miss Barnes, who is incontestably one of the most original writers of our time, that never has so much genius been combined with so little talent" (Field, *Djuna*, 222).
51 Eliot, "Introduction" to *Nightwood*, 232.
52 Quoted in Plumb, "Introduction" to *Nightwood*, xxv.
53 Eliot, "Introduction" to *Nightwood*, 228.
54 Eliot, "Introduction" to *Selected Poems*, 7.
55 *Ibid.*
56 *Ibid.*
57 T. S. Eliot, "Foreword" to *One-Way Song*, by Wyndham Lewis (London: Methuen, 1960), 10.
58 T. S. Eliot, "Introductory Note" to *Introducing James Joyce: A Selection of Joyce's Prose by T. S. Eliot* (London: Faber and Faber, 1942), 5, 6.
59 T. S. Eliot, "Critical Note" to *The Collected Poems of Harold Monro* (London: Cobden-Sanderson, 1933), xiii.
60 It also sounds remarkably like the literary underclass in Pound's ladder of literary reputation, the class which "contains the bulk of all writing," "the men who do more or less good style of a period" (a matter discussed at length in the previous chapter).
61 Eliot, "Critical Note," xv.
62 *Ibid.*, xiii.
63 *Ibid.*, xiv.
64 *Ibid.*
65 *Ibid.*
66 *Ibid.*
67 *Ibid.*
68 Commissioned by Caresse Crosby for the collected works and vanity-published after her husband's bizarre suicide.
69 T. S. Eliot, "Preface" to *Transit of Venus*, vi–vii.
70 *Ibid.*, i.
71 T. S. Eliot, "Introduction to *Selected Poems*," in *Marianne Moore: A Collection of Critical Essays*, ed. Charles Tomlinson (Englewood Cliffs, N. J.: Prentice Hall, 1969), 60.

72 T. S. Eliot, *After Strange Gods: A Primer of Modern Heresy* (London: Faber and Faber, 1934), 23.

73 Eliot, "Introduction to *Selected Poems* [of Marianne Moore]," 61, 65.

74 Eliot, "Introduction to *Selected Poems* [by Ezra Pound]," 13, 9–11.

75 Eliot, "Introduction to *Selected Poems* [of Marianne Moore]," 60–1.

76 Sandra Gilbert and Susan Gubar, *Sexchanges*, vol. II of *No Man's Land: The Place of the Woman Writer in the Twentieth Century* (New Haven: Yale University Press, 1989), xi.

77 Actually, Pound published the Gourmont translation and preface in 1921. It is a tempting slip, though, because it makes a particularly apt emblem for what was, for Pound, a colossally ill-conceived decade.

78 Canto 76: Ezra Pound, *The Cantos of Ezra Pound* (New York: New Directions, 1989), 472; Gilbert and Gubar, *Sexchanges*, xiv.

79 Ezra Pound, "Date Line," *Make It New* (Cambridge: Cambridge University Press, 1934), 11. Significantly, this is the only really new material in *Make It New*.

80 In *Mauberley*, Pound describes the England he has departed for less obstinate expatriate Paris in equally misogynistic language, a "botched civilization," an "old bitch gone in the teeth," the chief symptom of this disease being its unresponsiveness to authors: Ezra Pound, *Personae* (New York: New Directions, 1990), 188.

81 Beach, *Shakespeare*, 52; Ernest Hemingway, *A Moveable Feast* (New York: Scribner's, 1964), 28; Robert Graves, "These Are Your Gods, O Israel," in *The Crowning Privilege* (Freeport, N.Y.: Books for Libraries Press, 1970), 142–3; Ford Madox Ford, "Enter Ezra Pound," in *The Bodley Head Ford Madox Ford* (London: Bodley Head, 1962), 318.

82 *Punch* 136 (23 June 1909), 449; quoted in James G. Nelson, *Elkin Mathews: Publisher to Yeats, Joyce, Pound* (Madison: University of Wisconsin Press, 1989), 138–9.

83 *Punch* 141 (16 August 1911), 122–3; quoted in Ezra Pound and Dorothy Shakespear, *Ezra Pound and Dorothy Shakespear: Their Letters, 1909–1914*, ed. Omar Pound and A. Walton Litz (New York: New Directions, 1984), 46.

84 The design's genesis is contentious but critically important. In *Gaudier-Brzeska*, Pound indicates that the phallomorphosis was Gaudier-Brzeska's idea, writing in an oft-repeated sentence: "You understand it will not look like you, it *will*... *not*... *look*... like you. It will be the expression of certain emotions I get from your character": Ezra Pound, *Gaudier-Brzeska, A Memoir* (London: Laidlaw and Laidlaw, 1939), 52. Tellingly, Pound attributes the germ of the idea to the first impression given by an impromptu performance of "Sestina-Altaforte": "it was the 'Altaforte' that convinced him that I would do to be sculpted" (47). Jacob Epstein contended that Pound himself supplied the design, a view with which Gilbert and Gubar seem to concur. Pound's letters to Dorothy Shakespear suggest the former, see 3–10 March 1914 ("Brzx's column gets more gravely beautiful and more phallic each week," as does his reference to "my bust by Gaudier" as a means of insulting "Moeurs Contemporaines": Pound, *Letters*, 323; *Personae*, 176. In the Gaudier memoir, Pound can't resist writing that

"Gaudier has stiffened it [his character] up quite a lot" (52). See the chapter titled "The Stone," in *The Pound Era* (Berkeley: University of California Press, 1971), 248–60, for Kenner's meditations on the Hieratic Head and 260 especially for the fate of the sculpture after leaving London. For a good critical account of the sculpture as modernist promotional "event," complicated by a savvy account of its gender dynamics, see Lisa Tickner, "Now and Then: The Hieratic Head of Ezra Pound," *Oxford Art Journal* 16.2 (1993), 55–61.

85 Humphrey Carpenter, *A Serious Character: The Life of Ezra Pound* (London: Faber and Faber, 1988), 232.

86 Wayne Koestenbaum, *Double Talk: The Erotics of Male Literary Collaboration* (London: Routledge, 1989), 6. See also Lisa Tickner, "Men's Work? Masculinity and Modernism," in Norman Bryson, et al., eds., *Visual Culture: Images and Interpretations* (Middletown, Conn.: Wesleyan University Press, 1994).

87 Rupert Brooke, "Ezra Pound," *The Prose of Rupert Brooke*, Christopher Hassall, ed. (London: Sidgwick and Jackson, 1956), 111.

88 See Foster on F. T. Marinetti's will to be the phallus: "Marinetti does not embrace the technological in order to usurp the procreative, for . . . he desires not to be the mother but to be what she is said to desire": Hal Foster, "Prosthetic Gods," *Modernism/Modernity* 4.2 (April 1997), 13. It is, Foster writes, a "frenzied attempt to override sexual difference . . . played out hyperbolically." Hyperbolic self-promotion is, in effect, self-production without recourse to metaphors of female biology.

89 Ronald Bush, "Ezra Pound," in Scott, *The Gender of Modernism*, 353. See also Scott's discussion of the Pound–Moore letters in the context of Pound's gynophobic imaginary: Bonnie Kime Scott, *Refiguring Modernism*, vol. I, *The Women of 1928* (Bloomington: Indiana University Press, 1995), 84–112. As with Gilbert and Gubar, Pound's gendering of creative work strikes an appropriate chord of outrage in both Bush and Scott – it is "so outrageous," Bush writes, "one might view it as a bizarre joke did Pound not use it as the basis for an important statement of poetics . . . and then for a striking passage in Canto XXIX" (353). It is hardly surprising that Pound's letters to Moore are also tinged with racism. At one point, following an absurdly racist hunch, he asks Moore, "are you a jet black Ethiopian Othello-hued?" Learning that Moore is white, he replies: "I am glad that you are red-headed and not / woolled, dark, ethiopian. / It would have been a test case: / you dark, nubian ethiopian: could I / have risen to it; could I, / perceiving the intelligence for a distance, / have got over the Jim Crow law," etc. (363). Bush plots Pound's gender politics across the trajectory of "the darker side of his religion of Life," his eccentricities "becom[ing] coarser and more confused as his career progressed." Drawing on Robert Casillo's argument, he links Pound's gender politics of the twenties to thirties to the animus of Pound's attraction to Italian fascism, "renewing the chaotic and feminine morass of Western culture through male hierarchical order," as Mussolini drained the swamps. Yet, as Bush notes, Pound's gender politics, like his racism, change across his literary career (355–6).

90 Bush, "Ezra Pound," 362.

91 *Ibid.*, 359.
92 *Ibid.*, 360.
93 *Ibid.*, 362.
94 *Ibid.*, 364.
95 *Ibid.*, 363.
96 *Ibid.*, 361–2.
97 Koestenbaum, *Double Talk*, 3.
98 He tends to read hot subjectivity in a modernist promotional narrative where there are only cold objects: "A text is most precisely and satisfyingly collaborative if it is composed by two writers who admit the act by placing both their names on the title page. A double signature confers enormous interpretive freedom: it permits the reader to see the act of collaboration shadowing every word in the text. Collaborative works are intrinsically *different* than books written by one author alone; even if both names do not appear, or one writer eventually produces more material, the decision to collaborate determines the work's contours, and the way it can be read. Books with two authors are specimens of a relation, and show writing to be a quality of motion and exchange, not a fixed thing." (2) Koestenbaum, *Double Talk*, the "sublimation of erotic entanglement," he reads in Eliot's "use of hysterical discourse to invoke the corrective affections of another man," i.e., Pound, depends on presuming a shared hot signature in the work, when, in bibliographic terms, Pound's signature is structurally deferred into an apocrypha of promotion.
99 A counterexample to Pound's practice is the Hogarth colophon, "printed and published by Leonard and Virginia Woolf at the Hogarth Press."
100 Coyle, *Ezra Pound*, 12.
101 Koestenbaum, *Double Talk*, 120; also see Eliot, *Letters*, 498–9.
102 Koestenbaum, *Double Talk*, 121.
103 See Rainey, *Institutions*, 196, note 11. The 24 January 1922 letter is reprinted but expurgated in Pound, *Letters*, 233–5, and unexpurgated but misdated (see Rainey) in Valerie Eliot's edition of Eliot, *Letters*, 497–9. Koestenbaum includes the unexpurgated doggerel but trims off the final sentence, which helps frame it in the context of a forward-looking letter: "It is after all a grrrreat littttterary period / Thanks for the Aggymemnon" (499).
104 Eliot, *Letters*, 498.
105 "Hebrew eulogists" is certainly an anti-Semitic reference to the hapless Bodenheim, who reviewed Pound in the "Isolation of Carved Metal," appearing in January 1923 ("The massive isolation of Ezra Pound has probably not been surpassed by that of any poet in any other generation, and seldom equaled"): Maxwell Bodenheim, "Isolation of Carved Metal," *The Dial* 72 (January 1923), 87. The phrase may also refer to Gilbert Seldes, Scofield Thayer's representative in the *Dial*'s literary negotiations, who visited London and Europe at the time, and perhaps even to Virgil Geddes who in "Ezra Pound Today," appearing in November 1922, praised Pound's most recent work as "the complete and unalloyed disclosure of Ezra Pound": Virgil Geddes, "Ezra Pound Today," *Poetry* 21.2 (November 1922), 100. The most suggestive possibility, however,

may be Edmund Wilson, mistaken as a Jew. His "Poetry of Drouth," published in the same issue of *The Dial* as the *Dial* Prize announcement, cut Pound by calling him Eliot's "imitator," a poet "who presents only a bewildering mosaic with no central emotion to provide the key": Edmund Wilson, "The Poetry of Drouth," *The Dial* 71 (December 1922), 616. For Eliot's reaction to Wilson's piece, see Michael Kammen, *The Lively Arts: Gilbert Seldes and the Transformation of Cultural Criticism in the United States* (Oxford: Oxford University Press, 1996), 60–1.

106 Pound's gender theories derive from his sustained reading of Gourmont – an infamous passage in his Translator's Postscript begins with Pound attempting to explain in quasi-scientific terms that Gourmont's seemingly far-fetched ideas about brainwork are not only "possible" but "probable": Pound, "Translator's Postscript" to *The Natural Philosophy of Love*, by Rémy de Gourmont, trans. Pound (New York: Rarity, 1931), 169. Although biographers and Pound himself have indicated his surprise as the Hieratic Head took on its final phallic form, it is likely that Pound was versed enough in Gourmont's *Physique de l'amour* (1906) (perhaps having read it in the late 1910s in French) to need no exegesis. Pound also clearly connected these notions with literary promotion. In one of his *Blast* poems, he chides "Frates Minores" for getting too worked up about "the twitching of three abdominal nerves" (*Personae*, 78). The lines were not only notorious but also significant promotionally, because they were unsuccessfully censored, the lines being legible through the censor's blacking (*Ezra Pound and Dorothy Shakespear*, 311).

107 Pound, "Translator's Postscript," 171, 169.

108 *Ibid.*, 169.

109 *Ibid.*, 173.

110 *Ibid.*, 170–1.

111 See Foster, "Prosthetic Gods."

112 Pound, *Letters*, 143.

113 Ezra Pound, "A Retrospect," *Literary Essays*, 3 (New York: New Directions, 1968), 3.

114 Ezra Pound, "Harold Monro," *The Criterion* 11.45 (July 1932), 590.

115 Kenner, *Pound Era*, 178.

116 See, for example, Svarny: "Allowing for the elements of humour and rhetorical exaggeration in Pound's statement, [it suggests] that the work produced by Eliot between 1914 and 1922 has a specific historical consistency which can best be appreciated and analysed in the context of his association with Pound." Erik Svarny, *The Men of 1914: T. S. Eliot and Early Modernism* (Philadelphia: Open University Press, 1988), 1–2.

117 See Pound's *Paris Review* interview: Donald Hall, Interview with Pound, in *Writers at Work: The Paris Review Interviews*, 2nd series, George Plimpton, ed. (New York: Viking Press, 1963), 48.

118 See Eliot's *Paris Review* interview: Hall, *Paris Review Interviews*, 97.

119 Pound, *The Cantos*, 231.

120 G. W. Stonier, "The Mystery of Ezra Pound," *Purpose* 10.1 (January–March 1938), 21–2, 24.

121 T. S. Eliot, "On a Recent Piece of Criticism," *Purpose* 10.2 (April–June 1938), 92–3.

122 Pound, "On Criticism," 147–8.

123 T. S. Eliot, *The Waste Land: A Facsimile and Transcript of the Original Drafts Including the Annotations of Ezra Pound*, Valerie Eliot, ed. (New York: Harcourt Brace, 1971), vii.

124 *Ibid.*

125 Quoted in Bush, "Ezra Pound," 360.

126 Marianne Moore, *The Selected Letters of Marianne Moore*, eds. Celeste Goodridge, et al. (London: Faber and Faber, 1998), 123.

127 *Ibid.*, 122.

128 *Ibid.*, 499–501.

129 T. S. Eliot, "The Publishing of Poetry," *The Bookseller* 2450 (6 December 1952), 1,568.

130 Harold Monro, *Some Contemporary Poets* (London: Leonard Parsons, 1920), 21.

131 Ford, *Thus to Revisit: Some Reminiscences* (London: Chapman and Hall, 1921), 139. This passage is discussed in Robert H. Ross: *The Georgian Revolt: Rise and Fall of a Poetic Ideal, 1910–22* (London: Faber and Faber, 1967), 42–3. Following this passage, Ford gives an example of one of his walks with Pound: "Of what Mr. Pound talked I have no idea. He was expressing himself, in low tones, in some Transatlantic dialect. This Genius, however, was plain to hear. 'What the public wants is Me,' Pound said, 'because I am not an imbecile, like the component members of the public!' . . . I dare say he was right . . . at any rate our Public took *Blast*; Signor Marinetti and his immense noises, his lungs of brass; Mr. Epstein and his Rock Drill, with great seriousness and unparalleled avidity" (139–40). Yeats writes "in 1900 everybody got down off his stilts; henceforth nobody drank absinthe with his black coffee; nobody went mad; nobody committed suicide; nobody joined the Catholic church; or if they did I have forgotten": W. B. Yeats, *The Oxford Book of Modern Verse, 1892–1935* (New York: Oxford University Press, 1937), xi. Yet, as Ford's description makes plain, Yeats may have overlooked the transition rather than forgotten it. Modernists tempered the denunciation of late nineteenth-century aestheticism with crucial appropriations of dandyism. See the discussion of these ideas and, in particular, the realignment of dandiacal aestheticism and connoisseurship in the modernist attitudes to production in Mao, *Solid Objects*, 30–43.

132 Wyndham Lewis, ed., *Blast* 1 (Santa Rosa: Black Sparrow, 1997), 292.

133 Monro, *Some Contemporary Poets*, 15.

4 PROMOTIONAL NETWORKING

1 T. S. Eliot, *The Letters of T. S. Eliot*, Valerie Eliot, ed. (London: Faber and Faber, 1988), 499.

2 Harriet Monroe, *A Poet's Life* (New York: Macmillan, 1938), 386–7.

3 Cary Wolfe, *The Limits of American Literary Ideology in Pound and Emerson* (Cambridge: Cambridge University Press, 1993), 127; Frank Lentricchia, "Lyric in the Culture of Capitalism," *American Literary History* 1.1 (Spring 1989), 71.

4 Pound, "How to Read," in *Literary Essays of Ezra Pound* (New York: New Directions, 1968), 17–18.

5 *Ibid.*, 18.

6 Ezra Pound, *The Letters of Ezra Pound, 1967–1941,* D. D. Paige, ed. (New York: Harcourt, Brace, 1950), 47.

7 *Ibid.*, 45.

8 Yeats, *Oxford Book of Modern Verse*, xlii.

9 *Ibid.*

10 Wolfe, *The Limits of American Literary Ideology*, 101.

11 Q's *Oxford Book of English Verse* (1900) sold half a million copies during his lifetime: L. G. Wickham Legg and E. T. Williams, eds., *Dictionary of National Biography* (Oxford: Oxford University Press, 1959), 703.

12 Arthur [Q] Quiller-Couch, ed., *The Oxford Book of Victorian Verse* (Oxford: Clarendon, 1912), ix.

13 Advance copies went out in November, but the anthology (according to advertisements in *Poetry Review*) was to be ready 1 December.

14 Edward Marsh, "Prefatory Note," in *Georgian Poetry, 1911–12* (London: Poetry Bookshop, 1912), n.p.

15 War poetry anthologies clearly outnumber all other anthologies: see Catherine W. Reilly, *English Poetry of the First World War: A Bibliography* (London: George Prior, 1978), 1–33. War poetry anthologies figure at least partly within the broader context of the 1912 anthology "offensive," which for various reasons (about which more later) had already adopted an aggressive, militaristic idiom and which, after the outbreak of war in 1914, had no problem assimilating and capitalizing on its poetic output.

16 Edward Marsh, *A Number of People: A Book of Reminiscences* (London: Heinemann, 1939), 321.

17 John Drinkwater, *Discovery: Being the Second Book of an Autobiography, 1897–1913* (London: E. Benn, 1932), 11.

18 Marsh, *A Number of People*, 326–9. Also see Ross, *Georgian Revolt*, 127–9. For the relationship between modernism and the signs of patronage, see Wolfe, *American Literary Ideology*, 134–52; and, especially, Lawrence Rainey, *Institutions of Modernism: Literary Elites and Public Culture* (London: Yale University Press, 1998), 14–31, and the final two chapters.

19 Quoted in Ross, *Georgian Revolt*, 129.

20 Plowman captures the post-*Georgian Poetry* shift when, in his June 1913 review of Q's anthology, he writes, "Broadly speaking, Lascelles Abercrombie, Rupert Brooke, Harold Monro, James Stephens, and others found in this Victorian Anthology, have nothing whatever to do with Victorian poetry and should not have been included. No man can serve Victoria and George at the same time": Max Plowman, "Rev. of the Oxford Book of Victorian Verse," *Poetry and Drama* 1.2 (1913), 239.

21 Michael Roberts, "Introduction," in *Faber Book of Modern Verse* (London: Faber and Faber, 1936), 1.

22 Roberts includes H. D., Marianne Moore, Laura Riding, and Edith Sitwell.

23 Geoffrey Grigson, "Introduction," in *Poetry of the Present: An Anthology of the 'Thirties and After* (London: Phoenix House, 1949), 13.

24 Marsh, "Prefatory Note," n.p.

25 See Ross, *Georgian Revolt*, 212–13. Graves' letter to the *TLS* condemning anthology *ranch-brands* is an excellent example of the combative literary environment that the new anthology offensive helped to foster. Graves writes to "heartily commend" Eliot's denunciation of anthologies in the previous issue. Eliot's letter to the *TLS* complains of his unauthorized inclusion in Louis Untermeyer's *Modern American Poetry*: "On previous occasions, when compilers of such works have asked my consent, there have always been personal reasons for my willing compliance: here there would have been none . . . Some months ago I discussed the general question of anthologies with a poet . . . whose name is much more widely known than mine. We agreed that the work of any poet who has already published a book of verse is likely to be more damaged than aided by anthologies": Eliot, Letter, *TLS* (24 November 1921), 771. As subsequent letter-writers noted, Eliot and Graves were "reviling some of their best friends"; they had both participated and benefited from the first new anthologies – Eliot in *Others* and *Catholic Anthology*, Graves in *Georgian Poetry* 3; Adam Gowans, Letter, *TLS* (8 December 1921), 827. One letter-writer even speculates that he would have never heard of Eliot if not for the anthology system: "I bought Mr. T. S. Eliot's *Prufrock* entirely on account of the poems from it in *Catholic Anthology*": John Haines, Letter, *TLS* (15 December 1921), 844.

26 Marsh, *A Number of People*, 321.

27 See Brooke's letter to Marsh, 9 November 1912: Rupert Brooke, *The Letters of Rupert Brooke*, Geoffrey Keynes, ed. (London: Faber and Faber, 1968), 406.

28 Ross, *Georgian Revolt*, 124.

29 Brooke, *Letters*, 406.

30 H. G. Wells, *Tono-Bungay* (London: Collins Clear Type Press, n.d.), 124–5. The novel has a Dr. Strangelovian war-room for patent medicine: "My uncle had in his inner office a big map of England, and as we took up fresh sections of the local press and our consignments invaded new areas, flags for advertisements and pink underlines for orders showed our progress" (136).

31 Ross, *Georgian Revolt*, 124–6.

32 "The Death of Mr. Rupert Brooke," *The Times* (26 April 1915), 5e.

33 For example, *War Poems by Rupert Brooke (Sub-Lieutenant R.N.D., British Mediterranean Expeditionary Force, Died in the Ægean April 23rd, 1915)* in a small deluxe edition ("quarter vellum, marbled boards, lettered in gold on the side WAR POEMS. Edges untrimmed"), has seventeen blank pages for owners to write in additional poems. Are these pages space in expectation of more dead poet-soldiers? Geoffrey Keynes, *A Bibliography of the Works of Rupert Brooke*, 2nd edn. (London: Rupert Hart-Davies, 1959), 67. For brief overviews of the

Brooke hagiography, see Martin Taylor, Introduction to *Rupert Brooke's Death and Burial*, by J. Perdriel-Vaissières, trans. Vincent O' Sullivan (London: Imperial War Museum, 1992); and John Lehmann, *Rupert Brooke: His Life and His Legend* (London: Weidenfeld and Nicolson, 1980), 150–64.

34 Edward Marsh, ed., *Georgian Poetry, 1913–1915* (London: Poetry Bookshop, 1915), 61.

35 Wilfred Owen, *The Complete Poems and Fragments*, Jon Stallworthy, ed. (London: Chatto and Windus, 1983), 140.

36 In Marsh's memoir of Brooke, he writes that Brooke had already appointed him "literary agent or grass-executor": Rupert Brooke, *The Collected Poems of Rupert Brooke, with a Memoir by Edward Marsh*, vol. I (London: Sidgwick and Jackson, 1929), cx.

37 Pound, for example, instantly hit on Brooke's death as good literary publicity, writing Harriet Monroe, "Rupert Brooke is dead in the Dardanelles. I have some of his work, and will send the Post Mortem in a day or so, probably tonight. So it will reach you in time for the June number . . . He was the best of all that Georgian group": Pound, *Letters*, 59.

38 Christopher Hassall, *Rupert Brooke: A Biography* (London: Faber and Faber, 1964), 502–3.

39 Karen L. Levenback, "Virginia Woolf and Rupert Brooke: Poised between Olympus and the 'Real World,'" *Virginia Woolf Miscellany* 33 (Fall 1989), 5.

40 Lehmann, *Rupert Brooke*, 150.

41 Drinkwater, *Discovery*, 228.

42 Arundel del Re, "Italian Chronicle," *Poetry and Drama* 1.2 (1913), 236.

43 Marsh, *Number*, 295–6.

44 *Ibid.*, 295.

45 Marinetti visited England as early as 1910. The spring 1912 visit was far more triumphal: "After only six weeks in England, he [Marinetti] reported in mid-April [1912], the futurists had elicited 350 articles in newspapers and reviews and had earned more than 11,000 francs in sales of paintings": Rainey, *Institutions*, 28. According to Lemaire, Marinetti and other futurists appeared before the British public no less than ten times during 1913–14, including appearances at the Sackville Gallery (March 1913), the Marlborough Gallery (April 1913), three exhibitions at the Doré Galleries (between October 1913 and April 1914), a banquet at the Florence Restaurant (18 November 1913), and, the appearance which Rainey discussed at length, a week at the Coliseum music hall (mid-June 1914): Gérard-Georges Lemaire, *Futurisme* (Paris: Éditions du Regard, 1995), 166–7; Rainey, *Institutions*, 33–8. According to Monro, Marinetti's mid-November 1913 visit included the Florence dinner as well as engagements at the Poetry Bookshop, the Cabaret, the Poets' Club, Clifford's Inn Hall, and the Doré Galleries: Harold Monro, "The Origin of Futurism," *Poetry and Drama* 1.4 (1913), 389.

46 Monro, "Origin," 389.

47 Marsh, *A Number of People*, 295–6.

48 *Ibid.*, 377.

49 Harold Monro, "Futurism," *Poetry and Drama* 1.3 (1913), 262. He writes: "The first principles of *our* Futurism are: I. To forget God, Heaven, Hell, Personal Immortality, and to remember, always, earth. II. To lift the eyes from a sentimental contemplation of the past, and, through dwelling in the present, nevertheless, always, to *live*, in the future of the earth" (262).

50 Harold Monro, "Broadsides and Chap-Books," *Poetry and Drama* 1.3 (1913), 265.

51 Harold Monro, "Laureate's Bays," *Poetry and Drama* 1.3 (1913), 270.

52 Harold Monro, "The Bookshop," *Poetry Review* 1.11 (1912), 498.

53 *Ibid.*, 500.

54 *Ibid.*, 498–9.

55 *Ibid.*, 498. "In short," Monro writes, "we propose to establish an informal Guild" (499). Monro's hybridized, Anglicized "futurism" clearly also owes something to the notion of medieval modernism, elaborated by Michael T. Saler, *The Avant-Garde in Interwar England: Medieval Modernism and the London Underground* (Oxford: Oxford University Press, 1998). Monro's recourse to the continental avant-garde as a business model suggests that Saler's case for a wholly nativist – if not to say wholly indigenous – British avant-garde is more vexed than he lets on.

56 Monro stages his retreat in the issue following the futurist number, the intervening event being Marinetti's mid-November visit to England. In the editorial, Monro writes, we "had our minds cleared" about futurism's nationalist project, futurism was "avowedly Italian . . . for Italians": Monro, "Origin," 389.

57 H. Caldwell Cook, "Poetry Alive," *Poetry and Drama* 1.4 (1913), 327.

58 Advertisement for *Georgian Poetry, 1912–1913*, in *Poetry Review* 1.11 (1912), iii.

59 For examples, see Ross, *Georgian Revolt*, 141. Arthur Waugh's 1916 review of the first two volumes of *Georgian Poetry* collocates them with Pound's *Catholic Anthology* as dangerous signs of poetic sedition (the same infamous review which condemns Eliot's *Prufrock* for being "Cubist" verse, discussed in chapter two). Waugh identifies "E.M." as "one of the most conspicuous revolutionists of the new school": Timothy Rogers, ed., *Georgian Poetry, 1911–1922: The Critical Heritage* (London: Routledge and Kegan Paul, 1977), 142. Even allies of Marsh like Edmund Gosse tended to read *Georgian Poetry* along these lines, "at once" as "anthology and manifesto" (73).

60 Once more, divergence came later. Eventually, anti-Georgianism was a mainstay of both the Pound–Eliot–Leavis axis and the *Wheels*-group, particularly following the appearance of the third *Georgian Poetry* (which included poems by the rabidly anti-modernist editor of the *London Mercury*, J. C. Squire). In a sense, Pound's attack on "Georgianism" began *avant la lettre*, when he singled out Lascelles Abercrombie (later "Abercrumbie") for censure in *Poetry Review*: Ezra Pound, "Introductory Note, a Section from the Tempers," *Poetry Review* 1.10 (October 1912), 481; Pound, *Letters*, 12. By 1918, it was clearly a matter of "us" versus "the Poetry Bookshop and the Georgian Anthologies, Abercrombie, Eddie Marsh, etc.": Pound, *Letters*, 133. For a history of *Georgian*

Poetry's critical brush-off, and for particular specimens, see John Middleton Murry's and T. S. Eliot's reviews collected in Rogers, *Georgian Poetry*. These two related pieces set the tone for the bulk of subsequent dismissals, such as Leavis's famous characterization of "Georgianism" as a "Garden-Suburb ethos" or Orwell's remarks about "Georgianism" being the beer-and-cricket school of poetry (51). Roy Campbell's *Georgiad* (1931), of course, and the back-matter of Sitwell's *Wheels* anthologies are also notably rife with "Georgian" animus. While I am not interested in making any claims for the "Georgian" poetics en masse, I would, following Ross, draw attention to the substantial number of key "Georgian" texts which participate in modernist literary vernacular by Lawrence, Monro, Brooke ("Old Vicarage, Grantchester"), Masefield ("The Everlasting Mercy"), and others.

61 Letter of 19 October 1914: Pound, *Letters*, 84. On the former point, see especially Rainey, *Institutions*, ch. 1; on the latter, see Wolfe, *American Literary Ideology*, 51ff.

62 Del Re, "Italian Chronicle," 236.

63 Part of Pound's dissatisfaction with the trajectory of imagism(e) stemmed from Lowell's bid to decentralize (democratize, as it were) the anthology, to let each author select his or her own material: Richard Aldington, *Life for Life's Sake: A Book of Reminiscences* (London: Cassell, 1968), 127. Aldington describes how Lowell "proposed a Boston Tea Party for Ezra, the immediate abolition of his despotism and the substitution of pure democracy. There was to be no more of the Duce business, with arbitrary inclusions and exclusions and a capricious censorship . . . Each poet was to choose for himself what he considered best in his year's output, and the anthology would appear annually. To preserve democratic equality names would appear in alphabetical order" (127).

64 Eliot, "Disjecta Membra," *Egoist* 5.4 (April 1918), 55.

65 F. S Flint, *Imagism*, ed. Peter Jones, *Imagist Poetry* (London: Penguin, 1972), 129.

66 Ezra Pound, "Prefatory Note" to *The Complete Poetical Works of T. E. Hulme* (New York: New Directions, 1990), 59. In effect, these fragments (first conceived in the wake of futurism, late summer 1912, see Rainey, *Institutions*, 182–4) are part of Pound's attempt to establish a chronology of imagism that antedates futurism. Returning again to the "divergence later" pattern, Pound's need to regulate the history of his literary associations persists long after his departures. Just as with Eliot and the break with Amygism; so too, with Hulme and the alleged origins of imagism. In early 1921, Pound is still writing Ford to discuss a proposed history of imagism to be written by F. S. Flint, which upholds the events as Pound first advances them in the back-matter of *Ripostes* and *Des Imagistes*, and extends imagist trajectory through Pound's subsequent career: "Roughly = the cenacle. / Hulme. / Eng. Rev. / me – imagisme. / Various shades of symbolism – / your impressionism . . . / and my ticks for centre, intensity, vortex – hardness / hokku – as an aside": quoted in Brita Lindberg-Seyersted, *Pound / Ford: The Story of a Literary Friendship* (London: Faber and Faber, 1982), 51–2.

67 Jones, *Imagist Poetry*, 22.

68 F. T. Marinetti, "The Founding and Manifesto of Futurism," in Jane Goldman, et al., eds., *Modernism: An Anthology of Sources and Documents* (Chicago: University of Chicago Press, 1998), 251. In the *Figaro* manifesto of 1909, Marinetti describes a mythic founding scene in collaboration much like Gray's Inn of the "Georgians" or the "cenacle" of Pound ("arguing up the last confines of logic and blackening many reams of paper with our frenzied scribbling") but then leaves the meeting in a speeding automobile, connecting the first founding apocrypha with his subsequent car-crash into a ditch: "O maternal ditch, almost full of muddy water! Fair factory drain! I gulped down your nourishing sludge; and I remembered the blessed black breast of my Sudanese nurse . . . When I came up – torn, filthy, stinking – from under the capsized car, I felt the white-hot iron of joy deliciously pass through my heart!" (250).

69 I am counting "Michael Field" as a man rather than two women, Katherine Harris Bradley and Edith Emma Cooper, because Q, unlike later anthologists such as Yeats, does not make this identification.

70 F. T. Palgrave, *Golden Treasury of the Best Songs and Lyrical Poems in the English Language* (London: Macmillan, 1861), 324–6.

71 The Sitwell family alone – Edith, Osbert, and Sacheverell – account for two-fifths of the poems in the first volume.

72 Edith Sitwell, ed., *Wheels, Fifth Cycle* (London: Leonard Parsons, 1920), 123.

73 Richard Fifoot, *A Bibliography of Edith, Osbert and Sacheverell Sitwell*, 2nd edn. (London: Rupert Hart-Davis, 1971), 81–8.

74 Edith Sitwell, ed., *Wheels, Second Cycle* (Oxford: Blackwell, 1917), 110.

75 Quoted in Monroe, *Poet's Life*, 389; Marinetti, "Founding and Manifesto," 251.

76 Edith Sitwell, ed., *Wheels, Third Cycle* (Oxford: Blackwell, 1919), 100.

77 Nancy Cunard, "Wheels," in Wheels, ed. Edith Sitwell (Oxford: Blackwell, 1916), viii.

78 Sitwell, *Wheels, Second Cycle*, 105.

79 Edith Sitwell, *Selected Letters: 1919–1964*, ed. John Lehmann and Derek Parker (London: Macmillan, 1970), 21.

80 *Ibid.*

81 Wilfred Owen, *Collected Letters*, ed. Harold Owen and John Bell (London: Oxford University Press, 1967), 559–69.

82 Sitwell, *Letters* (Lehmann, ed.), 13.

83 *Ibid.*, 17.

84 *Ibid.*, 19.

85 *Ibid.*, 22.

86 F. R. Leavis, *New Bearings in English Poetry: A Study of the Contemporary Situation* (London: Penguin, 1982), 58.

87 Sitwell, *Wheels, Fifth Cycle*, 113.

88 Erin G. Carlston, *Thinking Fascism: Sapphic Modernism and Fascist Modernity* (Stanford, Calif.: Stanford University Press, 1998), 2.

89 Shari Benstock, *Women of the Left Bank: Paris, 1900–1940* (London: Virago, 1987), 4.

90 *Ibid.*
91 Caresse Crosby, *The Passionate Years* (London: Alvin Redman, 1955), 11.
92 Margaret Anderson, *My Thirty Years' War: An Autobiography* (London: Knopf, 1930), 3.
93 *Ibid.*, 243.
94 *Ibid.*, 251.
95 Bonnie Kime Scott, "Introduction," in *The Gender of Modernism: A Critical Anthology*, Bonnie Kime Scott, ed. (Bloomington: Indiana University Press, 1990), 10.
96 *Ibid.*, 2.
97 Quoted in Ken Garland, *Mr Beck's Underground Map* (Middlesex: Capital Transport, 1994), 17. Compare Janin Hadlaw, "The London Underground Map: Imagining Modern Time and Space," *Design Issues* 19.1 (Winter 2003), 25–35. Beck's map itself draws on distinctly modernist epistemological and aesthetic assumptions: "Above any consideration of the Diagram as a navigation aid was the optimistic vision it offered of a city that was not chaotic, in spite of appearances to the contrary, that knew what it was about and wanted its visitors to know it, too. Its bright, clean and colourful design exuded confidence in every line. Get a hang of this, it said, and the great metropolis is your oyster. . . . How did they all manage to get along before it burst on their delighted gaze?" (Garland, 7–9). The same can be said for the Yeats–Eliot–Pound–Woolf–Lewis–Joyce circuit of modernism: in Hadlaw's words, "the center puffs out, the margins crowd in" (32). Modernist "true scale," if we want it, would take full account of all aspects of its cultural production and generic heterogeneity and consequently won't fit neatly on a folded card.
98 Garland, *Mr Beck's Underground Map*, 7; Scott, "Introduction," 9.
99 Scott, "Introduction," 3. The anthology includes sources and documents of various genres – poetry, letters, criticism, journals, excerpted fiction – some previously published and others not, from twenty-six "modernist" authors; supplementing the "interchange" figures with May Sinclair, Nancy Cunard, Charlotte Mew, Katherine Mansfield, Gertrude Stein, Rose Macaulay, Nella Larsen, Anna Wickham, Antonia White, Sylvia Townsend Warner, Willa Cather, Hugh MacDiarmid, and Jean Rhys.
100 *Ibid.*

5 INSTITUTIONS, OUTRAGES, AND POSTCARDS

1 "Mortal Blow," *Time* (9 May 1938), 35.
2 Brenda R. Silver, *Virginia Woolf Icon* (Chicago: University of Chicago Press, 1999), 278.
3 *Ibid.*, 27; Daniel Boorstin, *The Image* (New York: Atheneum, 1987).
4 The head of retailing of the NPG, the source of Silver's information, takes a somewhat different view from her about the Woolf postcard, the sales of which occasioned a full-scale blitz of Woolf paraphernalia: "the fridge magnet . . . best

exemplifies the iconic status of Virginia Woolf. No product has come closer to representing the 'demystification' of works of art nor indeed the transformation in attitude towards commerce by galleries and museums . . . Virginia Woolf is not unique in inspiring sales of serious as well as more frivolous products . . . but she is by far and away the most varied and 'commercial' [personage in the NPG] both as a fashionable icon and as a serious subject of study. Sadly I have no evidence to show that Woolf mousemats and literary critiques sell to the same customers." (Silver, *Virginia Woolf Icon*, 278.)

5 "National Portraits," *The Times* (7 April 1932), 13d.
6 Paul Barlow, "Facing the Past and Present: The National Portrait Gallery and the Search for 'Authentic' Portraiture," in *Portraiture: Facing the Subject*, Joanna Woodall, ed. (Manchester: Manchester University Press, 1997), and "The Imagined Hero as Incarnate Sign: Thomas Carlyle and the Mythology of the 'National Portrait' in Victorian Britain," *Art History* 17.4 (December 1994), 517–45. See also Marcia Pointon, *Hanging the Head* (New Haven: Yale University Press, 1993), epilogue. For some of the ideology's influence on Pound, see my discussion above, pp. [139–41].
7 Thomas Carlyle, *Past and Present*, Richard D. Altick, ed. (New York: New York University Press: 1965), 124. For an extended reading of this scene, see Barlow, "Facing the Past and Present," 226–7.
8 Quoted in Charles Saumerez Smith, *The National Portrait Gallery* (London: National Portrait Gallery, 1997), 12.
9 Barlow, "Facing the Past and Present," 232, 219.
10 Barlow, "Facing the Past and Present," 221, 237. In the mid-1920s, British *Vogue* published its "Nominations for the Halls of Fame," "Some Portraits of Our Contemporaries," and "Galaxy of Stars of Today and Tomorrow" along much the same lines – replete with references to T. S. Eliot, Ezra Pound, James Joyce, Wyndham Lewis, Virginia Woolf, Edith Sitwell, and e. e. cummings, among others. I owe my awareness of this stirring of modernist promotion to Aurelea Mahood, "Mainstream Modernism" (paper presented at the Modernism and Popular Culture Seminar, Inaugural Modernist Studies Association Conference, Pennsylvania State University, 7 October 1999).
11 *Hansard's Parliamentary Debates* 140 (Jan.–Mar. 1856), 1778.
12 *Ibid.*, 1780–1.
13 Quoted in Smith, *National Portrait Gallery*, 12.
14 Terry Eagleton, *Ideology: An Introduction* (New York: Verso, 1991), 221.
15 Quoted in John Cooper, *National Portrait Gallery: A Visitor's Guide* (London: National Portrait Gallery, 2000), 7.
16 Barlow, "Facing the Past and Present," 224.
17 Thomas Carlyle, *On Heroes, Hero-Worship, and the Heroic in History* (Berkeley: University of California Press, 1993), 12.
18 Susan Foister, et al., *The National Portrait Gallery Collection* (London: National Portrait Gallery, 1988), 211.
19 Elizabeth Williamson, "Thinking Man's Calendar Girls," *The Daily Telegraph* (13 November 1989), 15.

20 Wyndham Lewis, *Rude Assignment: An Intellectual Autobiography*, Toby Foshay, ed. (Santa Barbara: Black Sparrow, 1984), 11–12.

21 *Ibid.*, 12.

22 Wyndham Lewis, "Preliminary Aside to the Read; Regarding Gossip, and its Pitfalls" [ca. 1937], *Modernism/Modernity* 4.2 (April 1997), 185.

23 Thomas R. Smith, "Introduction to 'Preliminary Aside to the Read; Regarding Gossip, and its Pitfalls,' by Wyndham Lewis," *Modernism/Modernity* 4.2 (April 1997), 182–3.

24 *Ibid.*, 181–2.

25 Hugh Kenner, *Wyndham Lewis* (Norfolk, Conn.: New Directions, 1954), xiii.

26 Wyndham Lewis, *The Letters of Wyndham Lewis*, W. K. Rose, ed. (Norfolk, Conn.: New Directions, 1963), 565.

27 Wyndham Lewis, introduction to *Wyndham Lewis and Vorticism* [exhibition at the Tate Gallery, July–August 1956] (London: Tate, 1956), 3.

28 Richard Cork, *Vorticism and its Allies* (London: Arts Council, 1974), 5.

29 See Rose, ed., *Letters of Wyndham Lewis,* 565–6, for an account of this episode sympathetic to Lewis, and see Cork, *Vorticism,* for a detailed but generally unsympathetic account.

30 William Roberts, *The Resurrection of Vorticism and the Apotheosis of Wyndham Lewis at the Tate* (London: Favil, 1956).

31 The scene recalls Pound's apocryphal invocations of the ur-imagist cenacle of 1909, discussed in chapter four.

32 See Cork, *Vorticism,* 106.

33 From the *Tate Collections* website.

34 Lewis, *Blast*. A second address listed – "5, Holland Place Chambers, Church Street, Kensington" – belongs to Ezra Pound.

35 *Ibid.,* 140. The advertisement is reprinted in both Paige Reynolds, "'Chaos Invading Concept': *Blast* as a Native Theory of Promotional Culture," *Twentieth Century Literature* (Summer 2000), 239; and Ezra Pound and Dorothy Shakespear, *Ezra Pound and Dorothy Shakespear: Their Letters, 1909–1914*, ed. Omar Pound and A. Walton Litz (New York: New Directions, 1984), 311. See Reynolds for a savvy analysis of *Blast* as a vehicle of avant-garde promotion (240). Reynolds cites the advance advertising for *Blast* "as a trenchant example of how modernist intellectuals deployed the tropes of commercial print advertising to publicize a nascent avant-garde movement and its organ of cultural and political expression" (268).

36 Virginia Woolf, "Mr. Bennett and Mrs. Brown," in *The Captain's Death Bed* (London: Hogarth, 1981), 91–2.

37 Pound, *Personae,* 186.

38 Wyndham Lewis, *Blasting and Bombardiering: An Autobiography, 1914–1926* (London: John Calder, 1982), 22.

39 Lewis, *Blasting and Bombardiering,* 35.

40 *Ibid.*, 32.

41 Susan Stanford Friedman, "Introduction to H. D.," in *The Gender of Modernism: A Critical Anthology*, Bonnie Kime Scott, ed. (Bloomington: Indiana University Press, 1990), 88.

42 Miriam Hansen, "T. E. Hulme, Mercenary of Modernism, or, Fragments of Avantgarde Sensibility on Pre-World War I Britain," *ELH* 47.2 (Summer 1980), 357; George Dangerfield, *The Strange Death of Liberal England* (New York: H. Smith and R. Haas, 1935). On the practical resemblances between Pound's engagements with *Blast*, A. R. Orage's *New Age* (where Pound "cut his political teeth"), and militant syndicalism, see David Kadlec, "Pound, Blast, and Syndicalism," *ELH* 60.4 (Winter 1993), 1,019.

43 Hansen, "T. E. Hulme," 357.

44 Woolf, "Mr. Bennett," 107–8.

45 Jane Goldman, "Virginia Woolf and Post-Impressionism: French Art, English Theory, and Feminist Practice," *Miscelánea* 20 (1999), 175.

46 Woolf, "Mr. Bennett," 108–10.

47 Goldman, "Virginia Woolf," 185.

48 Quoted in J. B. Bullen, ed., *Post-Impressionists in England* (New York: Routledge, 1988), 102.

49 Quoted in Paul O'Keeffe, *Some Sort of Genius: A Life of Wyndham Lewis* (London: Jonathan Cape, 2000), 101.

50 O'Keeffe, *Some Sort of Genius*, 106–7.

51 Tom Normand, *Wyndham Lewis the Artist: Holding the Mirror up to Politics* (Cambridge: Cambridge University Press, 1992), 68.

52 Jeffrey Meyers, *The Enemy: A Biography of Wyndham Lewis* (Routledge and Kegan Paul: London, 1980), 40.

53 Quoted in Paul Edwards, *Wyndham Lewis: Painter and Writer* (New Haven, Conn.: Yale University Press, 2000), 58.

54 O'Keeffe, *Some Sort of Genius*, 124.

55 A reviewer of *Laughing Woman*, in the *Daily Post*, for instance, comments that Lewis "at any rate allows himself pleasant colour if he deals in forms of nightmarish shape": quoted in O'Keeffe, *Some Sort of Genius*, 130. Clearly, something other than the familiar Fry/Bell formalist vocabulary is afoot with Lewis. Ironically, it was Bell himself who purchased *Laughing Woman*; for an account of the transaction and its relation to Lewis's eventual falling out with Omega Workshops Ltd. and Bloomsbury see 127–31.

56 Normand, *Wyndham Lewis*, 68.

57 Along with Hansen, a handful of scholars have picked up the undertones of suffragette militancy in *Blast*: Lyon notes *Blast*'s rhetorical similarities to Christabel Pankhurst's *Great Scourge* and their shared debts to the submerged politics of the manifesto form: Janet Lyon, *Manifestoes: Provocations of the Modern* (Ithaca, N.Y.: Cornell University Press, 1999). Reynolds notes common resemblances of both vorticist and suffragette propaganda with contemporary advertising: Reynolds, "Chaos Invading Concept."

58 A. E. Metcalfe, *Woman's Effort: A Chronicle of British Women's Fifty Year Struggle for Citizenship (1865–1914)* (Oxford: Blackwell, 1917), 243; Rowena Fowler, "Why Did Suffragettes Attack Works of Art?," *Journal of Women's History* 2.3 (Winter 1991), 121.

59 Lewis, *Blast,* 151. Reynolds reads this reference as evidence of "the vorticists' admiration for and anxiety about the ways in which advertising culture was

used for the women's cause": Reynolds, "'Chaos Invading Concept,'" 252. Rather than an anxiety and containment narrative, I see this as characteristic of modernism's cultural stance as it manifests the displacement of revolutionary politics – a reading that follows critical insights about modernism's hollowed-out revolutionary orientation made by a number of commentators (among others, Hansen, Lyon, Marianne DeKoven, Michael Tratner, and David Wier) and, indeed, Lewis himself, who writes about *Blast* that "[r]eally all this disorganized disturbance was Art behaving as if it were Politics. But I swear I did not know it. It may in fact have been politics. I see that now": Lewis, *Blasting and Bombardiering*, 32. Lewis recounts meeting Asquith in 1914: "He smelled politics beneath this revolutionary [vorticist] artistic technique. I, of course, was quite at a loss to understand what he was driving at" (51).

60 Lyon, *Manifestoes*, 109.
61 Fowler, "Why Did Suffragettes Attack," 125.
62 Lyon, *Manifestoes*, 110.
63 Quoted in Fowler, "Why Did Suffragettes Attack?" 120.
64 *Ibid.*, 112–13.
65 *Ibid.*, 124.
66 *Ibid.*, 117. James received 309 notes of condolence; for James's reaction to the symbolic mutilation, see Fowler.
67 *Ibid.*, 115.
68 *Ibid.*, 122.
69 "Militant with a Chopper," *The Times* (22 July 1914), 10e.
70 Barlow, "Facing the Past and Present," 234.
71 *Ibid.*, 220.
72 *Ibid.*, 236.
73 Woolf, "Mr. Bennett," 92. Thanks to Suzette Henke for directing my attention to Woolf's 1909 sketch about visiting the Carlyles' house: Virginia Woolf, "Carlyle's House," *Carlyle's House and Other Sketches*, David Bradshaw, ed. (London: Hesperus, 2003), 3–4.
74 Goldman, "Virginia Woolf," 188.
75 Diane Atkinson, *The Suffragettes in Pictures* (London: Sutton, 1996), 116.
76 Quoted in Atkinson, *The Suffragettes*, 116.
77 "Picture Outrages Renewed: Mutilation of Millais Portrait of Carlyle," *The Times* (18 July 1914), 5.
78 Quoted in Atkinson, *The Suffragettes*, 163.
79 According to Omar Pound and A. Walton Litz, *Blast* – despite being dated five days earlier on 20 June 1914 – made its first appearance five days later on 25 June 1914: Pound and Shakespear, *Letters,* 311.
80 Wyndham Lewis, Foreword to "'Guns by Wyndham Lewis,' Goupil Gallery, February 1919," in *Wyndham Lewis: Paintings and Drawings*, Walter Michel, ed. (Berkeley: University of California Press, 1971), 433.
81 For a detailed survey and examination of Lewis's portraits of modernist contemporaries, see Edwards, *Wyndham Lewis*, 245ff.

82 Hugh Kenner, "The Visual World of Wyndham Lewis," in *Wyndham Lewis: Paintings and Drawings*, Walter Michel, ed. (Berkeley: University of California Press, 1971), 39.

83 *Ibid.,* 38–9.

84 Wyndham Lewis, *Thirty Personalities and a Self-Portrait* (London: Desmond Harmsworth, 1932), 3.

85 *Ibid.,* 4.

86 Perhaps, some version of this structural discomfort led to the deliberately frag-mented and deformed gallery space of the modernist room in the recent reno-vations to the NPG.

87 Benjamin's collector is apposite here, who so dwells with the physiognomy of objects he "liberates [them] from the drudgery of being useful": Walter Benjamin, *The Arcades Project*, trans. Howard Eiland and Kevin McLaughlin (Cambridge: Harvard University Press, 1999), 209; see also "Unpacking My Library," in *Illuminations*, trans. Harry Zohn (New York: Schocken, 1968), 59–68.

EPILOGUE

1 Robert Sencourt, *T. S. Eliot: A Memoir* (London: Garnstone, 1971), 233.

2 In turn, this phenomenon also points to the rise of virtual and actual por-trait galleries in the nineteenth century and their structural transformation in the twentieth century, discussed at length in chapter five. The *meme*, however – the gallery of mixed worthies knowingly juxtaposing the elite and the popular – points to the kind of qualified (re)integration of high and low forms first undertaken by Gilbert Seldes.

3 *The New York Times* (5 January 1965), 1.

4 Max Horkheimer and Theodor W. Adorno, *The Dialectic of Enlightenment*, trans. John Cumming (New York: Continuum, 1988), 133.

5 Groucho Marx, *The Groucho Letters: Letters from and to Groucho Marx* (New York: Da Capo, 1994), 155.

6 Roland Barthes, *Mythologies* (New York: Noonday, 1988), 11.

7 Walter Benjamin, "The Task of the Translator," *Illuminations*, trans. Harry Zohn (New York: Schocken, 1968), 78.

8 The mural was painted by commercial artist Gary Kelley and commissioned by the bookseller in the early 1990s for its Rockefeller Center outlet in New York City. Thanks to Mary Ellen Keating, Barnes and Noble's Senior Vice President of Corporate Communications, for this information. As before, there are many ways to reshuffle the deck. Gender: more than three times as many men as women – twenty-three to seven. Major genres: more novelists than poets, more poets than playwrights. No Dickens. No Shakespeare. No romantic besides Mary Shelley. No writer older than Shelley (b. 1792); none more contempo-rary than Pablo Neruda (b. 1904). The twentieth century fares better than the nineteenth century: nineteen (including Shaw, Kipling, and Tagore) to eleven

(including Hardy, Wharton, and James). American: sixteen, counting Eliot, James, Chandler, Nabokov, and Singer. British: eleven, counting Wilde, Shaw, and Joyce. Only four in languages other than English (Neruda, Tagore, Kafka, and Singer), three of color (Tagore, Hughes, and Hurston), and two from third continents (Neruda and Tagore).

9　E. M. Forster, *Aspects of the Novel* (New York: Harcourt, Brace, Jovanovich, 1985), 9.

10　*Ibid.*, 14.

11　*Ibid.*, 13–14.

12　*Ibid.*, 13.

13　Thomas M. Disch, "The Man Who Read a Book," *The Hudson Review* 47.1 (Spring 1994).

14　After a year's hiatus, Winfrey returned to book recommending in mid-2003, promising to focus on "great books that have stood the test of time," "three to five choices a year, with the books likely written by both living and dead authors," especially, "'classic' authors such as William Faulkner and Ernest Hemingway": "Oprah's Book Club: Take Two," CBSNews.com (13 June 2003), <http://www.cbsnews.com/ stories/2003/06/18/entertainment/main559257.shtml>. The first selection was John Steinbeck's *East of Eden*.

15　Richard Lacayo and Andrea Sachs, "Oprah Turns the Page," *Time* (15 April 2002), 63.

16　Forster, *Aspects,* 14.

17　Lacayo and Sachs, "Oprah," 63.

Index

Abbott, Bernice, 97
Abercrombie, Lascelles, 142, 145, 147
Achebe, Chinua, 17
Acton, Harold, 74–5, 79, 215
adjective(s)
  authorial, 84–7
  Beckett as, 60
  Eliot as, 61, 72–80, 87
  Hemingway and, 58, 59–60
  Lawrence as, 86–7
  Pound and, 58–60, 61–2, 66
  Shakespeare as, 87
Adorno, Theodor, 200, 218
Aeschylus, 70
Aldington, Richard, 63
  Eliot and, 104
  Stepping Heavenward, 50
Anderson, Margaret, 99, 161–2, 163, 166
  Eliot and, 107
  My Thirty Years' War, 97, 162–3
Anderson, Perry, 41, 42
anonymity, 50–2, 54
anthologies, 8, 97, 100–2, 137–9, 186
  brands and, 4, 102, 135–6, 137–8, 144–6, 159, 168
  Eliot and, 139, 227
  gender issues with, 138–9, 141, 148, 154, 159
  imprimaturs and, 152, 159
  literary movements and, 135, 152–3, 159
apocrypha, 97, 101–3, 178–9
Apuleius, 70
Arlen, Michael, 17, 74
Arnold, Matthew, 76, 143
Asquith, Anthony, 197
Atkinson, Laurence, 155, 156
Auden, W. H., 42, 47, 70, 71
Austen, Jane, 69
authenticity, Carlyle's theory of, 192, 194–5
author classifications, 10
  anthologies and, 4, 138
  Barnes and Noble and, 201–4, 237–8

Eliot and, 69, 71
Foucault and, 52–3
"hero-archy" and, 204
Kenner and, 71
Leavis on, 70, 71
Pound and, 9, 67–9, 71, 106, 213–14
authorial adjectives. *See under* adjective(s)
authorship, 8–9
  anonymity and, 50–2, 54
  Barthes on, 51, 52
  Beebe on, 46
  collaboration and, 95, 119
  commodification and, 33, 90–1
  écriture and, 56–7
  Eliot on, 54–5, 119
  fetishized, 90–1
  Foucault on, 50–4
  immanence and, 15–16, 39, 47
  imprimaturs and, 20
  in extremis, 12, 23, 119–20, 169–70
  James on, 23–6
  Koestenbaum on, 124
  Richards on, 84–7
  as thought experiments, 50–7
  Waugh on, 47–50

Barlow, Paul, 172, 174, 192
Barnes, Djuna, 3, 100–2
  anthologies and, 160, 161–2, 164–5
  Eliot and, 107, 108–9, 111, 112–14, 119, 120
  Muir and, 105
  Nightwood, 108–9, 111, 112–14
Barnes and Noble booksellers, 201–4, 237–8
Barney, Natalie, 161, 162
Barthes, Roland, 51, 52, 201
Basic English, 63–5
  Joyce and, 63, 64, 65, 213
  Pound and, 64–5, 67, 68–9
Bataille, Georges, 207
Baudelaire, Charles, 70, 132, 207

Gosse, Edmund, 145, 158, 159, 229
gossip, 105–6, 163, 175–6, 177–9
Gourmont, Rémy de, 93
  gender issues and, 129
  Natural Philosophy of Love, 120, 124, 127, 141, 224
Goux, Jean-Joseph, 9–10, 11, 14
Graham, Freda, 188, 190
Grant, Duncan, 187
Graves, Robert, 63, 102, 148
  on branding, 144, 227
  "These are Your Gods, O Israel," 122
Green, Henry, 17
Gresham's law, 11–12
Grierson, Herbert, 79
Grigson, Geoffrey, 143–4
Grock (clown), 199

H. D. *See* Doolittle, Hilda
Haigh-Wood, Vivienne, 18
Hall, Donald, 131
Hamilton, Cuthbert, 179
Hansen, Miriam, 184
Hardy, Thomas, 145
Harmsworth, Alfred Charles William, 89
Harwood, John, 12, 88
heap, jane, 161–2, 163
Hemingway, Ernest, 70, 71, 95, 100, 163
  adjectives and, 58, 59–60
  Kerouac and, 17
  A Moveable Feast, 58, 122
  Pound and, 58
"hero-archy," 204
hero-worship, 170
  Carlyle and, 171–2, 174, 193, 196
  romanticism and, 37, 39
Herrick, Robert, 68
hierarchy, 9–10
Hogarth Press, 72, 74, 223
Homer, 67, 70
homosexuality. *See* queer theory
Hopkins, Gerard Manley, 69, 143
Horkheimer, Max, 200
Housman, A. E., 145
Hoyt, Helen, 139, 143
Hughes, Glenn, 142
Hulme, T. E., 153
Hunt, Violet, 122
Huxley, Aldous, 49, 104, 156
Huyssen, Andreas, 19, 88

icons, 170–1, 175
ideograms, 58–9, 61–2
imagism, 4, 66, 135
  anthologies of, 137–8, 142, 154
  branding of, 135–6, 152–3

futurism and, 152
  gender issues with, 153–4
  Pound and, 121, 130, 133–4
impersonalization, 4
  Eliot and, 55, 118–19
  Ford and, 16
  Woolf and, 16
imprimaturs, 1–3, 18–22, 55–7, 200–1, 204
  anthologies and, 152, 159
  authorial adjectives and, 60
  collaboration and, 102
  cultural capital and, 10, 14, 176–7
  definition of, 20
  Eliot's, 200–1
  functions of, 20
  interdependent, 137
  Isherwood's, 50
  James's, 25–6, 31, 33
  Joyce's, 33, 34–5, 36, 38, 165
  maintenance of, 165
  paradox of, 26
  stipulations for, 25–6, 28–9, 31
  synecdoche and, 30–1
  Waugh's, 48–9
influence. *See* promotion
introductions, 8, 101, 102, 103–6, 144, 168
  by Eliot, 106–20, 125, 131
  gender issues with, 109
  by Lewis, 175–6, 177–8
  reputations and, 106, 109–10, 119
Iser, Wolfgang, 29
Isherwood, Christopher
  Eliot and, 107
  imprimatur of, 50
  James, Henry, and, 43
  Lions and Shadows, 50, 80
  Prater Violet, 22, 39, 42–50, 56
  Waugh and, 47, 48
Isis (journal), 75–6, 78

James, Henry, 22–33, 38, 52, 69
  on artistic success, 26, 27–8
  on authorship, 23–6
  career of, 21–2
  creative sources for, 22–3
  "Death of a Lion," 23–6, 31–2
  "Figure in the Carpet," 23–6, 29–30, 31–2
  finances of, 21
  imprimatur of, 25–6, 31, 33, 48
  Isherwood and, 43
  "John Delavoy," 21, 31–3
  Joyce and, 38–9
  New York Edition of, 22–3
  "Next Time," 21, 28, 31–2
  "Private Life," 31–2
  "Spoils of Poynton," 22